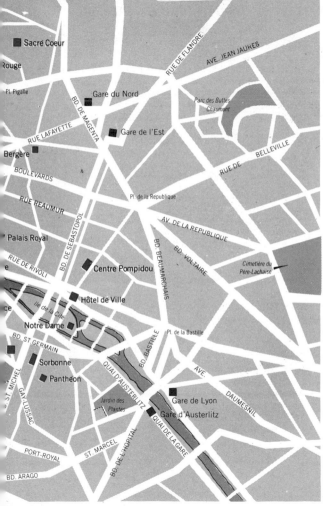

Sacré Coeur

Rouge

Pl. Pigalle

Gare du Nord

RUE DE FLANDRE

AVE. JEAN JAURES

BD. DE MAGENTA

Gare de l'Est

Parc des Buttes
Chaumont

RUE LAFAYETTE

Bergère

BOULEVARDS

BELLEVILLE

RUE DE

RUE REAUMUR

Pl. de la Republique

AV. DE LA REPUBLIQUE

Palais Royal

BD. DE SEBASTOPOL

BD. BEAUMARCHAIS

BD. VOLTAIRE

RUE DE RIVOLI

e

Centre Pompidou

Cimetière du
Pere-Lachaise

Hôtel de Ville

ce

Ile de la Cité

Notre Dame

Pl. de la Bastille

BD. ST. GERMAIN

BD. BASTILLE

Sorbonne

Panthéon

AVE.

ST. MICHEL

GAY-LUSSAC

QUAI D'AUSTERLITZ

DAUMESNIL

Jardin des
Plantes

Gare de Lyon

Gare d'Austerlitz

PORT-ROYAL

ST. MARCEL

BD. DE L'HOPITAL

QUAI DE LA GARE

BD. ARAGO

USEFUL PHONE NUMBERS

FRANCE
Emergencies (in Paris):

Ambulance	(1) 45 67 50 50
Anti-poison squad	(1) 42 05 63 29
Dentist, 24-hour	(1) 47 07 33 68
Fire	18
Police	17

Other important numbers:

U.S. Embassy	(1) 42 96 12 02
American Hospital	(1) 47 47 53 00
Hertford British Hospital	(1) 47 58 13 12
Time	36 99
Weather: (in Paris and suburbs)	36 65 02 02
(in Ile de France and Normandy)	36 65 00 00
(in all of France)	36 65 01 01
Railroads (information in English)	45 82 08 41
Road and traffic conditions	48 99 33 33

CANADA
Emergencies (in Quebec City):

Ambulance	911
Anti-poison squad	(1) 800-463-5060
	or (418) 656-8090
Health information	(418) 648 2626
Fire	911
Police	911

Other important numbers:

U.S. Consulate	(418) 692-2095
Weather	(418) 872-6088
Railroads (from U.S.)	1-800-361-3663
Road and traffic conditions	(418) 643-6830
Quebec Province Information	1-800-363-7777

FRENCH
AT A GLANCE

PHRASE BOOK & DICTIONARY FOR TRAVELERS

FRENCH
AT A GLANCE
PHRASE BOOK & DICTIONARY FOR TRAVELERS

BY GAIL STEIN, M.A.
Teacher of French
Department of Foreign Languages
Martin Van Buren High School
New York

HEYWOOD WALD, Coordinating Editor
Former Chairman, Department of Foreign Languages
Martin Van Buren High School
New York

SECOND
EDITION

BARRON'S

BARRON'S EDUCATIONAL SERIES, INC.

Cover and Book Design   Milton Glaser, Inc.
Illustrations   Juan Suarez
Travel Tips revised by Janet Celesta Lowe

All inquiries should be addressed to:
Barron's Educational Series, Inc.
250 Wireless Boulevard
Hauppauge, New York 11788

Library of Congress Catalog Card No. 92-26539

Paper Edition
International Standard Book No. 0-8120-1394-8

Library of Congress Cataloging in Publication Data

Stein, Gail.
    French at a glance : phrase book & dictionary for travelers / by
Gail Stein.
       p.   cm.
    ISBN 0-8120-1394-8
    1. French language—Conversation and phrase books—English.
    2. French language—Dictionaries—English.   I. Title.
PC2129.E5S764   1992
448.3'421—dc20   92-26539
                                                                CIP

PRINTED IN THE UNITED STATES OF AMERICA
    5   9770   109

CONTENTS

PREFACE

So you're taking a trip to one of the many fascinating countries of the world. That's exciting! This phrase book, part of Barron's popular *At a Glance* series, will prove an invaluable companion.

In these books we present the phrases and words that a traveler most often needs for a brief visit to a foreign country, where the customs and language are often different. Each phrase book highlights the terms particular to that country, in situations that the tourist is most likely to encounter. This revision includes dialogues using words and expressions for each situation. Travel tips found throughout the book have been updated. With a specially developed key to pronunciation, this book will enable you to communicate quickly and confidently in colloquial terms. It is intended not only for beginners with no knowledge of the language, but also for those who have already studied it and have some familiarity with it.

Some of the unique features and highlights of the Barron's series are:

■ Easy-to-follow *pronunciation keys* and complete phonetic transcriptions for all words and phrases in the book.

■ Compact *dictionary* of commonly used words and phrases—built right into this phrase book so there's no need to carry a separate dictionary.

■ Useful phrases for the *tourist*, grouped together by subject matter in a logical way so that the appropriate phrase is easy to locate when you need it.

■ Special phrases for the *business traveler*, including banking terms, trade and contract negotiations, and secretarial services.

■ Thorough section on *food and drink*, with comprehensive food terms you will find on menus.

■ *Emergency phrases* and terms you hope you won't need: legal complications, medical problems, theft or loss of valuables, replacement or repair of watches, camera, etc.

- *Sightseeing itineraries*, shopping tips, practical travel tips, and regional food specialties to help you get off the beaten path and into the countryside, to the small towns and cities, and to the neighboring areas.
- Dialogues coordinated with each situation.
- A *reference section* providing: important signs, conversion tables, holidays, abbreviations, telling time, days of week and months of year.
- A brief *grammar section*, with the basic elements of the language quickly explained.

Enjoy your vacation and travel with confidence. You have a friend by your side.

ACKNOWLEDGMENTS

We would like to thank the following individuals and organizations for their assistance on this project:
Nora Brossard, Assistant Director Public Relations, French National Tourist Office, New York, New York; Professor Pierre François, SUC New Paltz, New York; Marie-Charlotte Iszkowski, Foreign Service Institute, Washington, D.C.; Michel Lalou, Phonelab, New York, New York; George Lang, George Lang, Inc., New York, New York; Dr. Gladys Lipton, Coordinator of Foreign Languages and ESOL, Anne Arundel County Public Schools, Annapolis, Maryland; François Mead, Alliance Française, New York, New York; Professor Henry Urbanski, Chairman, Department of Foreign Languages, SUC New Paltz, New York; Herta Erville; and Andrée Katz.

Also, Air France, Association of American Travel Writers, French National Tourist Office, *New York Times, Signature Magazine, Travel-Holiday Magazine, Travel and Leisure Magazine*, U.S. Tour Operators, and U.S. Travel Data Center.

QUICK PRONUNCIATION GUIDE

Although all the phrases in this book are presented with an easy-to-use key to pronunciation, you will find speaking French quite a bit easier if you learn a few simple rules. Below are some tables which give the sounds represented by each French letter along with the symbols used to indicate them in this book. Although a French sound is quite different from ours, with a little practice and repetition you will be able to make yourself understood by native French speakers.

After studying the phonetic pronunciation system below, begin to practice the vocabulary words and then progress to the longer phrases. Bonne chance! *Bohn shah<u>nss</u>*

STRESS

As an aid to pronunciation, words in this book have been divided into syllables. Since all French syllables have approximately the same amount of stress, pronounce each syllable with equal emphasis and put a slightly stronger emphasis on the last syllable of a word group.

CONSONANTS

In French, final consonants are usually silent, except for final C, R, F, and L (as in CaReFuL), which are usually pronounced.

FRENCH LETTER	ENGLISH SOUND	SYMBOL	EXAMPLE
b, d, f, k, l, m, n,	same as English		
p, s, t, v, z	same as English		
c (before e, i, y)	SS (S at beginning of word)	S	cigare *see-gahr*
ç (before a, o, u)	SS (S at beginning of word)	S	garçon *gahr-ssoh<u>n</u>*
c (before a, o, u)	K	K	comme *kohm*

FRENCH LETTER	ENGLISH SOUND	SYMBOL	EXAMPLE
g (before e, i, y)	S as in plea_s_ure	ZH	rouge *roozh*
ge (before a, o)	S as in plea_s_ure	ZH	mangeons *mahn-zhohn*
g (before a, o, u)	G	G	gant *gahn*
gn	nyuh as in o_ni_on	NY	oignon *oh-nyohn*
h	always silent		hôtel *oh-tehl*
j	S as in plea_s_ure	ZH	je *zhuh*
qu, final q	K	K	cinq *sank*
r	Roll the R at the top back of the mouth as if you were gargling or spitting.	R	rue *rew*
ss	S	SS	poisson *pwah-ssohn*
s	beginning of word	S	six *sees*
	next to consonant	SS	disque *deessk*
s	between vowels	Z	poison *pwah-zohn*
th	T	T	thé *tay*
x	S in these words only	SS	six *seess*, dix *deess*, soixante *swah-ssahnt*
x	X	KSS	excellent *ehkss-eh-lahn*

NOTE: When combined with a word beginning with a vowel or *h*, *x* has a *z* sound. Before a word beginning with a consonant, it is silent.

VOWELS

FRENCH LETTER	ENGLISH SOUND	SYMBOL	EXAMPLE
a, à, â	A as in yacht or A in after	AH	la *lah*
é, final er, final ez, et	A as in day	AY	musée *mew-zay*
e+2 consonants e+final pronounced consonant e, ê, è	E as in ever	EH	sept *seht*
e	sometimes like E of early with no R sound	UH	le *luh*
i (î), y	EE as in meet	EE	île *eel*
i+ vowel or ll	Y as in yes	EE	famille *fah-mee*
o+final pronounced consonant	O as in for	OH	homme *ohm*
o, o before se, o last sound in word, au, eau	O as in open	OH	au *oh*
ou	OO as in tooth	OO	où *oo*
oy, oi	WA as in watch	WAH	trois *trwah*
U	There is none. Round lips and say E and U at same time.	EW	du *dew*
U + vowel	WEE as in wee	WEE	huit *weet*

NASAL SOUNDS

Nasal sounds are produced through the mouth and the nose at the same time. Nasal sounds occur when N or M follow a vowel in the same syllable. There is NO nasal sound for VOWEL + NN, VOWEL + MM, VOWEL + N + VOWEL, VOWEL + M + VOWEL. NOTE: n means there is a nasalized pronunciation of the "N" sound. The tip of the tongue does not touch the roof of the mouth.

FRENCH LETTER	ENGLISH SOUND	SYMBOL	EXAMPLE
AN, AM, EN, EM	similar to on	AHN	France *Frahnss*
IN, IM, AIN, AIM	similar to an	AN	pain *pan*
IEN	similar to yan of Yankee	YAN	bien *byan*
ON, OM	similar to on of long.	OHN	bon *bohn*
UN, UM	similar to un of under.	UHN	un *uhn*

LIAISON and ELISION

Liaison and elision are two linguistic devices that add to the beauty and fluidity of the French language.

Liaison means linking. In French, the final consonant of a word is usually not pronounced. Sometimes, however, when the final consonant of one word is followed by a beginning vowel or "H" of the next word, liaison occurs.

EXAMPLE:

Nous arrivons. *noo zah-ree-vohn*

With the following words in French, the final vowel is dropped if the next word starts with a vowel or "H". The dropped vowel is replaced by an apostrophe. This is called elision.

EXAMPLE:

la auto = l'auto *(loh-toh)*

le homme = l'homme *(lohm)*

THE BASICS FOR GETTING BY

MOST FREQUENTLY USED EXPRESSIONS

The expressions in this section are the ones you'll use again and again—the fundamental building blocks of conversation, the way to express your wants or needs, and some simple question forms which you can use to construct all sorts of questions. It's a good idea to practice these phrases until you know them by heart.

yes	**oui**	*wee*
no	**non**	*nohn*
maybe	**peut-être**	*puh-teh-truh*
please	**s'il vous plaît**	*seel voo pleh*
thank you very much	**merci beaucoup**	*mehr-ssee boh-koo*
you're welcome	**de rien**	*duh ryan*
	Je vous en prie	*zhuh voo zahn pree*
Excuse me.	**Excusez-moi.**	*ehkss-kew-zay mwah*
	Pardon	*pahr-dohn*
I'm sorry.	**Je suis désolé(e).**	*zhuh swee day-zoh-lay*
Just a second.	**Un moment.**	*uhn moh-mahn*
That's all right, O.K.	**Ça va.**	*sah-vah*
	D'accord.	*dah-kohr*
	Bien entendu.	*byan nahn-tahn-dew*
It doesn't matter.	**Ça ne fait rien.**	*sah nuh feh ryan*
Good morning (afternoon).	**Bonjour.**	*bohn-zhoor*
Good evening (night).	**Bonsoir.**	*bohn-swahr*
	Bonne nuit.*	*bohn nwee*

NOTE: Used on leaving for the night

Sir	**Monsieur**	*muh-ssyuh*
Madame	**Madame**	*mah-dahm*
Miss	**Mademoiselle**	*mahd-mwah-zehl*
Good-bye.	**Au revoir.**	*oh ruh-vwahr.*
See you later (so long).	**À tout à l'heure.**	*ah toot ah luhr.*
See you tomorrow.	**À demain.**	*ah duh-man*
Do you speak English?	**Parlez-vous anglais?** *pahr-lay voo ahn-gleh*	
I speak a little French.	**Je parle un peu le français.** *zhuh pahrl uhn puh luh frahn-sseh*	
Do you understand?	**Comprenez-vous? (Vous comprenez?)** *voo kohn-pruh-nay (voo kohn-pruh-nay)*	
I understand.	**Je comprends.** *zhuh kohn-prahn*	
I don't understand.	**Je ne comprends pas.** *zhuh nuh kohn-prahn pah*	
What?	**Quoi?** *kwah*	
What did you say?	**Qu'est-ce que vous avez dit?** *kehss kuh voo zah-vay dee*	
How do you say _____ in French?	**Comment dit-on _____ en français?** *koh-mahn dee tohn _____ ahn frahn-sseh*	
What does this (that) mean?	**Que veut dire ceci (cela)?** *kuh vuh deer suh-see (suh-lah)*	
Please repeat.	**Répétez, s'il vous plaît.** *Ray-pay-tay, seel voo pleh*	
I'm American.	**Je suis américain/américaine (f).** *zhuh swee zah-may-ree-kan/zah-may-ree-kehn*	

My name is ____.	**Je m'appelle ____.** *zhuh mah-pehl*
What's your name?	**Comment vous appelez-vous?** *koh-mahn voo zah-play voo*
How are you?	**Comment allez-vous?** *koh-mahn tah-lay voo*
How's everything?	**Comment ça va?** *koh-mahn sah vah*
Very well, thanks. And you?	**Très bien, merci. Et vous?** *treh byan mehr-ssee. ay voo*
Where is ____?	**Où est ____?** *oo eh*
■ the bathroom	**les toilettes** *lay twah-leht*
■ the dining room	**la salle à manger** *lah sahl ah mahn-zhay*
■ the entrance	**l'entrée** *lahn-tray*
■ the exit	**la sortie** *lah sohr-tee*
■ the taxi	**le taxi** *luh tak-ssee*
■ the telephone	**le téléphone** *luh tay-lay-fohn*
I'm lost.	**Je suis perdu(e).** *zhuh swee pehr-dew*
We're lost.	**Nous sommes perdus(ues).** *noo sohm pehr-dew*
Where are my friends?	**Où sont mes amis?** *oo sohn may zah-mee*
Where is the bus?	**Où est le bus?** *Oo eh luh bewss*
Which way did they go?	**Par où sont-ils allés?** *Pahr oo sohn teel zah-lay*
■ to the left	**à gauche** *ah gohsh*
■ to the right	**à droite** *ah drwaht*
■ straight ahead	**tout droit** *too drwah*
How much is it?	**C'est combien?** *Seh kohn-byan*

I'd like ____.	**Je voudrais ____.**	*zhuh voo-dreh*
Please bring me ____.	**Apportez-moi, s'il vous plaît ____.** *ah-pohr-tay mwah seel voo pleh*	
Please show me ____.	**Montrez-moi, s'il vous plaît ____.** *Mohn-tray mwah, seel voo pleh*	
I'm hungry.	**J'ai faim.** *zhay fan*	
I'm thirsty.	**J'ai soif.** *zhay swahf*	
I'm tired.	**Je suis fatigué(e)** *zhuh swee fah-tee-gay*	
What's that?	**Qu'est-ce que c'est?** *kehss-kuh-seh*	
What's up?	**Qu'est-ce qui se passe?** *kehss kee suh pahss*	
	Quoi de neuf? *kwah duh nuhf*	
I (don't) know.	**Je (ne) sais (pas).** *zhuh (nuh) seh (pah)*	

QUESTIONS

Where is ____?	**Où est ____?**	*oo eh*
When?	**Quand?**	*kahn*
How much?	**Combien?**	*kohn-byan*
Who?	**Qui?**	*kee*
Why?	**Pourquoi?**	*poor-kwah*
How?	**Comment?**	*koh-mahn*
What?	**Quoi?**	*kwah*

EXCLAMATIONS, SLANG, COLLOQUIALISMS

Ouch!	**Aïe!**	*ahy*
That hurts!	**Oh, ça fait mal!**	*oh sah feh mahl*
Wow! Man alive! (expressing surprise)	**Oh là là!**	*oh lah lah*
Darn it! (expressing annoyance)	**Zut alors!**	*zewt ah-lohr*
How about that! (Well!)	**Eh bien, mon vieux!**	*eh byan mohn vyuh*
How beautiful!	**Magnifique!** **Quelle merveille!**	*mah-nyee-feek* *kehl mehr-vehy*
Ugh!	**Pouah!**	*pwah*
Phew!	**Ouf!**	*oof*
That's awful!	**C'est affreux!**	*seh-tah-fruh*
Great! Wonderful!	**Formidable!**	*fohr-mee-dah-bluh*
That's it!	**C'est ça!**	*seh sah*
My goodness!	**Mon Dieu!**	*mohn dyuh*

Good Heavens!	**Mon Dieu!**	*mohn dyuh*
For heaven's sake!	**Par exemple!**	*Pahr ehg-zahn-pluh*
Bottoms up! Cheers!	**Santé.** **À votre santé!**	*sahn-tay* *ah voh-truh sahn-tay*
Quiet!	**Silence!**	*see-lahnss*
Shut up!	**Tais-toi!**	*teh-twa*
That's enough!	**Ça suffit!**	*sah sew-fee*
	C'est assez!	*seh tah-ssay*
Never mind!	**N'importe.**	*nan-pohrt*
Of course!	**Bien sûr!**	*byan sewr*
With pleasure!	**Avec plaisir!**	*ah-vehk pleh-zeer*
Let's go!	**Allons-y!**	*ah-lohn zee!*
What a shame (pity)!	**Quel dommage!**	*kehl doh-mahzh*
What a nuisance (showing annoyance)!	**Que c'est ennuyeux!**	*keh seh tahn-nwee-yuh*
Nonsense! No way!	**C'est ridicule!** **Allons, donc.**	*seh ree-dee-kewl* *ah-lohn dohnk*
Don't be stupid!	**Ne sois pas bête!**	*nuh swah pah beht*
Are you crazy?	**Êtes-vous fou/folle?**	*eht voo foo/fohl*
What a fool!	**Quel imbécile!**	*kehl an-bay-sseel*
Good luck!	**Bonne chance!**	*bohn shahnss*

PROBLEMS, PROBLEMS, PROBLEMS (EMERGENCIES)

| Hurry up! | **Dépêchez-vous!** | *day-peh-shay voo!* |
| Look! | **Regardez!** | *ruh-gahr-day* |

Watch out! Be careful!	**Faites attention!** *feht zah-tah<u>n</u>-ssyoh<u>n</u>*
	Soyez prudent(e)! *swah-yay prew-dah<u>n</u> (t)*
Listen!	**Écoutez!** *ay-koo-tay*
Wait!	**Attendez!** *ah-tah<u>n</u>-day*
Fire!	**Au feu!** *oh fuh*
I have lost ___.	**J'ai perdu ___.** *zheh pehr-dew*
What's the matter with you?	**Qu'est-ce que vous avez?** *kehss kuh voo zah-vay*
What (the devil) do you want?	**Que (diable) voulez-vous?** *kuh (dee-ah-bluh) voo-lay voo*
Stop bothering me!	**Laissez-moi tranquille!** *leh-ssay mwah trah<u>n</u>-keel*
Go away!	**Allez-vous-en!** *ah-lay voo zah<u>n</u>*
	Va-t-en (fam.)! *Vah-tah<u>n</u>*

Scram! Beat it!	**Fiche-moi la paix!**	*feesh mwah lah peh*
Leave me alone!	**Laissez-moi tranquille!**	*leh-ssay mwah trah<u>n</u>-keel*
Help, police!	**Au secours, police!**	*oh suh-koor, poh-leess*
I'm going to call a cop!	**Ja vais appeler la police!**	*zhuh veh zah-play lah poh-leess*
Get out!	**Sortez!**	*sohr-tay!*
That guy is a thief!	**Ce type est un voleur!**	*suh teep eh tuh<u>n</u> voh-luhr*
He has stolen _____.	**Il a volé _____.**	*eel ah voh-lay*
■ my car	**ma voiture**	*mah vwah-tewr*
■ my passport	**mon passeport**	*moh<u>n</u> pahss-pohr*
■ my purse	**mon sac**	*moh<u>n</u> sahk*
■ my suitcase	**ma valise**	*mah vah-leez*
■ my wallet	**mon portefeuille**	*moh<u>n</u> pohr-tuh-fuhy*
■ my watch	**ma montre**	*mah moh<u>n</u>-truh*
This young man is annoying me.	**Ce jeune homme m'embête.**	*suh zhuhn ohm mah<u>n</u>-beht*
	m'ennuie.	*mah<u>n</u>-nwee*
He keeps following me.	**Il n'arrête pas de me suivre!**	*eel nah-reht pah duh muh swee-vruh*
Stop that boy!	**Arrêtez ce garçon!**	*Ah-reh-tay suh gahr-ssoh<u>n</u>*
I haven't done anything.	**Je n'ai rien fait.**	*zhuh nay rya<u>n</u> feh*
It's a lie!	**C'est un mensonge.**	*seh tuh<u>n</u> mah<u>n</u>-ssoh<u>n</u>zh*
It's not true!	**Ce n'est pas vrai!**	*suh neh pah vreh*

I'm innocent.	**Je suis innocent(e)** *zhuh swee zee-noh-sahn(t)*	
I want a lawyer.	**Je voudrais parler à un avocat.** *zhuh voo-dreh pahr-lay ah uhn nah-voh-kah*	
I want to go _____.	**Je voudrais aller _____.** *zhuh voo-dreh zah-lay*	
■ to the American consulate	**au consulat américain** *oh kohn-sew-lah ah-may-ree-kan*	
■ to the police station	**au commissariat de police** *oh koh-mee-ssah-ryah duh poh-leess*	
I need help, quick!	**Vite. Aidez-moi.** *veet eh-day mwah*	
	Vite, au secours! *veet oh suh-koor*	
Can you help me, please?	**Pouvez-vous m'aider, s'il vous plaît?** *poo-vay voo meh-day seel voo pleh*	
Does anyone here speak English?	**Y a-t-il quelqu'un ici qui parle anglais?** *ee ah teel kehl-kuhn ee-ssee kee pahrl ahn-gleh*	
I need an interpreter.	**Il me faut un interprète.** *eel muh foh tuhn nan-tehr-preht*	

NUMBERS

You will use numbers the moment you land in France, whether it be to exchange money at the airport, purchase a bus ticket for a ride into town, or describe the length of your stay to a customs official. We list here first the cardinal numbers, then follow with ordinal numbers, fractions, and other useful numbers.

CARDINAL NUMBERS

0	**zéro**	*zay-roh*
1	**un**	*uhn*

2	**deux**	*duh*
3	**trois**	*trwah*
4	**quatre**	*kah-truh*
5	**cinq**	*sa_n_k*
6	**six**	*seess*
7	**sept**	*seht*
8	**huit**	*weet*
9	**neuf**	*nuhf*
10	**dix**	*deess*
11	**onze**	*oh_nz_*
12	**douze**	*dooz*
13	**treize**	*trehz*
14	**quatorze**	*kah-tohrz*
15	**quinze**	*ka_nz_*
16	**seize**	*sehz*
17	**dix-sept**	*dee-seht*
18	**dix-huit**	*dee-zweet*
19	**dix-neuf**	*deez-nuhf*
20	**vingt**	*va_n_*
21	**vingt et un**	*va_n_-tay-uh_n_*
22	**vingt-deux**	*va_n_-duh*
23	**vingt-trois**	*va_n_-trwah*
24	**vingt-quatre**	*va_n_-kah-truh*
25	**vingt-cinq**	*va_n_-sa_n_k*
26	**vingt-six**	*va_n_-seess*
27	**vingt-sept**	*va_n_-seht*
28	**vingt-huit**	*va_n_-tweet*

29	**vingt-neuf**	*van-nuhf*
30	**trente**	*trahnt*
31	**trente et un**	*trahn-tay-uhn*
32	**trente-deux**	*trahnt-duh*
40	**quarante**	*kah-rahnt*
41	**quarante et un**	*kah-rahn-tay-uhn*
42	**quarante-deux**	*kah-rahnt-duh*
50	**cinquante**	*san-kahnt*
51	**cinquante et un**	*san-kahn-tay-uhn*
52	**cinquante-deux**	*san-kahnt-duh*
60	**soixante**	*swah-ssahnt*
61	**soixante et un**	*swah-ssahn-tay-uhn*
62	**soixante-deux**	*swah-ssahnt-duh*
70	**soixante-dix**	*swah-ssahnt-deess*
71	**soixante et onze**	*swah-ssahn-tay-ohnz*
72	**soixante-douze**	*swah-ssahnt-dooz*
73	**soixante-treize**	*swah-ssahnt-trehz*
74	**soixante-quatorze**	*swah-ssahnt-kah-tohrz*
75	**soixante-quinze**	*swah-ssahnt-kanz*
76	**soixante-seize**	*swah-ssahnt-sehz*
77	**soixante-dix-sept**	*swah-ssahnt-dee-seht*
78	**soixante-dix-huit**	*swah-ssahnt-dee-zweet*
79	**soixante-dix-neuf**	*swah-ssahnt-deez-nuhf*

80	quatre-vingts	*kah-truh-van*
81	quatre-vingt-un	*kah-truh-van-uhn*
82	quatre-vingt-deux	*kah-truh-van-duh*
90	quatre-vingt-dix	*kah-truh-van-deess*
91	quatre-vingt-onze	*kah-truh-van-ohnz*
92	quatre-vingt-douze	*kah-truh-van-dooz*
100	cent	*sahn*
101	cent un	*sahn-uhn*
102	cent deux	*sahn-duh*
110	cent dix	*sahn-deess*
120	cent vingt	*sahn-van*
200	deux cents	*duh-sahn*
201	deux cent un	*duh-sahn-uhn*
330	trois cent trente	*trwah-sahn-trahnt*
1000	mille	*meel*
1001	mille un	*meel-uhn*
1100	{ mille cent onze cents	*meel-sahn* *ohnz-sahn*
1200	{ mille deux cents douze cents	*meel-duh-sahn* *dooz-sahn*
1350	{ mille trois cent cinquante treize cent cinquante	*meel-trwah-sahn-san-kahnt* *trehz-sahn-san-kahnt*
2000	deux mille	*duh-meel*
5000	cinq mille	*sank-meel*
10,000	dix mille	*dee-meel*

100,000	**cent mille**	*sahn-meel*
1,000,000	**un million**	*uhn-mee-lyohn*
198_	**mille neuf cent quatre-vingt_**	*meel-nuhf-sahn kah-truh van*

ORDINAL NUMBERS

first	**premier/première (1ᵉʳ)**	*pruh-myay/pruh-myehr*
second	**deuxième (2ᵉ)**	*duh-zyehm*
third	**troisième**	*trwah-zyehm*
fourth	**quatrième**	*kah-tree-yehm*
fifth	**cinquième**	*san-kyehm*
sixth	**sixième**	*see-zyehm*
seventh	**septième**	*seh-tyehm*
eighth	**huitième**	*wee-tyehm*
ninth	**neuvième**	*nuh-vyehm*
tenth	**dixième**	*dee-zyehm*

QUANTITIES

a half	**une moitié**	*ewn mwah-tyay*
half a	**un/une demi/e**	*uhn/ewn duh-mee*
half of	**la moitié de**	*lah mwah-tyay duh*
a quarter	**un quart**	*uhn kahr*
three quarters	**trois quarts**	*trwah kahr*
a third	**un tiers**	*uhn tyehr*
two thirds	**deux tiers**	*duh tyehr*
a cup of	**une tasse de**	*ewn tahss duh*
a dozen of	**une douzaine de**	*ewn doo-zehn duh*
a kilo of	**un kilo de**	*uhn kee-loh duh*

a liter of	**un litre de**	*uhn lee-truh duh*
a little bit of	**un peu de**	*uhn puh duh*
a lot of	**beaucoup de**	*boh-koo duh*
a pair of	**une paire de**	*ewn pehr duh*
enough of	**assez de**	*ah-ssay duh*
too much of	**trop de**	*troh duh*

TRAVEL TIP

Touring on a budget? Then it pays to do your home-work. Look for hotels or bed-and-breakfast establish-ments that include a morning meal in the price of a room. Often the breakfast is hearty enough to allow a light lunch. Carry nutrition bars from home in your tote bag for snacking when only expensive airport or restaurant food is available. Use public transportation whenever possible. Rail and air passes are sold for Europe and other regions but often can only be purchased in the U.S. before departure. If you must rent a car and have booked one from home, double-check local prices. Sometimes better deals can be arranged on the spot. When you first arrive in a country, check with a visitors' bureau. Agents there will explain discount cards or money-saving packets offered by local governments or merchants. The discount plans often cover transportation, food, lodging, muse-ums, concerts, and other entertainment.

WHEN YOU ARRIVE

PASSPORT AND CUSTOMS

In France at last! Your vacation can't begin until you've shown your passport to the proper authorities and passed through customs.

The following chart shows what duty-free items visitors may bring into France.

DUTY-FREE ITEMS	OUTSIDE EUROPE	COMMON MARKET (EEC)	NON-COMMON MARKET
cigarettes	400	300 OR	200
cigars	100	75 OR	50
pipe tobacco	500 g	400 g	250 g
wine	2L	3L. AND	2L
over 38 proof sp.	1L	1½L	1L
perfume	50 g	75 g	50 g
toilet water	25 cl	25 cl	25 cl

Generally all items for personal use enter the country duty-free and most tourists have little trouble passing through customs. Baggage in hand, you must follow the sign that applies to you: *Articles à déclarer* or *Rien à déclarer* (Nothing to declare). Good luck! You're on your way!

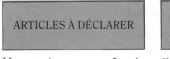

ARTICLES À DÉCLARER

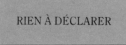

RIEN À DÉCLARER

My name is ____	**Je m'appelle** ____ *zhuh mah-pehl*
I'm American Canadian, British, Australian.	**Je suis américain(e) canadien(ne), anglais(e), australien(ne).** *zhuh swee zah-may-ree-kahn (kehn) kah-nah-dyan (dyehn), ahn-gleh (glehz), ohs-trah-lyan (yehn)*

My address is _____	**Mon adresse est** _____ *mohn nah-drehss eh*
I'm staying at _____	**Je loge à** _____ *zhuh lohzh ah*
Here is (are) _____.	**Voici** _____. *vwah-ssee*
■my documents	**mes papiers** *may pah-pyay*
■my passport	**mon passeport** *mohn pahss-pohr*
■my identification card	**ma carte d'identité** *mah kahrt dee-dahn-tee-tay*
I'm _____.	**Je suis** _____. *zhuh swee*
■on a business trip	**en voyage d'affaires** *zahn vwah-yahzh dah-fehr*
■on vacation	**en vacances** *zahn vah-kahnss*
■on a visit	**en visite** *zahn vee-zeet*
I'll be staying here _____.	**Je resterai ici** _____. *zhuh rehss-tray ee-ssee*
■a few days	**quelques jours** *kehl-kuh zhoor*
■a few weeks	**quelques semaines** *kehl-kuh suh-mehn*
■a week	**huit jours** *wee zhoor*
■two weeks	**quinze jours** *kanz zhoor*
■a month	**un mois** *uhn mwah*
I'm travelling _____.	**Je voyage** _____. *zhuh vwah-yahzh*
■alone	**seul** *suhl*
■with my husband	**avec mon mari** *ah-vehk mohn mah-ree*
■with my wife	**avec ma femme** *ah-vehk mah fahm*
■with my family	**avec ma famille** *ah-vehk mah fah-mee*
These are my bags.	**Voici mes bagages.** *vwah-ssee may bah-gahzh*

I have nothing to declare.	**Je n'ai rien à déclarer.** *zhuh nay ryan ah day-klah-ray*
I only have a carton of cigarettes.	**J'ai seulement une cartouche de cigarettes.** *zhay suhl-mahn ewn kahr-toosh duh see-gah-reht*
■ a bottle of whisky	**une bouteille de whisky** *ewn boo-tehy duh wheess-kee*
They're gifts.	**Ce sont des cadeaux.** *suh sohn day kah-doh*
They're for my personal use.	**Ils sont pour usage personnel.** *eel sohn poor ew-zazh pehr-soh-nehl*
Do I have to pay duty?	**Dois-je payer des droits de douane?** *dwahzh peh-yay day drwah duh dwahn*
May I close my bag now?	**Puis-je fermer ma valise maintenant?** *pweezh fehr-may mah vah-leez mant-nahn*

IDENTITY CARD

Upon entering the country you will be required to fill out an identity card, usually with the following information.

Nom de famille _____ Last name _____

Prénom _____ First name _____

Nationalité _____ Nationality _____

Date de naissance _____ Birthdate _____

Profession _____ Profession _____

Adresse _____ Address _____

Passeport (de) _____ Passport (from) _____

BAGGAGE AND PORTERS

If you can find a porter to help you with your luggage, it is customary to give him/her a tip of about five to seven francs per bag. It will probably be simpler and less expensive, however, to avail yourself of the hand carts now in use at most airports and railway stations. You can usually wheel them right through customs and into the street.

Where can I find a baggage cart?	**Où puis-je trouver un chariot à bagages?** *oo pweezh troo-vay uhn shah-ryoh ah bah-gahzh*
(I need a) porter.	**(Il me faut un) porteur.** *(eel muh foh tuhn) pohr-tuhr*
These are our (my) bags.	**Voici nos (mes) valises.** *vwah-ssee noh (may) vah-leez*
■ that big one	**cette grande** *seht grahnd*
■ these two little ones	**ces deux petites** *say duh puh-teet*
Put them here (there).	**Mettez-les ici (là).** *meh-tay lay zee-ssee (lah)*
Be careful with that one!	**Faites attention avec celle-là!** *feht zah-tahn-ssyohn ah-vehk sehl lah*
I'll carry this one myself.	**Je porterai celle-ci moi-même.** *zhuh pohr-tray sehl see mwah mehm*

I'm missing a suitcase.	**Il me manque une valise.** *eel muh mahnk ewn vah-leez*
How much do I owe you?	**Combien est-ce que je vous dois?** *kohn-byan ehss kuh zhuh voo dwah*
Thank you (very much).	**Merci (beaucoup).** *mehr-ssee (boh-koo)*
This is for you.	**C'est pour vous.** *seh poor voo*

AIRPORT TRANSPORTATION

Where can I get a taxi?	**Où puis-je trouver un taxi?** *oo pweezh troo-vay uhn tahk-ssee*
What buses go into town?	**Quels bus vont en ville?** *kehl bews vohn tahn veel*
Where is the bus stop?	**Où est l'arrêt de bus?** *oo eh lah-reh duh bews*
How much is the fare?	**Quel est le tarif?** *kehl eh luh tah-reef*
Can I rent a car?	**Puis-je louer une voiture?** *pweezh loo-ay ewn vwah-tewr*

TRAVEL TIP

Luggage is sometimes lost or arrives long after you do. To avoid problems, some people travel light and carry on everything. At the very least, take one complete change of clothing, basic grooming items, and any regular medication aboard with you. Because airlines will not replace valuable jewelry when paying for lost luggage, it should be carried on your person. Safer yet, select one set of basic, simple jewelry than can be worn everywhere—even in the shower—and wear it during your whole trip. Remember, carry-on bags must be small enough to fit in overhead bins or to slide under your seat.

BANKING AND MONEY MATTERS

BANKS

Banks generally open between 8:15 and 9:00 and close between 3:00 and 4:45. Some banks close between noon and 1:30, especially during the summer. All banks close at noon the day preceding a holiday. Banks will change foreign currency into francs at the most favorable rate of exchange. *Bureaux de change* at airports or railway stations give a less favorable exchange rate. Some *bureaux de change* on the streets of Paris give very favorable exchange rates. Many hotels will exchange money and travelers' checks, but the rate will be the least favorable.

BANKING TERMS

amount	**le montant**	*luh mohn-tahn*
bad	**mauvais**	*moh-veh*
bad check	**le chèque sans provision**	*luh shehk sahn proh-vee-zyohn*
banker	**le banquier**	*luh bahn-kyay*
bill	**le billet**	*luh bee-yeh*
borrow (to)	**emprunter**	*ahn-pruhn-tay*
cashier	**le caissier**	*luh kehss-yay*
capital	**le capital**	*luh kah-pee-tahl*
cashier's office	**la caisse**	*lah kehss*
checkbook	**le carnet de chèques**	*luh kahr-neh duh shehk*
endorse (to)	**endosser**	*ahn-doh-ssay*
income	**le revenu**	*luh ruh-vuh-new*
interest rate	**le taux d'intérêt**	*luh toh dan-tay-reh*

investment	**le placement**	*luh plahss-mahn*
lend (to)	**prêter**	*preh-tay*
loss	**la perte**	*la pehrt*
make change (to)	**faire de la monnaie**	*fehr duh la mohneh*
mortgage	**l'hypothèque (f.)**	*lee-poh-tehk*
open an account (to)	**ouvrir un compte**	*oo-vreer uhn kohnt*
poster	**l'affiche (f.)**	*lah-feesh*
premium	**la prime**	*lah preem*
profit	**le bénéfice**	*luh bay-nay-feess*
secretary	**le (la) secrétaire**	*luh (lah) seh-kray-tehr*
safe	**le coffre-fort**	*luh koh-fruh fohr*
signature	**la signature**	*lah see-nyah-tewr*
window	**le guichet**	*luh gee-sheh*

MONEY

The franc is the basic unit of French currency. The franc consists of 100 centimes. French money is issued in the following denominations:

- Five (*un sou*), ten and twenty copper-colored centime coins.
- Fifty centime (one-half franc), one franc, two franc, and five franc silver-colored coins.
- Ten franc, dark, copper-colored coin that is replacing the ten franc note which is still in circulation.
- There are 20, 50, 100, 200, and 500 franc bills.

EXCHANGING MONEY

Where can I (change) _____?	**Où puis-je (changer) _____?**	*oo pweezh (shahn-zhay)*
■ money	**de l'argent**	*duh lahr-zhahn*
■ dollars	**des dollars**	*day doh-lahr*
■ travelers' checks	**des chèques de voyage**	*day shehk duh vwah-yahzh*
■ cash a personal check	**toucher un chèque personnel**	*too-shay uhn shehk pehr-soh-nehl*
Where is there a bank?	**Où se trouve une banque?**	*Oo suh troov ewn bahnk*
■ money exchange	**un bureau de change**	*uhn bew-roh duh shahnzh*
At what time do they open (close)?	**À quelle heure ouvre (ferme)-t-on?**	*ah kehl uhr oo-vruh (fehrm) tohn*
Where is the cashier's window?	**Où est la caisse?**	*oo eh la kehss*

The current exchange rates are available in the banks which exchange money, and are also published daily in the newspapers. Since the rates fluctuate from day to day, you may find it helpful to convert the following amounts in francs into their equivalent in your own currency.

FRENCH FRANCS	YOUR CURRENCY
1	
5	
10	
50	
100	
500	

BELGIAN FRANCS	YOUR CURRENCY
10	
20	
50	
100	
500	
1000	

SWISS FRANCS	YOUR CURRENCY
1	
2	
5	
10	
20	
50	
1000	

What's the current exchange rate?	**Quel est le cours (du change) le plus récent?** *kehl eh luh koor (dew shahnzh) luh plew ray-sahn*
I'd like to cash this check.	**Je voudrais toucher ce chèque.** *zhuh voo-dreh too-shay suh shehk*

Where do I sign?	**Où dois-je signer?** *oo dwahzh see-nyay*
Where do I endorse it?	**Où est-ce que je l'endosse?** *oo ehss kuh zhuh lahn-dohss*
I'd like the money in (large) bills.	**Je voudrais l'argent en grosses coupures.** *zhuh voo-dreh lahr-zhahn ahn grohss koo-pewr*
■ in small change	**en petite monnaie** *ahn puh-teet moh-nay*
Give me two twenty-franc bills.	**Donnez-moi deux billets de vingt francs.** *doh-nay mwah duh bee-yeh duh van frahn*
■ fifty	**cinquante** *san-kahnt*
■ one hundred	**cent** *sahn*
Do you accept credit cards?	**Acceptez-vous les cartes de crédit?** *ahk-ssehp-tay voo lay kahrt duh kray-dee*

TIPPING

In many instances, service charges are included in the price of the service rendered. These usually come to about 10 to 15% and should be indicated on the bill.

Usually a customer will leave some small change in addition to any charge that has been included if the service has been satisfactory. At times, a set amount should be given.

The following table is merely a suggested guide. Tips will vary from time to time due to inflation and other factors. It is therefore advisable to ask some knowledgeable person (hotel manager, tour director, etc.) once you get to the country, for proper tipping information, or you should check the rate of exchange.

SERVICE	TIP
Waiter	12–15%
Bellboy, porter	5–6 francs/bag
Chambermaid	8–10 francs/day
Usher	3–4 francs
Taxi driver	10–15% of the fare
Guide	10%
Barber, hairdresser	10–15%
Shoeshine	small change
Bathroom attendant	1–2 francs

TIPPING AT HOTELS

Check to see whether the service charge (usually 10–15%) is included in the room price. The words "service compris" or "toutes taxes comprises" indicate that your tipping obligations have been fulfilled except for the bellboy carrying your luggage and the concierge who may perform special services for you. Should any other employee go out of his way to help you, then a small additional tip would be in order.

TRAVEL TIP

There are many theories on how to survive jet lag— the adjustment to a long trip into a different time zone. Some multinational corporations take jet lag so seriously they do not allow employees to make business decisions on the first day abroad. Most experts agree on several techniques: avoid alcohol but drink plenty of other fluids while flying to avoid dehydration; take frequent strolls around the plane to keep your blood circulating; if possible, get some rest on the flight; ear plugs, an eye mask and an inflatable neck collar make sleep easier; if you arrive early in the morning, take an after-lunch nap, get up for some exercise and dinner, then go to bed at the regular new time; if you arrive at your destination in afternoon or later, skip the nap and let yourself sleep late the next morning; in countries where massage or saunas are standard hotel service, indulge yourself on the evening of arrival to help you sleep soundly that night.

AT THE HOTEL

LODGING

Accommodations are varied, plentiful and are available in different price ranges. If you have not made a reservation and are looking for a place to stay, it is best to go to a tourist information center called le Syndicat d'Initiative (SI) or Office du Tourisme (OT). Someone there will gladly help you find a room to suit your needs and your budget. You will find yourself staying at one of the following:

HOTEL

Although there are hotel rooms in every price range, it is best to make an advance reservation. Festivals, exhibitions, shows and trade fairs attract many visitors and rooms are quickly filled. The French government rates hotels by using a star system ranging from * inexpensive to **** expensive (*luxe*). A hotel receives its rating based on room price and the conveniences it provides: size of room, telephone availability, bathroom facilities. A continental breakfast, consisting of rolls, butter and jam and coffee or tea is often included in the price of the room. English is spoken in the larger, more exclusive hotels, and American style breakfasts are usually available there.

MOTEL

Motels have recently spread to France. They are located near main roads outside towns and cities and at the airport.

PENSION

Pensions resemble rooming houses where the visitor pays for a room and all or part of his meals.

AUBERGE (LOGIS)

This is usually a small, modest and inexpensive country inn found off the main roads in rural areas.

CHAMBRES D'HÔTE

In towns or villages rooms are made available in the homes of local families who will supply bed and breakfast for a fee.

GÎTES RURAUX

If you visit the countryside, you may rent a gîte, a private residence—house or apartment.

You should be aware that in France, especially outside of Paris, it is customary and expected that a guest eat dinner at his hotel. Many smaller hotels will charge you for dinner whether you eat it or not, or refuse to rent the room unless you eat in the hotel. You may inquire about this at the desk.

GETTING TO YOUR HOTEL

I'd like to go to the ____ Hotel.	**Je voudrais aller à l'hôtel ____ .** *zhuh voo-dreh zah-lay ah loh-tel*
Is it near (far)?	**C'est près (loin) d'ici?** *seh preh (lwan) dee-ssee*
Where can I get a taxi?	**Où puis-je trouver un taxi?** *oo pweezh troo-vay uhn tahk-see*
How much is the fare?	**Quel est le tarif?** *kehl eh luh tah-reef*
Where is the bus stop?	**Où est l'arrêt de bus?** *oo eh lah-reh duh bews*

CHECKING IN

When you register, it will be necessary to fill out a form (une fiche) with your name, address and passport number at the registration desk of any establishment.

I'd like a single (double) room for tonight ____.	**Je voudrais une chambre à un lit (à deux lits) pour ce soir ____ .** *zhuh voo-dreh zewn shahn-bruh ah uhn lee (ah duh lee) poor suh swahr*

■ with a shower	**avec douche** *ah-vehk doosh*
■ with a bath	**avec salle de bains** *ah-vehk sahl duh banh*
■ with a balcony	**avec balcon** *ah-vehk bahl-kohn*
■ facing the ocean	**qui donne sur l'océan** *kee dohn sewr loh-ssay-ahn*
■ facing the street	**qui donne sur la rue** *kee dohn sewr lah rew*
■ facing the court-yard	**qui donne sur la cour** *kee dohn sewr lah koor*
Does it have ____?	**Y a-t-il ____?** *ee ah teel*
■ air conditioning	**la climatisation** *lah klee-mah-tee-zah-ssyohn*
■ hot water	**l'eau chaude** *loh shohd*
■ television	**une télévision** *ewn tay-lay-vee-zyohn*
■ a private bathroom	**une douche et des toilettes privées** *ewn doosh ay day twah-leht pree-vay*
■ shower	**une douche** *ewn doosh*
I (don't) have a reservation.	**J'ai (Je n'ai pas) retenu (réservé)** *zhay (zhuh nay pah) ruh-tuh-new·ray-ssehr-vay·wn (duh) shahn-bruh*
Could you call another hotel to see if they have something?	
May I see the room?	**Puis-je voir la chambre?** *pweezh vwahr lah shahn-bruh*
I (don't) like it.	**Elle me plaît.** *ehl muh pleh*
	Elle ne me plaît pas. *ehl nuh muh pleh pah*

Do you have something ____?	**Avez-vous quelque chose ____?** *ah-vay voo kehl-kuh shohz*
■ better	**de meilleur** *duh meh-yuhr*
■ larger	**de plus grand** *duh plew grahn*
■ smaller	**de plus petit** *duh plew puh-tee*
■ cheaper	**de meilleur marché** *duh meh-yuhr mahr-shay*
On what floor is it?	**C'est à quel étage?** *seht ah kehl ay-tahzh*
Is there an elevator?	**Y a-t-il un ascenseur?** *ee ah teel uhn nah-sahn-suhr*
How much do you charge for ____?	**Quel est le tarif ____?** *kehl eh luh tah-reef*
■ the American plan	**pension complète** *pahn-ssyohn kohn-pleht*
■ bed and breakfast	**petit déjeuner compris** *puh-tee day-zhuh-nay kohn-pree*

■ breakfast and dinner	**en demi-pension** *ahn duh-mee pahn-ssyohn*
■ the room without meals	**pour la chambre sans repas** *poor lah shahn-bruh sahn ruh-pah*
Is it necessary to eat here?	**Faut-il manger ici?** *foh-teel man-zhay ee-see*
Is everything included?	**Est-ce que tout est compris?** *ehss kuh too teh kohn-pree*
The room is very nice. I'll take it.	**Cette chambre me plaît. Je la prends.** *seht shahn-bruh muh pleh. Zhuh lah prahn*
I prefer a room in the back.	**Je préfère une chambre sur la cour.** *zhuh pray-fehr ewn shahn-bruh sewr lah koor*
Is there a reduction for children?	**Accordez-vous des réductions aux enfants?** *ah-kohr-day voo day ray-dewk-ssyohn oh zahn-fahn*
Could you put another bed in the room?	**Pourriez-vous mettre un autre lit dans la chambre?** *poo-ree-yay voo meh-truh uhn noh-truh lee dahn lah shahn-bruh*
Is there a charge? How much?	**Faut-il payer pour cela? Combien?** *foh teel peh-yay poor suh-lah? kohn-byan*

OTHER ACCOMMODATIONS

I'm looking for _____.	**Je cherche _____.** *zhuh shehrsh*
■ a boarding house	**une pension** *ewn pahn-ssyohn*
■ a private house	**une maison particulière** *ewn meh-zohn pahr-tee-kew-lyehr*
I want to rent an apartment.	**Je voudrais louer un appartement.** *zhuh voo-dreh loo-ay uhn nah-pahr-tuh-mahn*

| I need a living room, bedroom and kitchen. | **Il me faut un salon, une chambre à coucher et une cuisine.** *eel muh foh tuhn sah-lohn, ewn shah-bruh ah koo-shay ay ewn kwee-zeen* |

| Do you have a furnished room? | **Avez-vous une chambre meublée? (garnie?)** *ah-vay voo zewn shahn-bruh muh-blay (gahr-nee)* |

| How much is the rent? | **C'est combien le loyer?** *seh kohn-byan luh lwah-yay* |

| I'll be staying here for _____. | **Je resterai ici _____.** *zhuh rehss-tray ee-ssee* |

| ■ two weeks | **quinze jours** *kahnz zhoor* |

| ■ one month | **un mois** *uhn mwah* |

| ■ the whole summer | **tout l'été** *too lay-tay* |

| I want a place that's centrally located near public transportation. | **Je voudrais (avoir) une résidence située au centre de la ville près des transports publics.** *zhuh voo-dreh zah-vwahr ewn ray-zee-dahnss see-tew-ay oh sahn-truh duh lah veel preh deh trahnss-pohr pew-bleek* |

| Is there a youth hostel around here? | **Y a-t-il une auberge de jeunesse par ici?** *ee ah teel ewn oh-behrzh duh zhuh-nehss preh dee-ssee* |

ORDERING BREAKFAST

The French or Continental breakfast is usually simple—coffee or chocolate, a croissant or brioche with jam or marmalade. At the larger hotels you will be able to order an English-style breakfast (juice, eggs, bacon, toast). You may enjoy having breakfast in your room.

| We'll have breakfast in the room. | **Nous prendrons le petit déjeuner dans la chambre.** *noo prahn-drohn luh puh-tee day-zhuh-nay dahn lah shahn-bruh* |

Please send up ____	**Faites monter ____ s'il vous plaît** *feht mohn-tay seel voo pleh*
■ One (two) coffee(s)	**Un (deux) café(s)** *uhn (duh) kah-fay*
■ Tea	**Un thé** *uhn tay*
■ Chocolate	**Un chocolat** *uhn shoh-koh-lah*
■ A (some) croissant(s)	**Un (des) croissant(s)** *uhn (day) krwah-ssahn*
■ Fruit	**Des fruits** *day frwee*
■ Fruit juice	**Du jus de fruit** *dew zhew duh frwee*
I'll (we'll) eat breakfast in the dining room.	**Je (nous) prendrai (prendrons) le petit déjeuner dans la salle à manger.** *zhuh (noo) prahn-dray (prahn-drohn) luh puh-tee day-zhuh-nay dahn lah sahl ah mahn-zhay*
We'd like ____	**Nous voudrions ____** *noo voo-dree-yohn*
■ Scrambled (fried) (boiled) eggs	**Des oeufs brouillés (au plat) (à la coque)** *day zuh broo-yay (oh plah) (ah lah kohk)*
■ Toast	**Du pain grillé** *dew pan gree-yay*
■ Jam	**De la confiture** *duh lah kohn-fee-tewr*

NOTE: See Food section (pp. 77–107) for more phrases for ordering meals

HOTEL SERVICE

Where is ____?	**Où sont ____?** *oo sohn*
■ the dining room	**la salle à manger** *lah sahl ah mahn-zhay*
■ the bathroom	**les toilettes** *lay twah-leht*

■the elevator	**l'ascenseur** *lah-ssahn-ssuhr*
■the phone	**le téléphone** *luh tay-lay-fohn*
What is my room number?	**Quel est le numéro de ma chambre?** *kehl eh luh new-may-roh duh mah shahn-bruh*
May I please have my key?	**Pourrais-je avoir la clef?** *poo-rehzh ah-vwahr lah klay*
I need _____.	**Il me faut _____.** *eel muh foh*
■a bellboy	**un chasseur** *tuhn shah-ssuhr*
■a chambermaid	**une femme de chambre** *tewn fahm duh shahn-bruh*
Please send me _____.	**Veuillez m'envoyer _____.** *vuh-yay mahn-vwah-yay*
■breakfast	**le petit déjeuner** *luh puh-tee day-zhuh-nay*
■a towel	**une serviette** *ewn sehr-vyeht*
■a bar of soap	**une savonnette** *ewn sah-voh-neht*
■some hangers	**des cintres** *day san-truh*
■a pillow	**un oreiller** *uhn noh-reh-yay*
■a blanket	**une couverture** *ewn koo-vehr-tewr*
■some ice	**de la glace** *duh lah glahss*
■ice cubes	**des glaçons** *day glah-ssohn*
■some ice water	**de l'eau glacée** *duh loh glah-ssay*
■an ashtray	**un cendrier** *uhn sahn-dree-yay*
■toilet paper	**un rouleau de papier hygiénique** *uhn roo-loh duh pah-pyay ee-zhyay-neek*
■a bottle of mineral water	**une bouteille d'eau minérale** *ewn boo-tehy doh mee-nay-rahl*

■ a reading lamp — **une lumière pour lire** *ewn lew-myehr poor leer*

■ an electric adaptor — **un transformateur** *uhn trahnss-fohr-mah-tuhr*

NOTE: Electrical current is usually 220 volts. A European-style adaptor plug or an adaptable appliance is necessary for electric hair dryers or clocks. Large international hotels may have an adaptor plug at the reception desk, but smaller hotels or pensions are unlikely to be able to provide one.

Just a minute.	**Un moment.** *uhn moh-mahn*	
Come in.	**Entrez.** *ahn-tray*	
Put it on the table.	**Mettez-ça sur la table.** *meh-tay sah sewr lah tah-bluh*	
Will you wake me?	**Voulez-vous bien me réveiller?** *voo-lay voo byan muh ray-veh-yay*	
Please wake me to-morrow at ___	**Réveillez-moi demain matin à ___, s'il vous plaît.** *ray-veh-yay mwah duh-man mah-tan ah seel voo pleh*	
There is no ___.	**Il n'y a pas ___.** *eel nyah pah*	

■ running water — **d'eau courante** *doh koo-rahnt*

■ hot water — **d'eau chaude** *doh shohd*

■ electricity — **d'électricité** *day-lehk-tree-ssee-tay*

The ___ doesn't work. — **___ ne fonctionne pas.** *nuh fohnk-ssyohn pah*

■ air conditioning — **le climatiseur** *luh klee-mah-tee-zuhr*

■ fan — **le ventilateur** *luh vahn-tee-lah-tuhr*

■ faucet — **le robinet** *luh roh-bee-neh*

■ lamp — **la lampe** *lah lahnp*

■ light — **la lumière** *lah lew-myehr*

- radio **la radio** *lah rah-dyoh*
- socket **la prise de courant** *lah preez duh koo-rah<u>n</u>*
- switch **le commutateur** *luh koh-mew-tah-tuhr*
- television **la télévision** *lah tay-lay-vee-zyoh<u>n</u>*

Can you fix it? **Pouvez-vous la réparer** *poo-vay voo lah ray-pah-ray*

- now **maintenent** *ma<u>n</u>t-nah<u>n</u>*
- as soon as possible **aussitôt que possible** *oh-ssee-toh kuh poh-ssee-bluh*

The room is dirty. **La chambre est sale.** *lah shah<u>n</u>-bruh eh sahl*

Are there any ____ for me? **Y a-t-il ____ pour moi.** *ee ah teel poor mwah*

- letters **des lettres** *day leh-truh*
- messages **des messages** *day meh-ssahzh*
- packages **des colis** *day koh-lee*
- post cards **des cartes postales** *day kahrt pohss-tahl*

Did anyone call for me? **Est-ce que quelqu'un m'a téléphoné?** *ehss kuh kehl kuh<u>n</u> mah tay-lay-foh-nay*

Who is it? **Qui est-ce?** *kee ehss*

Can you make a phone call for me? **Pouvez-vous faire un appel téléphonique pour moi?** *poo-vay voo fehr uh<u>n</u> nah-pehl tay-lay-foh-neek poor mwah*

I'd like to put this in the hotel safe. **Je voudrais mettre ceci dans le coffre-fort de l'hôtel.** *zhuh voo-dreh meh-truh ssuh-ssee dah<u>n</u> luh koh-fruh-fohr duh loh-tehl*

CHECKING OUT

I'd like the bill, please.	**Je voudrais la note, s'il vous plaît.** *zhuh voo-dreh lah noht-ssyohn seel voo pleh*
I'm leaving today (tomorrow).	**Je pars aujourd'hui (demain).** *zhuh pahr oh-zhoor-dwee (duh-man)*
Please send someone up for the baggage.	**Faites monter quelqu'un pour les valises, s'il vous plaît.** *feht mohn-tay kehl-kuhn poor lay vah-leez seel voo pleh*

TRAVEL TIP

Most airlines allow passengers to select a seat location and the type of meal preferred at the time reservations are made. Especially on overseas flights, good choices mean the difference between a pleasant or a miserable trip. To get some sleep, choose a window seat well away from the galley (kitchen area). If you like to walk around, request an aisle seat. To watch the movie, avoid the row facing the bulkhead. If you don't smoke, ask to be placed well away from the smokers. The reservations agent will know the aircraft being used and can help you pick the best location. Among the meal options are vegetarian, kosher, and low-fat menus. If you have other special dietary needs, ask the reservations agent if those can be met. Be sure to confirm your seat assignment and meal choice when checking in for the flight.

GETTING AROUND TOWN

In villages or out in the country you may want to stroll around to do your sightseeing. Although walking in the city is also rewarding, you'll want to be familiar with the types of public transportation available.

For information on plane, train or boat travel, see pp. 53–58.

THE SUBWAY

The subway (LE MÉTRO), is the clean, inexpensive and efficient underground train system in Paris. A big "M" indicates a metro stop. Large subway maps help you locate the correct line to take. For convenience and economy, a book of 10 tickets (**un carnet**) is available for regular riders. Daily and weekly passes for unlimited rides can be purchased at reasonable rates. Frequent riders may purchase an orange card (**carte orange**) which permits unlimited rides for a month. The Métro closes at 1:30 AM and at 2:00 AM on Fridays and Saturdays.

Is there a subway in this city?	**Y a-t-il un métro dans cette ville?** *ee ah teel uhn may-troh dahn seht veel*
Where is there a subway station?	**Où se trouve une station de métro?** *oo suh troov ewn stah-ssyohn duh may-troh*
How much is the fare?	**Quel est le prix du trajet?** *kehl eh luh pree dew trah-zheh*
Where can I buy a ticket?	**Où puis-je acheter un billet?** *oo pweezh ahsh-tay uhn bee-yeh*
Which line goes to _____?	**Quelle ligne va à _____?** *kehl lee-nyuh vah ah*
Does this train go to _____?	**Est-ce que ce train va à _____?** *ehss kuh suh tran vah ah*

How many more stops?	**Il nous reste combien d'arrêts?** *eel noo rehsst koh<u>n</u>-bya<u>n</u> dah-reh*
What's the next station?	**Quelle est la prochaine station?** *kehl eh lah proh-shehn stah-ssyoh<u>n</u>*
Where should I get off to go to ____?	**Où dois-je descendre pour aller à ____?** *oo dwahzh day-sah<u>n</u>-druh poor ah-lay ah*
Do I have to change?	**Faut-il prendre une correspondance?** *foh teel prah<u>n</u>-druh ewn koh-rehss-poh<u>n</u>-dah<u>n</u>ss*
Please tell me when we get there.	**S'il vous plaît, dites-moi quand nous y arriverons.** *seel voo pleh, deet mwah kah<u>n</u> noo zee ah-ree-v roh<u>n</u>*

Défense de cracher	No spitting

In the trains, buses, and metro, certain seats with numbers are reserved. You may sit in one of those seats if there are enough seats vacant. A war veteran may come up to you and show you his ID card, and in that case, you have to give him your seat. You may see the following notices posted:

LES PLACES NUMÉROTÉES SONT RÉSERVÉES:	NUMBERED SEATS ARE RESERVED FOR:
1. Aux invalides de guerre	Disabled veterans
2. Aux invalides civils	Handicapped persons
3. Aux femmes enceintes	Pregnant women
4. Aux personnes accompagnées d'enfants de moins de 4 ans	Persons with children under 4 years of age.

THE BUS (STREETCAR, TRAM)

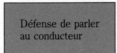

European Express and Europabus serve major European cities. They are less expensive, but slower, than trains. If you plan to travel around the city by bus, you may purchase a discount book of tickets *(un carnet)*. Be sure to have some small change on entering the bus.

Défense de parler au conducteur	Do not speak to the driver

Where is the bus stop? (bus terminal)?	**Où est l'arrêt de bus?/le terminus?** *oo eh lah-reh duh bewss/luh tehr-mee-newss*
Which bus do I take to get to ____?	**Quel bus faut-il prendre pour aller à ____?** *kehl bewss foh teel prahn-druh poor ah-lay ah*
In which direction do I have to go?	**Dans quel sens dois-je aller?** *dahn kehl sahnss dwahzh ah-lay*
How often do the buses run?	**Quelle est la fréquence des bus?** *kehl eh lah fray-kahnss day bewss*
Do you go to ____?	**Est-ce que vous allez à ____?** *ehss kuh voo zah-lay ah*
I want to go to ____.	**Je voudrais aller à ____.** *zhuh voo-dreh zah-lay ah*
Is it far from here?	**C'est loin d'ici?** *seh lwan dee-ssee*
How many stops are there?	**Il y a combien d'arrêts?** *eel yah kohn-byan dah-reh*
Do I have to change?	**Faut-il changer de bus?** *foh teel shahn-zhay duh bewss*
How much is the fare?	**Quel est le prix du trajet?** *kehl eh luh pree dew trah-zheh*

Could you tell me where to get off?

Pourriez-vous me dire quand je dois descendre? *poo-ree-yay voo muh deer kahn zhuh dwah day-sahn-druh*

Where do I get off?

Où dois-je descendre? *oo dwahzh day-sahn-druh*

TAXIS

Taxis, except for certain ones making trips to and from the airport, which give a flat rate, are metered. Look for the sign **Stationnement de Taxis** indicating a taxi stand. You cannot hail a taxi on the street within 100 meters of a stand. There is a supplement (indicated on the meter) after 11 p.m.

Is there a taxi stand around here?

Y a-t-il une station de taxis près d'ici? *ee ah teel ewn stah-ssyohn duh tahk-ssee preh dee-ssee*

Where can I get a taxi?

Où puis-je trouver un taxi? *oo pweezh troo-vay uhn tahk-ssee*

Taxi! Are you available?

Taxi! Êtes-vous libre? *tahk-ssee eht voo lee-bruh*

Take me (I want to go) ____.

Conduisez-moi (Je voudrais aller) ____. *kohn-dwee-zay mwah (zhuh voo-dreh zah-lay)*

■ to the airport

à l'aéroport *ah lahy-roh-pohr*

■ to this address

à cette adresse *ah seht ah-drehss*

■ to the hotel

à l'hôtel *ah loh-tehl*

■ to the station

à la gare *ah lah gahr*

■ to ____ Street

à la rue ____ *ah lah rew*

Do you know where it is?

Savez-vous où ça se trouve? *sah-vay voo oo sah suh troov*

How much is it to ____?

C'est combien pour aller à ____? *seh kohn-byan poor ah-lay ah*

Faster! I'm in a hurry.	**Allez plus vite! Je suis pressé(e)!** *ah-lay plew veet zhuh swee preh-ssay*
Please drive slower.	**Conduisez plus lentement, s'il vous plaît.** *koh<u>n</u>-dwee-zay plew lah<u>n</u>t-mah<u>n</u> seel voo pleh*
Don't go so fast.	**Ne conduisez pas si vite, s'il vous plaît.** *Nuh koh<u>n</u>-dwee-zay pah see veet seel voo pleh*
Stop here at the corner.	**Arrêtez-vous ici, au coin.** *ah-reh-tay voo zee-ssee, oh kwa<u>n</u>*
Stop at the next block.	**Arrêtez-vous à la prochaine rue.** *ah-reh-tay voo ah lah proh-shehn rew*
Wait for me. I'll be right back.	**Attendez-moi, s'il vous plaît. Je reviens tout de suite.** *ah-tah<u>n</u>-day mwah seel voo pleh zhuh ruh-vya<u>n</u> toot sweet*
How much do I owe you?	**Combien est-ce que je vous dois?** *koh<u>n</u>-bya<u>n</u> ehss kuh zhuh voo dwah*
This is for you.	**Voilà pour vous.** *vwah-lah poor voo*

Where is the Tourist Office? | **Où est le Syndicat d'Initiative?** *oo eh luh sa**n**-dee-kah dee-nee-ssyah-teev*

I need an (English speaking) guide. | **J'ai besoin d'un guide (qui parle anglais).** *zhay buh-zwa**n** duh**n** geed (kee pahrl ah**n**-gleh)*

How much does he charge _____? | **Quel est le prix _____?** *kehl eh luh pree*
C'est combien _____? *seh koh**n**-bya**n***

■ per hour | **à l'heure** *ah luhr*

■ per day | **à la journée** *ah lah zhoor-nay*

There are two (four, six) of us. | **Nous sommes deux (quatre, six).** *noo sohm duh (kah-truh, seess)*

Where can I buy a guide book? (a map) | **Où puis-je acheter un guide touristique? (une carte)** *oo pweez ahsh-tay uh**n** geed too-reess-teek (ewn kahrt)*

What are the main attractions? | **Qu'est-ce qu'il y a de plus intéressant?** *kehss keel yah duh plew za**n**-tay-reh-ssah**n***

What are things of interest here? | **Qu'est-ce qu'il y a d'intéressant à voir par ici?** *kehss keel yah da**n**-tay-reh-ssah**n** ah vwahr pahr ee-ssee*

Are there trips through the city? | **Y a-t-il des visites guidées à travers la ville?** *ee ah teel day vee-zeet gee-day ah trah-vehr lah veel*

Where do they leave from? | **D'où partent-elles?** *doo pahr tehl*

We want to see _____. | **Nous voudrions voir _____.** *noo vood-ree-yoh**n** vwahr*

■ the botanical garden | **le jardin botanique** *luh zhahr-da**n** boh-tah-neek*

■ the business center | **le quartier des affaires** *luh kahr-tyay day zah-fehr*

■ the castle | **le château** *luh shah-toh*

■ the cathedral	**la cathédrale** *lah kah-tay-drahl*
■ the church	**l'église** *lay-gleez*
■ the concert hall	**la salle de concert** *lah sahl duh kohn-ssehr*
■ the downtown area	**le centre de la ville** *luh sahn-truh duh la veel*
■ the fountains	**les fontaines** *lay fohn-tehn*
■ the library	**la bibliothèque** *lah bee-blee-oh-tehk*
■ the main park	**le parc principal** *luh pahrk pran-ssee-pahl*
■ the main square	**la place principale** *lah plahss pran-ssee-pahl*
■ the market	**le marché** *luh mahr-shay*
■ the mosque	**la mosquée** *lah mohss-kay*
■ the museum (of fine arts)	**le musée des beaux arts** *luh mew-zay day boh zahr*
■ a nightclub	**une boîte de nuit** *ewn bwaht duh nwee*
■ the old part of town	**la vieille ville** *lah vyehy veel*
■ the opera	**l'opéra** *loh-pay-rah*
■ the palace	**le palais** *luh pah-leh*
■ the stadium	**le stade** *luh stahd*
■ the synagogue	**la synagogue** *lah see-nah-gohg*
■ the university	**l'université** *lew-nee-vehr-ssee-tay*
■ the zoo	**le zoo** *luh zoh*
Is it all right to go in now?	**Peut-on entrer maintenant?** *puh tohn ahn-tray mant-nahn*
Is it open?	**C'est ouvert?** *seh too-vehr*
Is it closed?	**C'est fermé?** *seh fehr-may*

At what time does it open?	**À quelle heure ouvre -t-il / elle?** *ah kehl uhr oo-vruh teel/ tehl*
At what time does it close?	**À quelle heure ferme-t-il/elle?** *ah kehl uhr fehrm teel/tehl*
What are the visiting hours?	**Quelles sont les heures de visite?** *kehl sohn lay zuhr duh vee-zeet*
What's the admission price?	**Combien coûte un billet d'entrée?** *kohn-byan koot uhn bee-yeh dahn-tray*
How much do children pay?	**C'est combien pour les enfants?** *seh kohn-byan poor lay zahn-fahn*
Can they go in free? Until what age?	**Est-ce gratuit pour les enfants? Jusqu'à quel âge?** *ehss grah-twee poor lay zahn-fahn. zhewss-kah kehl ahzh*
Is it all right to take pictures?	**Peut-on prendre des photos?** *puh tohn prahn-druh day foh-toh*

A SIGHTSEEING ITINERARY

France is a country overwhelmingly rich in places and things to be seen. Its cities and countryside overflow with sites and institutions redolent of historic, intellectual and artistic tradition. Few indeed are the areas not commemorated by a general's triumph, a king's passage, an artist's inspiration or a philosopher's wit. To attempt an exhaustive tour in the usual short vacation span would be foolhardy. We try here simply to suggest, in broad outline, some of the highlights, the best-known and most popular attractions to which visitors are drawn. Modern France has an extensive and sophisticated system of public transportation, enabling the traveler to get quickly to whatever area most interests him.

PARIS

Paris is the cultural, economic, political and social center of France. Among its museums are: The *Louvre,* which contains the Venus de Milo and the Mona Lisa, and also Leoh Ming Pei's controversial new Pyramid, as well as art and antiquities from all over Europe; the *Army Museum* by the *Invalides* with Napoleon's tomb; the *Panthéon*, commemorating illustrious French people; and the *Cluny Museum* with beautiful medieval art. For a glimpse of the future, there's the new *Cité des Sciences* in northern Paris, with its geodesic dome and giant-screen science movies.

Those with an interest in church sculpture and architecture will be particularly interested in the Cathedral of *Notre-Dame*. Its spires, portals, stained glass windows and flying buttresses make it a milestone in Gothic architecture. Vividly colored stained glass windows dating back to the 13th century and portraying over 1,000 biblical scenes make the *Sainte-Chapelle* church unique. *Sacré-Coeur,* the domed white church dominating Montmartre, resembles a mosque and is decorated on the interior with mosaics. The 18th-19th century church of the *Madeleine* with its colonnade is also of some interest.

Noted public squares frequented by tourists include: the *Place de la Concorde,* where many historical figures, including Louis XVI and Marie Antoinette, were guillotined during the French Revolution. The obelisk in the middle of the square comes from the ruins of the temple at Luxor in Egypt and is covered with hieroglyphics. The *Place Vendôme* is the site of the Vendôme column, which has scenes depicting Napoleon's military campaigns at its center. On top of the column is a statue of the emperor. The *Place de l'Opéra,* dominated by the Opéra, is the home of the national opera and ballet companies and renowned for its architecture and decor. The *Place de la Bastille* is the site of the once famous prison, since destroyed, where the first shots of the Revolution are commemorated every July 14. The *Place Charles de Gaulle,* upon which stands the *Arc de Triomphe,* is one of France's best known landmarks. Under the arch is the tomb of the Unknown Soldier. Twelve avenues fan out from the arch, creating the pattern of a star. Leading to the arch, the Champs Elysées is lined with trees, cafés and luxurious shops.

The *Centre National d'Art et de Culture Georges Pompidou,* on the site of the old Les Halles market, is a national museum with frequent expositions and a voluminous research library. From the observation deck on the roof you can see all of Paris.

The *Eiffel Tower* stands over 1,000 feet tall and acts as a radio and television transmitter. From any of its three different levels one gets a panoramic view of Paris. At its base there is a popular restaurant. Walking along the *quais* of the *Seine* you will find the parapets lined with quaint bookshops. *Montmartre,* or the "Butte," as it is commonly known, is a center of artistic life where bohemianism may be said to have its roots. The *Latin Quarter* is the home of the Sorbonne University and an intellectual hub.

At the *Palais de Justice,* the seat of the courts and all the judicial system, you will see the *Conciergerie* which served as a prison during the Revolution. Also not to be missed are *La Bourse* or Stock Exchange, and *Le Marché aux puces,* the Paris flea market.

When your feet hurt and you want to take a break, relax in the *Tuileries* gardens, beside the Seine. Statues, figures and decorative vases line these formal French gardens. The *Bois de Boulogne* is a vast park containing ornamental lakes, flower gardens, cafés, restaurants, two racetracks and a children's amusement park. Best, however, not to frequent it at night. The *Bois de Vincennes* contains museums and a zoo. The *Luxembourg* gardens, on the left bank, are much used by students.

Just outside of Paris is *Versailles,* the luxurious palace known for its architecture, style, and gardens. A bus tour from Paris to Versailles might also include side trips to *Fontainebleau* and *Chantilly* castles. The *Basilica of Saint Denis,* and the small city of *Sèvres,* known for its multicolored porcelain, are also not far from the capital.

FARTHER AFIELD

A bus tour of the *Loire* valley enables one to visit many splendid castles, among them *Chambord* and *Chenonceaux.* This tour might include a trip to the *Chartres* cathedral, which contains sculptures representing biblical personages. The stained glass windows of the cathedral are unique, drawing visitors who travel to France just to see them.

The beaches of *Normandy,* where the Allies landed in 1944, will be of special interest to history buffs.

Mont-Saint-Michel, a monastery surrounded by a medieval

fortress, is situated on a small island in the English Channel, between Normandy and Brittany.

A visit to the *wine country,* the regions of Bordeaux, Champagne and Languedoc, will be interesting and informative.

Strasbourg, an industrial city, has a cathedral famous for its astronomical clock. It also contains the offices of the EEC, the European Economic Community known as the Common Market.

The cities of *Chamonix* and *Grenoble,* and the *French Alps,* are extremely popular and offer a wide variety of winter activities.

Nice, capital of the *Riviera,* vacation spot of the jet-set and refuge from the ravages of winter, has pebble beaches and a casino. If you prefer a sand beach, *Cannes,* also on the *Côte d'Azur,* is a pleasant alternative.

On a side trip to *Monaco,* a visit to Prince Rainier's palace provides a view of the harbor and the yachts moored there. The casino at *Monte Carlo* is its principal attraction.

In *Avignon* there is the *Palace of the Popes* and the *Bridge of St. Bénézet. Nîmes* and *Arles,* quaint cities noted for their Roman ruins, have amphitheaters still in their original form. *Lourdes* has a shrine that attracts religious pilgrims and those seeking relief from illness or injury.

OUTSIDE FRANCE

For a glimpse of France closer to the United States, visit *Québec* with its magnificent beaches, parks, mountains, forests and lakes. Participate in your favorite summer or winter sport. See the old and the new cities and visit the charming castles.

If you prefer a tranquil vacation, visit a tropical island. Rest in the shade of the palm and coconut trees of *Martinique* or *Guadeloupe* in the Lesser Antilles. Enjoy the beaches, the languorous life style and the fruit-flavored daiquiris. In Martinique, tour the capital, *Fort-de-France,* see the ruins of *Saint-Pierre* and *Mt. Pelée,* and the luxuriant rain forest. In Guadeloupe, the town of *Gosier* is the heart of vacation life. At *Le Moule,* the horseshoe beach is one of the island's most popular attractions. Or visit *Haiti,* on the island of Hispaniola, in the Greater Antilles. Horseback ride to the famed *Citadelle,* tour *Port-au-Prince,* the capital, relax by the *waterfalls of Cayes* and lie on the beautiful beaches of *Port Salut*.

AMUSEMENT PARKS

Two amusement parks not far from Paris will delight children and adults as well.

Just 20 miles east of Paris at Marne-La-Vallée is *Euro-Disney*'s new $4 billion theme park, complete with Mickey Mouse, Donald Duck, and their friends. Its 29 attractions in five different "lands" and the six hotels, artificial lakes, and entertainment grounds cover an area one fifth the size of Paris. The admission price is the equivalent of $40 for adults and $20 for children. The park is serviced by the R.E.R. (Réseau Express Régional), the suburban railroad line that makes Paris a mere 45 minutes away. The T.G.V. (train à grande vitesse), the high-speed French train, will also include a stop on its lines to accommodate tourists. Although the Disney Company remains adamant in its decision not to serve traditional French wine, it boasts that the quality of food in Euro-Disneyland surpasses that of its other theme parks.

But if it's typical French amusement that you seek, try *Parc Astérix*, 20 miles north of Paris. A giant roller coaster, a dolphin lake, and a replica of a Romano-Gallic village dominate this park, based on the exploits of Astérix le Gaulois, the famous and much-loved comic-book character, whose fictional exploits took place 2,000 years ago during the Roman invasion of France.

TRAVEL TIP

Packing for a trip abroad is an art. Porters may sometimes be hard to find, so never take more luggage than you can handle alone. Wrap shampoo, mouthwash, or anything that can leak in recycled plastic bags or small plastic bottles. To prevent wrinkling, pack suits, dresses, etc. in dry cleaning bags.

PLANNING A TRIP

During your stay, you may want to plan some longer excursions. In France you can get around by moped (**mobylette**), bicycle or even hiking. For more extensive trips, boats, planes, and trains are all readily available, as are rental cards (see Driving a Car). You may even rent a barge to travel through France on an elaborate canal system.

AIR SERVICE

When is there a flight to ____?	**Quand y a-t-il un vol pour ____?** *kahn tee ah teel uhn vohl poor*
I would like a round trip (one way) ticket in tourist class (first class).	**Je voudrais un aller et retour (un aller) en seconde classe (première classe).** *zhuh voo-dreh zuhn ah-lay ay ruh-toor (uhn nah-lay) ahn suh-gohnd klahss (pruh-myehr klahss)*
A seat ____.	**Une place ____.** *ewn plahss*
■ in the smoking section	**dans la section fumeurs.** *dahn lah sehk-ssyohn few-muhr*
■ in the non-smoking section	**dans la section non-fumeurs** *dahn lah sehk-ssyohn nohn few-muhr*
■ next to the window	**à côté de la fenêtre** *ah koh-tay duh lah fuh-neh-truh*
■ on the aisle	**côté couloir** *koh-tay koo-lwahr*
What is the fare?	**Quel est le tarif?** *kehl eh luh tah-reef*
Are meals served?	**Sert-on des repas?** *sehr tohn day ruh-pah*
At what time does the plane leave?	**À quelle heure part l'avion?** *ah kehl uhr pahr lah vyohn*
At what time do we arrive?	**À quelle heure arrivons-nous?** *ah kehl uhr ah-reev-ohn noo*

When do we land in _____?	**Quand est-ce que l'avion atterrit en _____?** *kahn tehss kuh lah-vyohn ah-teh-ree ahn*
What is my flight number?	**Quel est le numéro de mon vol?** *kehl eh luh new-may-roh duh mohn vohl*
What gate do we leave from?	**De quelle porte partons-nous?** *duh' kehl pohrt pahr-tohn noo*
I want to confirm (cancel) my reservation for flight _____.	**Je voudrais confirmer (annuler) ma réservation pour le vol numéro _____.** *zhuh voo-dreh kohn-feer-may (ah-new-lay) mah ray-zehr-vah-ssyohn poor luh vohl new-may-roh*
I'd like to check my bags.	**Je voudrais enregistrer mes bagages.** *zhuh voo-dreh zahn-ruh-zheess-tray may bah-gahzh*
I have only carry-on baggage.	**J'ai seulement des bagages à main.** *zhay suhl-mahn day bah-gazh ah man*
Please pass my film (camera) through by hand.*	**Passez mon film (appareil) à la main, s'il vous plaît.** *pah-ssay mohn film (ah-pah-rehy) ah lah man seel voo pleh*

NOTE: Some high-speed film can be damaged by airport security X-rays. It is best to pack film in your suitcase, protected in a lead insulated bag. If you have film in your camera or carry-on baggage, avoid problems and ask the guard to pass it through by hand instead. If the guard refuses, bow to his wishes.

SHIPBOARD TRAVEL

Where is the dock?	**Où est le dock?** *oo eh luh dohk*
When does the next boat leave for _____?	**Quand part le prochain bateau pour _____?** *kahn pahr luh proh-shan bah-toh poor*

How long does the crossing take?	**La traversée dure combien de temps?** *lah trah-vehr-ssay dewr kohn-byan duh tahn*
Do we stop at any ports?	**Dans quels ports est-ce qu'on fait escale?** *dahn kehl pohr ehss kohn feh ehss-kahl*
How long will we remain in the port?	**L'escale dure combien de temps?** *lehss-kahl dewr kohn-byan duh tahn*
When do we land?	**Quand est-ce qu'on y arrive?** *kahn tehss kohn nee ah-reev*
At what time do we have to be back on board?	**À quelle heure faut-il retourner au bateau?** *ah kehl uhr foh teel ruh-toor-nay oh bah-toh*
I'd like a _____ ticket.	**Je voudrais un billet _____.** *zhuh voo-dreh zuhn bee-yeh*
■ first class	**de première classe** *duh pruh-myehr klahss*
■ tourist class	**de deuxième classe** *duh duh-zyehm klahss*
■ cabin	**de cabine** *duh kah-been*

I don't feel well.	**Je ne me sens pas bien.** *zhuh nuh muh sah<u>n</u> pah bya<u>n</u>*
Can you give me something for sea sickness?	**Pouvez-vous me donner quelque chose contre le mal de mer?** *poo-vay voo muh doh-nay kehl-kuh shohz koh<u>n</u>-truh luh mahl duh mehr*

TRAIN SERVICE

The French railway system is extensive, serving small as well as large cities. Trains have first and second class. The new TGV makes the regions of Rhône-Alps, Savoy, Rhône Valley, Provence, Languedoc and even western Switzerland only a few hours' journey from Paris. There are also special tourist trains (CEVENOL) running from Paris to Marseilles.

TYPES OF TRAINS

TEE (Trans-Europ-Express)	Has only first-class seating, plus supplementary charge.
TGV (Très grande vitesse)	High speed train with first and second class seating.
Rapide	Express that stops only at major stations. Luxury accommodations are available.
Express	Long-distance train.
Omnibus	Local train.

If you have to sleep on a train you will find the following expressions useful:

Wagon-lit	A first-class private sleeping compartment for one or two (with sink and mirror).
Couchette	A second-class sleeping compartment with 6 bunks. If you are not a party of six, you may have to share it with

strangers. You sleep in your clothes.

Coach

You sleep, if possible, fully dressed, sitting in your first or second class seat.

EATING ON A TRAIN

You can get anything from a full meal to a light snack and drinks on the train. Use the **wagon-restaurant** (dining car). Also, when the train pulls into a large station, call out the window to the vendors of sandwiches, cheeses and drinks. You may, if you prefer, carry on your own meals and refreshments, as the dining car can be very expensive.

STATION

Where is the train station? (the ticket office)	**Où est la gare? (le guichet)** *oo eh lah gahr (luh gee-sheh)*
I'd like to see the schedule.	**Je voudrais voir l'horaire.** *zhuh voo-dreh vwahr loh-rehr*
A first class (second class) ticket to _____, please.	**Un billet de première classe (seconde classe) pour _____, s'il vous plaît.** *uhn bee-yeh duh pruh-myehr klahss (suh-gohnd klahss) poor _____ seel voo pleh*
■ half-price ticket	**un billet de demi-tarif** *uhn bee-yeh duh duh-mee tah-reef*
■ one-way (round-trip) ticket	**un aller simple (aller et retour)** *uhn nah-lay san-pluh (nah-lay ay ruh-toor)*
I would like a (no) smoking compartment.	**Je voudrais un compartiment (non-) fumeurs.** *zhuh voo-dreh zuhn kohn-pahr-tee-mahn (nohn) few-muhr*
When does the train arrive (leave)?	**À quelle heure est-ce que le train arrive (part)?** *ah kehl uhr ehss kuh luh tran ah-reev (pahr)*

From what platform does it leave (arrive)?
Dé (À) quel quai (De quelle voie) part (arrive) -t-il? *duh (ah) kehl kay (duh kehl vwah) pahr (ah-reev) teel*

Does this train stop at _____?
Est-ce que ce train s'arrête à _____? *ehss kuh suh tran sah-reht ah*

Is the train late?
Est-ce que le train a du retard? *ehss kuh luh tran ah dew ruh-tahr*

How long does it stop?
Il s'arrête pendant combien de temps? *eel sah-reht pan-dan kohn-byan duh tahn*

Is there time to get a bite?
A-t-on le temps de prendre quelque chose? *ah tohn luh tahn duh prahn-druh kehl-kuh shohz*

Do we have to stand in line?
Faut-il faire la queue? *foh teel fehr lah kuh*

All aboard!
En voiture, s'il vous plaît! *ahn vwah-tewr seel voo pleh*

Is there a dining car (sleeping car)?
Y a-t-il un wagon restaurant (un wagon-lit)? *ee ah teel uhn vah-gohn rehss-toh-rahn (uhn vah-gohn lee)*

Is it a _____?
Est-ce _____? *ehss*

■ a through train
un rapide *uhn rah-peed*

■ a local
un omnibus *uhn nohm-nee-bewss*

■ an express
un express *uhn nehkss-prehss*

Do I have to change trains?
Dois-je changer de train? *dwahzh shahn-zhay duh tran*

Is this seat taken?
Est-ce que cette place est occupée? *ehss kuh seht plahss eh toh-kew-pay*

Where are we now?
Où sommes-nous maintenant? *oo sohm noo mant-nahn*

Will we arrive on time? (late)?
Arriverons-nous à l'heure? (en retard?) *ah-reev-rohn noo ah luhr? (ahn ruh-tahr)*

ENTERTAINMENT AND DIVERSION

MOVIES

Movies are generally shown from 2 p.m. to 10 p.m. with late night schedules on Saturday. "Pariscope" and "L'Officiel des Spectacles" are two guides to the movies in Paris, indicating the time and place of the film showing. The abbreviation V. O. (**version originale**) means that the original version of the movie in the language in which it was made is being shown. V. F. (**version française**) means that the movie is dubbed in French. In the movies or theater it is customary to tip the usher or usherette. Movies generally change on Wednesday. The bigger, more expensive, more comfortable movie houses are on the Champs-Elysées in Paris.

Let's go to the ____.	**Allons au ____.**	*ah-lohn zoh*
■movies	**cinéma**	*see-nay-mah*
■museum	**musée**	*mew-zay*
■theater	**théâtre**	*tay-ah-truh*
What are they showing today?	**Qu'est-ce qu'on joue aujourd'hui?**	*kehss kohn zhoo oh-zhoor-dwee*
It's a ____.	**C'est ____.**	*seh*
■mystery	**un mystère**	*tuhn mee-sstehr*
■comedy	**une comédie**	*tewn koh-may-dee*
■drama	**un drame**	*tuhn drahm*
■musical	**une comédie musicale**	*tewn koh-may-dee mew-zee-kahl*
■romance	**une histoire d'amour**	*tewn eess-twahr dah-moor*
■Western	**un western**	*tuhn wehss-tehrn*

■war film	**un film de guerre** *tuhn feelm duh gehr*
■science fiction film	**une histoire de science fiction** *tewn eess-twahr duh see-yahnss feek-ssyohn*
Is it in English?	**Est-ce en anglais?** *ehss ahn nahn-gleh*
Are there English subtitles?	**Y-t-il des sous-titres en anglais?** *ee ah teel day soo-tee-truh ahn nahn-gleh*
Where is the box office (time schedule)?	**Où est le bureau de location (l'horaire)?** *oo eh luh bew-roh duh loh-kah-ssyohn (loh-rehr)*
What time does the (first) show begin?	**À quelle heure commence le (premier) spectacle?** *ah kehl uhr koh-mahnss luh (pruh-myay) spehk-tah-kluh*
What time does the (last) show end?	**À quelle heure se termine le (dernier) spectacle?** *ah kehl uhr suh tehr-meen luh (dehr-nyay) spehk-tah-kluh*
I'd like to speak to an usher.	**Je voudrais parler à une ouvreuse.** *zhuh voo-dreh pahr-lay ah ewn oo-vruhz*

THEATER

France has several national theaters like the **Comédie Française** or the **Théâtre National de l'Odéon**. There are also about fifty private playhouses. Theaters are closed one day a week. The day is listed in the newspapers. Booking offices are generally open from 11 AM to 6 PM. Most of the theaters are closed one month in the summer, usually August.

For entertainment information in Paris call (1) 42 25 03 20.

I need tickets for tonight.	**Il me faut des billets pour ce soir.** *eel muh foh day bee-yeh poor suh swahr*
Two ____ seats	**Deux places ____** *duh plahss*

■ orchestra	**à l'orchestre**	*ah lohr-kehss-truh*
■ balcony	**au balcon**	*oh bahl-koh<u>n</u>*
■ first balcony	**au premier balcon**	*oh pruh-myay bahl-koh<u>n</u>*
■ mezzanine	**au parterre**	*oh pahr-tehr*

OPERA-BALLET-CONCERT

We would like to attend ____.	**Nous voudrions assister à ____.**	*noo voo-dree-yoh<u>n</u> ah-sseess-tay ah*
■ a ballet	**un ballet**	*uh<u>n</u> bah-leh*
■ a concert	**un concert**	*uh<u>n</u> koh<u>n</u>-ssehr*
■ an opera	**un opéra**	*uh<u>n</u> noh-pay-rah*
Is there a ____ nearby?	**Y a-t-il par ici ____?**	*ee ah teel pahr ee-ssee*
■ concert hall	**une salle de concert**	*ewn sahl duh koh<u>n</u>-ssehr*
■ opera house	**un opéra**	*uh<u>n</u> noh-pay-rah*
■ ballet	**un ballet**	*uh<u>n</u> bah-leh*
What are they playing?	**Que joue-t-on?**	*kuh zhoo toh<u>n</u>*
Who is the conductor?	**Qui est le chef d'orchestre?**	*kee eh luh shehf dohr-kehss-truh*
I prefer ____.	**Je préfère ____.**	*zhuh pray-fehr*
■ classical music	**la musique classique**	*lah mew-zeek klah-sseek*
■ modern music	**la musique moderne**	*lah mew-zeek moh-dehrn*
■ folk dances	**les danses folkloriques**	*lay dahnss fohl-kloh-reek*

Are there any seats for tonight's performance?

Y a-t-il des places pour ce soir? *ee ah teel day plahss poor suh swahr*

When does the season end?

Quand se termine la saison théâtrale? *kahn suh tehr-meen lah seh-zohn tay-ah-trahl*

Should I get the tickets in advance?

Faut-il acheter les billets d'avance? *foh teel ahsh-tay lay bee-yeh dah-vahnss*

Do I have to dress formally?

La tenue de soirée est-elle de rigueur? *lah tuh-new duh swah-ray eh tehl duh ree-guhr*

How much are the front row seats?

Combien coûtent les places au premier rang? *kohn-byan koot lay plahss oh pruh-myay rahn*

What are the least expensive seats?

Quelles sont les places les moins chères? *kehl sohn lay plahss lay mwan shehr*

May I have a program?

Un programme, s'il vous plaît. *uhn proh-grahm seel voo pleh*

What opera are they putting on?	**Quel opéra jouent-ils?** *kehl oh-pay-rah zhoo teel*
Who's singing?	**Qui chante?** *kee shahnt*
Who's playing the lead?	**Qui joue le rôle principal?** *kee zhoo luh rohl pra<u>n</u>-ssee-pahl*
Who are the members of the cast?	**Qui sont les membres de la troupe?** *kee soh<u>n</u> lay mah<u>n</u>-bruh duh lah troop*
Who is _____?	**Qui est _____?** *kee eh*
■ the tenor	**le ténor** *luh tay-nohr*
■ the baritone	**le baryton** *luh bah-ree-toh<u>n</u>*
■ the soprano	**le soprano** *luh soh-prah-noh*
■ the bass	**la basse** *lah bahss*

NIGHT CLUBS

If it's entertainment you want, try the bars, nightclubs and discos in the major cities. Paris, of course, offers the widest selection of things to do. Nightclubs, providing dinner and a show, are very expensive. A late night drink at a jazz spot or bar might interest you. Discos abound with the latest song hits and special lighting effects.

Let's go to a night-club!	**Allons dans une boîte de nuit!** *ah-loh<u>n</u> dah<u>n</u> zewn bwaht duh nwee*
Is a reservation necessary?	**Faut-il réserver?** *foh teel ray-zehr-vay*
I feel like dancing.	**J'ai envie de danser.** *zhay ah<u>n</u>-vee duh dah<u>n</u>-ssay*
Is there a disco-theque here?	**Y a-t-il une discothèque par ici?** *ee ah teel ewn deess-koh-tehk pahr ee-ssee*
Is there a dance at the hotel?	**Y a-t-il un bal à l'hôtel?** *ee ah teel uh<u>n</u> bahl ah loh-tehl*

I'd like a table near the dance floor.	**Je voudrais avoir une table près de la piste (de danse).** *zhuh voo-dreh zah-vwahr ewn tah-bluh preh duh lah peesst (duh dahnss)*
Is there a minimum (cover charge)?	**Y a-t-il un prix d'entrée?** *ee ah teel uhn pree dahn-tray*
Where is the checkroom?	**Où est le vestiaire?** *oo eh luh vehss-tyehr*
At what time does the floor show go on?	**À quelle heure commence le spectacle?** *ah kehl uhr koh-mahnss luh spehk-tah-kluh*

DANCING

May I have this dance?	**M'accordez-vous cette danse?** *mah-kohr-day voo seht dahnss*
Yes, all right. With pleasure.	**Oui, d'accord. Avec plaisir.** *wee dah-kohr. ah-vehk pleh-zeer*
Would you like a cigarette (a drink)?	**Voudriez-vous une cigarette (une boisson)?** *voo-dree-yay voo zewn see-gah-reht (ewn bwah-ssohn)*
Do you have a light?	**Avez-vous du feu?** *ah-vay voo dew fuh*
Do you mind if I smoke?	**Ça vous dérange si je fume?** *sah voo day-rahnzh see zhuh fewm*
May I take you home?	**Puis-je vous raccompagner chez vous?** *pweezh voo rah-kohn-pah-nyay shay voo*

CASINOS

While on the Côte d'Azur you must visit the world-famous Casino of Monte-Carlo in Monaco. Unlike most other casinos, admission is free. There are other casinos throughout France. All are licensed, regulated and monitored by the French government. A passport is needed to enter. Admission is restricted to adults (over 21 years of age).

QUIET RELAXATION

Do you want to play cards?	**Voulez-vous jouer aux cartes?** *voo-lay voo zhoo-ay oh kahrt*
■bridge	**au bridge** *oh breedzh*
■black jack	**au black-jack** *oh blahk zhahk*
■poker	**au poker** *oh poh-kehr*
I have the highest card.	**J'ai la meilleure carte.** *zhay lah meh-yuhr kahrt*
■an ace	**un as** *uhn nahss*
■a king	**un roi** *uhn rwah*
■a queen	**une dame** *ewn dahm*
■a jack	**un valet** *uhn vah-leh*
Do you want to cut?	**Voulez-vous couper les cartes?** *voo-lay voo koo-pay lay kahrt*
Where can I get a deck of cards?	**Où puis-je obtenir des cartes à jouer?** *oo pweezh ohp-tuh-neer day kahrt ah zhoo-ay*
Do you want to shuffle?	**Voulez-vous battre les cartes?** *voo-lay voo bah-truh lay kahrt*
I pass.	**Je passe** *zhuh pahss*
Do you have clubs, hearts, spades, diamonds?	**Avez-vous du trèfle, du coeur, du pique ou du carreau?** *ah-vay voo dew treh-fluh, dew kuhr, dew peek oo dew kah-roh*
It's your turn to deal.	**À vous de donner.** *ah voo duh doh-nay*
Who opens?	**Qui commence?** *kee koh-mahnss*
What's your score?	**Combien de points avez-vous?** *kohn-byan duh pwan ah-vay voo*

I win (lose).	**Je gagne (Je perds).** *zhuh gah-nyuh (zhuh pehr)*	
You win (lose).	**Vous gagnez (Vous perdez).** *voo gah-nyay (voo pehr-day)*	
Do you want to play ____?	**Voulez-vous jouer ____?** *voo-lay voo zhoo-ay*	
■ checkers	**aux dames** *oh dahm*	
■ chess	**aux échecs** *oh zay-shehk*	
■ dominoes	**aux dominos** *oh doh-mee-noh*	
We need a board (dice).	**Il nous faut un échiquier (des dés).** *eel noo foh tuhn nay-shee-kyay (day day)*	
We need the pieces.	**Il nous faut les pièces.** *eel noo foh lay pee-yehss*	
■ the king	**le roi** *luh rwah*	
■ the queen	**la reine** *lah rehn*	
■ the rook	**la tour** *lah toor*	
■ the bishop	**le fou** *luh foo*	
■ the knight	**le cavalier** *luh kah-vah-lyay*	
■ the pawn	**le pion** *luh pee-yohn*	
Checkmate.	**Échec et mat.** *ay-shehk ay maht*	
Check.	**Échec.** *ay-shehk*	

SPORTS

Golf, tennis, swimming, cycling, skiing, basketball, ice-skating, fishing, hiking and sailing are recreational activities in which you can participate throughout the country.

Boxing and wrestling matches, soccer, rugby and pelote (jai alai) matches draw large crowds of spectators.

Two special events that attract natives and tourists alike are Le Tour de France, a three week bicycle race across France (held each June) and Le Mans, a 24 hour Formula One auto race (also in June).

SPECTATOR SPORTS

SOCCER

I'd like to see a soccer match.	**Je voudrais voir un match de football.** *zhuh voo-dreh vwahr uhn mahtch duh foot-bohl*
Where's the stadium?	**Où est le stade?** *oo eh luh stahd*
When does the first half begin?	**Quand commence la première mi-temps?** *kahn koh-mahnss lah pruh-myehr mee-tahn*
When are they going to kick off?	**Quand vont-ils donner le coup d'envoi?** *kahn vohn teel doh-nay luh koo dahn-vwah*
What teams are going to play?	**Quelles équipes vont jouer?** *kehl zay-keep vohn zhoo-ay*
Who is playing _____?	**Qui joue _____?** *kee zhoo*
■ center	**au centre** *oh sahn-truh*
■ fullback	**à l'arrière** *ah lah-ryehr*
■ halfback	**en demi** *ahn duh-mee*
■ wing	**à l'aile** *ah lehl*
What was the score?	**Quel a été le score?** *kehl ah ay-tay luh skohr*

JAI ALAI

Are you a jai alai fan?	**Êtes-vous un fana de la pelote (basque)?** *eht voo zuhn fah-nah duh lah puh-loht (bahssk)*

I'd like to see a jai alai match.	**Je voudrais voir un match de pelote.** *zhuh voo-dreh vwahr uhn mahtch duh puh-loht*
Where can I get tickets?	**Où puis-je me procurer des billets?** *oo pweezh muh proh-kew-ray day bee-yeh*
Where is the jai alai court?	**Où est le fronton?** *oo eh luh frohn-tohn*
Who are the players?	**Qui sont les joueurs?** *kee sohn lay zhoo-uhr*
Each team has a forward end (a back end).	**Chaque équipe a un avant (un arrière).** *shahk ay-keep ah uhn nah-vahn (uhn nah-ryehr)*
I bet that the blue team will win.	**Je parie que l'équipe bleue va gagner.** *zhuh pah-ree kuh lay-keep bluh vah gah-nyay*
Where do I place my bet?	**Où fait-on les paris?** *oo feh-tohn lay pah-ree*
At that window.	**À ce guichet.** *ah suh gee-sheh*

HORSE RACING

Is there a racetrack here?	**Y a-t-il un champ de courses par ici?** *ee ah teel uhn shahn duh koorss pahr ee-ssee*
I want to see the horse races.	**Je voudrais voir les courses de chevaux.** *zhuh voo-dreh vwahr lay koorss duh shuh-voh*

ACTIVE SPORTS

TENNIS

Do you play tennis?	**Jouez-vous au tennis?** *zhoo-ay voo oh teh-neess*

I like the game.	**J'aime bien ce sport.** *zhehm byan suh spohr*
I (don't) play very well.	**Je (ne) joue (pas) bien.** *zhuh (nuh) zhoo (pah) byan*
I need practice.	**Je dois m'entraîner.** *zhuh dwah mahn-treh-nay*
Do you know where there is a (good) court?	**Savez-vous où se trouve un bon court de tennis?** *sah-vay voo oo suh troov uhn bohn koohr duh teh-neess*
Can I rent rackets and balls?	**Puis-je louer des raquettes et des balles?** *pweezh loo-ay day rah-keht ay day bahl*
How much do they charge per hour (per day)?	**Quel est le tarif à l'heure/à la journée?** *kehl eh luh tah-reef ah luhr/ ah lah zhoor-nay*
I serve (You serve) first.	**C'est à moi (à vous) le premier service.** *seh tah mwah (tah voo) luh pruh-myay sehr-veess*
You play very well.	**Vous jouez très bien.** *voo zhoo-ay treh byan*
You've won.	**Vous avez gagné.** *voo zah-vay gah-nyay*
I've won.	**J'ai gagné.** *zhay gah-nyay*
It's a tie.	**Match nul.** *mahtch newl*

BEACH OR POOL

Oh! It's hot.	**Oh là là! Quelle chaleur!** *oh lah lah kehl shah-luhr*
Let's go to the beach (to the pool).	**Allons à la plage (à la piscine).** *ah-lohn zah lah plahzh (ah lah pee-sseen)*

Is it a sand beach? **Est-ce une plage de sable?** *ehss ewn plahzh duh sah-bluh*

How do you get there? **Comment y va-t-on?** *koh-mahn tee vah tohn*

Which bus will take us to the beach? **Quel bus faut-il prendre pour aller à la plage?** *kehl bewss foh teel prahn-druh poor ah-lay ah lah plahzh*

Is there a pool in the hotel? **Y a-t-il une piscine à l'hôtel?** *ee ah teel ewn pee-sseen ah loh-tehl*

Is it an indoor (outdoor) pool? **Est-ce une piscine couverte (en plein air)?** *ehss ewn pee-sseen koo-vehrt (ahn pleh nehr)*

I (don't) know how to swim well. **Je (ne) sais (pas) bien nager.** *zhuh (nuh) seh (pah) byan nah-zhay*

I just want to stretch out in the sand. **Je voudrais tout simplement m'allonger sur le sable.** *zhuh voo-dreh too san-pluh-mahn mah-lohn-zhay sewr luh sah-bluh*

Is it safe to swim here? **Peut-on nager ici sans danger?** *puh-tohn nah-zhay ee-ssee sahn dahn-zhay*

Are the waves big? **Y a-t-il de grandes vagues?** *ee ah teel duh grahnd vahg*

Are there sharks? **Y a-t-il des requins?** *ee ah teel day ruh-kan*

Is there any danger for children? **Y a-t-il du danger pour les enfants?** *ee ah teel dew dahn-zhay poor lay zahn-fahn*

Is there a lifeguard? **Y a-t-il un maître-nageur?** *ee ah teel uhn meh-truh nah-zhuhr*

I'm going in the water now. **Je vais entrer dans l'eau maintenant.** *zhuh veh zahn-tray dahn loh mant-nahn*

Where can I get ____?	**Où puis-je obtenir ____?** *oo pweezh ohp-tuh-neer*
■ an air mattress	**un matelas pneumatique** *uhn maht-lah pnuh-mah-teek*
■ a bathing suit	**un maillot de bain** *uhn mah-yoh duh ban*
■ a beach ball	**un ballon de plage** *uhn bah-lohn duh plahzh*
■ a beach chair	**une chaise longue pour la plage** *ewn shehz lohng poor lah plahzh*
■ a beach towel	**une serviette de plage** *ewn sehr-vyeht duh plahzh*
■ a chaise longue	**une chaise longue** *ewn shehz lohng*
■ sunglasses	**des lunettes de soleil** *day lew-neht duh soh-leh*
■ suntan lotion	**la lotion pour bronzer** *lah loh-ssyohn poor brohn- zay*
■ a surfboard	**une planche de surf** *ewn plahnsh duh sewrf*
■ water skis	**des skis nautiques** *day skee noh-teek*

ON THE SLOPES

Which ski area do you recommend?	**Quelle station de ski recomman-dez-vous?** *kehl stah-ssyohn duh skee ruh-koh-mahn-day voo*
I am a novice (intermediate, expert) ski-er.	**Je suis un(e) débutant(e) (un skieur moyen; un expert).** *zhuh swee zuhn (zewn) day-bew-tahn(t) (zuhn skee-uhr mwah-yan/uhn ehks-pehr)*

What kind of lifts are there?	**Quel type de téléski y a-t-il?** *kehl teep duh tay-lay-sskee ee-yah-teel*
How much does the lift cost?	**Combien coûte le trajet?** *kohn-byan koot luh trah-zheh*
Do they give lessons?	**Donne-t-on des leçons?** *dohn-tohn day luh-ssohn*
Where can I stay at the summit?	**Où puis-je loger au sommet?** *oo pweezh loh-zhay oh soh-meh*
Is there any cross country skiing?	**Est-ce qu'on fait du ski de fond?** *ehss-kohn feh dew skee duh fohn*
Is there enough snow this time of year?	**Y a-t-il assez de neige en ce moment?** *ee ah teel ah-ssay duh nehzh ahn suh moh-mahn*
How would I get to that place?	**Comment aller à cet endroit-là?** *koh-mahn tah-lay ah seht ahn-drwah lah*

Can I rent ___ there?	**Peut-on y louer ___?** *puh-tohn nee loo-ay*
■ equipment	**un équipement de ski** *uhn nay-keep-mahn duh skee*
■ poles	**des bâtons** *day bah-tohn*
■ skis	**des skis** *day skee*
■ ski boots	**des chaussures de ski** *day shoh-ssewr duh skee*

ON THE LINKS

Is there a golf course here?	**Y a-t-il un terrain de golf par ici?** *ee ah teel uhn teh-ran duh gohlf pahr ee-ssee*
Can one rent clubs?	**Peut-on louer des clubs?** *puh tohn loo-ay day kluhb*

CAMPING

Campgrounds are located all over France. They are often crowded, especially in the month of August when most Frenchmen are on vacation. Arrive early to insure a spot. Campsites are rated by stars; the fewer the stars, the less desirable the site. Most sites have adequate facilities. Students are sometimes offered discounts. A camping permit is sometimes required. You may camp unofficially in a suitable place as long as you have permission from the land owner. Be sure to leave the property in the same condition as you found it.

Is there a camping site near here?	**Y a-t-il un terrain de camping par ici?** *ee ah teel uhn teh-ran duh kahn-peeng pahr ee-ssee*
Can you show me how to get there?	**Pouvez-vous m'indiquer comment y aller?** *poo-vay voo man-dee-kay koh-mahn tee ah-lay*

Where is it on the map?	**Où se trouve-t-il sur la carte?** *oo suh troov teel sewr lah kahrt*
Where can we park our trailer?	**Où pouvons-nous installer notre caravane?** *oo poo-vohn noo an-stah-lay noh-truh kah-rah-vahn*
Can we camp for the night?	**Pouvons-nous camper cette nuit?** *poo-vohn noo kahn-pay seht nwee*
Where can we spend the night?	**Où pouvons-nous passer la nuit?** *oo poo-vohn noo pah- ssay lah nwee*
Is there _____?	**Y a-t-il _____?** *ee ah teel*

- drinking water

  de l'eau potable *duh loh poh-tah-bluh*

- running water

  de l'eau courante *duh loh koo-rahnt*

- gas

  du gaz *dew gahz*

- electricity

  de l'électricité *duh lay-lehk-tree-ssee-tay*

- a children's playground

  un terrain de jeu pour enfants *uhn teh-ran duh zhuh poor ahn-fahn*

- a grocery store

  une épicerie *ewn ay-peess-ree*

Are there _____?	**Y a-t-il _____?** *ee ah teel*

- toilets

  des toilettes *day twah-leht*

- showers

  des douches *day doosh*

- washrooms

  des lavabos *day lah-vah-boh*

- tents

  des tentes *day tahnt*

- cooking facilities

  des installations pour faire la cuisine *day zan--stah-lah-ssyohn poor fehr lah kwee-zeen*

How much do they charge per person? (per car)?	**Quel est le tarif par personne/pour une caravane?** *kehl eh luh tah-reef pahr pehr-ssohn/poor ewn kah-rah-vahn*

| We intend staying ____ days/weeks. | **Nous pensons rester ____ jours/semaines.** *noo pahn-ssohn rehss-tay ____ zhoor/suh-mehn* |

IN THE COUNTRYSIDE

I'd like to drive through the countryside.	**Je voudrais conduire dans la campagne.** *zhuh voo-dreh kohn-dweer dahn lah kahn-pah-nyuh*
Where can I rent a car for the day?	**Où puis-je louer une voiture à la journée?** *oo pweezh loo-ay ewn vwah-tewr ah lah zhoor-nay*
Are there tours to the country?	**Y a-t-il des excursions à la campagne?** *ee ah teel day zehkss-kewr-zyohn ah lah kahn-pah-nyuh*
When do they leave?	**Quand sont les départs?** *kahn ssohn lay day-pahr*
From where do they leave?	**D'où partent-elles?** *doo pahrt-ehl*
Is there anyone who can take me?	**Y a-t-il quelqu'un qui puisse me conduire?** *ee ah teel kehl kuhn kee pweess muh kohn-dweer*
What a beautiful landscape!	**Quel beau paysage!** *kehl boh pay-zahzh*
Look at ____.	**Regardez ____.** *ruh-gahr-day*
■ the barn	**la grange** *lah grahnzh*
■ the bridge	**le pont** *luh pohn*
■ the farm	**la ferme** *lah fehrm*
■ the fields	**les champs** *lay shahn*
■ the flowers	**les fleurs** *lay fluhr*
■ the forest	**la forêt** *lah foh-reh*
■ the hill	**la colline** *lah koh-leen*

■ the lake	**le lac** *luh lahk*
■ the mountains	**les montagnes** *lay mohn-tah-nyuh*
■ the ocean	**l'océan (m.)** *loh-ssay-ahn*
■ the plants	**les plantes** *lay plahnt*
■ the pond	**l'étang (m.)** *lay-tahn*
■ the river	**la rivière** *lah ree-vyehr*
■ the stream	**le ruisseau** *luh rwee-ssoh*
■ the trees	**les arbres** *lay zahr-bruh*
■ the valley	**la vallée** *lah vah-lay*
■ the village	**le village** *luh vee-lahzh*
■ the waterfall	**la cascade** *lah kahss-kahd*
Where does this _____ lead to?	**Où mène _____?** *oo mehn*
■ road	**ce chemin** *suh shuh-man*
■ path	**ce sentier** *suh sahn-tyay*
■ highway	**cette grande route** *seht grahnd root*
How far away is _____?	**À quelle distance est _____?** *ah kehl deess-tahnss eh*
■ the city	**la ville** *lah veel*
■ the crossroads	**le carrefour** *luh kahr-foor*
■ the inn	**l'auberge (f.)** *loh-behrzh*
How long does it take to get to _____?	**Combien de temps faut-il pour aller à _____?** *kohn-byan duh tahn foh teel poor ah-lay ah*
I'm lost.	**J'ai perdu mon chemin.** *zhay pehr-dew mohn shuh-man*
Can you show me the way to _____?	**Pouvez-vous m'indiquer le chemin pour _____?** *poo-vay voo man-dee-kay luh shuh-man poor*

FOOD AND DRINK

The world has only a few truly great cuisines, and French is one of them. Respected for its extensive selection of dishes, its inventive uses of ingredients, and its exactness in preparation, French food is always reliably appetizing. French people are inherently great cooks, for they have been developing the elements of good taste since childhood. Wherever you eat in France, whether it be in Paris or Lyons, in the country or in the city, the food you will be offered will be carefully and lovingly prepared.

The past masters—especially Carême and Escoffier—defined and codified French food, so that you will not find the variations in ingredients or preparations that you notice in most other foods; a hollandaise sauce, for example, will always be made with egg yolks, into which are whisked butter and a dash of vinegar or lemon juice; it will be the same sauce, whether you are enjoying it in a Paris bistro or a country inn. What will vary will be particularly the regional dishes—dishes from the provinces of France that are made chiefly by the cooks in small restaurants and inns.

France's restaurants are famous, and they alone are worth a trip to that country. The most famous ones are those graded with one, two, or three (best) stars in the red Michelin guide. There are other ratings, too, especially from Gault & Millau, which tend to favor restaurants whose chefs prepare the nouvelle cuisine dishes. Three-star restaurants are also among the most expensive and the most formal, for these are the towers of **haute cuisine,** and all other restaurants strive to be in that category some day.

Eating in France is a somewhat structured affair. To make your stay enjoyable and to gather a bit of the French flavor, we suggest you follow the French manner of eating. First, here are the types of restaurants you are likely to encounter.

Auberge, Relais, Hostellerie	a country inn.
Bistro	a small neighborhood restaurant in town, similar to a pub or tavern and usually very informal.

Brasserie	a large café which serves quick meals throughout the day or evening; most meals involve only the entrée, such as a steak or chop.
Cabaret	a nightclub where you may also eat a meal.
Café	a neighborhood spot to socialize, either indoors or out, where you can linger over a coffee or glass of wine or beer and perhaps have a little snack. Cafés also serve breakfast (usually a **croissant** and **café au lait**) and later in the day serve soft drinks and ice cream.
Casse-croûte	a restaurant specializing in sandwiches.
Crêperie	a small stand specializing in the preparation of crêpes—thin pancakes dusted with sugar or covered with jam and rolled up.
Fast-food place	a small place to eat an American-style snack, mostly hamburgers and French fries; most are in Paris along the Champs-Elysée and many are American chains such as McDonald's and Burger King.
Restaurant	can range from a small, family-owned inn, where mom seats you, dad cooks the meal, and the children serve you, to a formal, three-star palace where you receive the most elegant service and most beautifully garnished foods.
Self	a cafeteria, popular with students and mostly located near a university.
Troquet	a wine shop where you can also have a snack.

By law, all establishments serving food must post a menu showing the prices. Most often, you will see posted two menus—one which is a listing of the *à la carte* offerings, and the other as one, two, or three different *prix fixe* meals. You can, of course, order the dishes you wish following the *à la carte* menu, but the resulting cost will be higher than if you choose one of the menus. The menus are a good choice since they always feature a freshly prepared entrée and usually reflect the specialty of the chef. When there is more than one menu from which to choose, they will differ depending upon the number of courses or the relative value of the entrée; lower-priced menus usually include a grilled steak or chicken dish as entrée, while the higher-priced might feature an additional cheese course or perhaps both fish and meat courses. In some regions, especially those that receive a number of tourists, you'll often see a special "tourist" menu, which will feature a specialty of the region—cassoulet in Languedoc or truffles in Perigord, for example. Wherever you eat, look for the **plat du jour** (day's specialty) or the **spécialités de la maison** (chef's specialties).

Most menus include a line at the bottom stating that the service charge is included in the price of the meal; it is usually about 12%. It is also customary to leave some small change on the table for the waiter, usually what would round off your bill. If you order a wine other than the house wine, you should also tip the steward, although the service for wine is sometimes also included in the bill. Oftentimes, especially in very casual restaurants, the wine is included in the menu **(boisson comprise)**. If you want a simple, inexpensive wine, select the house wine, which will usually be a regional wine; if you want advice in a casual restaurant, ask the waiter—as a Frenchman, he will have been brought up to know wines and will recommend one that you will enjoy with what you are eating (see also pages on wine, 104–107).

MEALS OF THE DAY

Most tourists will have their breakfast in the hotel, so much of the information that follows applies to lunch and dinner. Breakfast, **le petit déjeuner,** is usually small, consisting of a croissant or part of a loaf of day-old French bread, with butter and jam. It is usually served with **café au lait**—a large cup or bowl of hot coffee mixed half-and-half with steamed milk; this breakfast is called **café complet** and it is what you will most often be served, especially if breakfast is included in the cost of your room. You may also order hot tea or hot chocolate for breakfast.

Lunch and dinner in France are about the same in character and courses. Lunch, referred to as **le déjeuner,** is usually served between 12:30 and 3 p.m. Especially in smaller towns or on the road, be sure to stop early (by 12:15 to secure a table for lunch; many local spots have reserved tables for residents—you'll even see their napkins saved from the previous day).

In warm weather, do what many French people do for lunch—picnic. Especially if you are sightseeing and don't want to take the time for a lengthy lunch, buy some French bread in a **boulangerie,** then go next door to the *charcuterie* for 100 grams of *pâté de campagne;* stop in an *épicerie* for some salads or sliced tomatoes and some cheese, and also pick up a bottle of wine or mineral water. Take your goods to a park or stop along the road in a field and enjoy your lunch. In France, you'll find the roads are vacated by 12:30, and everyone has pulled over, set up tables, and begun to eat. In town, they will go to the **Jardin des Plantes** or **Bois de Boulogne.**

Dinner **(dîner)** is a bit more formal than lunch and usually served more graciously. In Paris, people eat late—8 p.m. is the earliest—while in the country, you can properly begin by 7:30. It is a time for the enjoyment of food and wine, and therefore a meal can carry on for at least two hours. Most French people do not begin their meal with a cocktail, but sometimes will have an apéritif. The meal consists of the following courses, in this order: cold or hot hors d'oeuvres; soup; fish; meat or poultry with accompanying vegetables; cheese; dessert. In recent years, lighter eating patterns have cut down on the number of courses, and you can of course decline to have a particular course.

In the specialty restaurants—those particularly noted for their food—you will often see a **menu dégustation** or a **menu gastronomique.** The former is a dinner whereby you receive a sampling of a large number of items on the menu, so

as to try many of the chef's dishes—this is most popular in
nouvelle cuisine restaurants. The latter is a special menu for
food-lovers, which features rare items or very difficult dishes to
prepare.

TYPES OF FRENCH COOKING

The basics of French food were established centuries ago,
but there have been developments in recent years that have
released this food from its straitjacket. The following is a
breakdown of the types of food you are likely to encounter.

Haute Cuisine	This is classic French cooking, offered in the top (Michelin starred) restaurants. The food is refined and exquisitely presented.
Cuisine Bourgeoise	This is the country food of France, made for centuries in everyday kitchens, and it is from this that **haute cuisine** was developed. This is the food you'll have in most bistros and small restaurants.
Nouvelle Cuisine	Developed in the seventies and now less respected, this food represented a break from traditional flour-based sauces and rigid rules. In this style, fruits were combined with meats and fish, sauces were reduced until thickened, and salads with elaborate arrangements were developed. This cuisine was promoted by such leaders as Paul Bocuse, Roger Vergé, and the Troisgros brothers; its influences are still apparent in most restaurants.
Cuisine Minceur	A special diet-conscious cuisine developed by Michel Guérard.

Nowadays, you'll find that menus will include a mixture of
dishes—some considered *nouvelle cuisine* and others more
along the line of traditional provincial food.

EATING OUT

Do you know a good restaurant?	**Connaissez-vous un bon restaurant?** *koh-neh-ssay voo uhn bohn rehss-toh-rahn?*
It is very expensive?	**C'est très cher?** *seh treh shehr*
Do you know a restaurant that serves regional dishes?	**Connaissez-vous un restaurant de cuisine régionale?** *koh-neh-ssay voo uhn rehss-toh-rahn duh kwee-zeen ray-zhyoh-nahl*
I'd like to make a reservation _____.	**Je voudrais retenir une table _____.** *zhuh voo-dreh ruh-tuh-neer ewn tah-bluh*
■ for tonight	**pour ce soir** *poor suh swahr*
■ for tomorrow evening	**pour demain soir** *poor duh-man swahr*
■ for two (four) persons	**pour deux (quatre) personnes** *poor duh (kah-truh) pehr-ssohn*
■ at 8 (8:30 P.M.)	**à vingt heures (vingt heures trente)** *ah van-tuhr (van-tuhr trahnt)*
Waiter!	**Garçon!** *gahr-ssohn!*
Miss!	**Mademoiselle** *mahd-mwah-zehl*
A table for two in the corner (near the window).	**Une table pour deux dans un coin (près de la fenêtre).** *ewn tah-bluh poor duh dahn zuhn kwan (preh duh lah fuh-neh-truh)*
We'd like to have lunch (dinner) now.	**Nous voudrions déjeuner (dîner) maintenant.** *noo voo-dree-yohn day-zhuh-nay (dee-nay) mant-nahn*
The menu, please.	**La carte (Le menu), s'il vous plaît.** *lah kahrt (luh muh-new) seel voo pleh*

I'd like the fifty-franc menu.	**Je voudrais le menu à cinquante francs.** *zhuh voo-dreh luh muh-new ah san-kahnt frahn*
What's today's special?	**Quel est le plat du jour?** *kehl eh luh plah dew zhoor*
What do you recommend?	**Qu'est-ce que vous me recommandez?** *kehss kuh voo muh ruh-koh-mahn-day*
What's the house specialty?	**Quelle est la spécialité de la maison?** *kehl eh lah spay-ssyah-lee-tay duh lah meh-zohn*
Do you serve children's portions?	**Servez-vous des demi-portions pour les enfants?** *sehr-vay voo day duh-mee pohr-ssyohn poor lay zahn-fahn*
I'm (not) very hungry.	**J'ai (Je n'ai pas) très faim.** *zhay (zhuh nay pah) treh fan*
To begin with, bring us ____.	**Pour commencer, apportez-nous ____.** *poor koh-mahn-ssay, ah-pohr-tay noo*

- an apéritif — **un apéritif** *uhn nah-pay-ree-teef*
- a cocktail — **un cocktail** *uhn kohk-tehl*
- some white (red, rosé) wine — **du vin blanc (rouge, rosé)** *dew van blahn (roozh, roh-zay)*
- some water — **de l'eau** *duh loh*
- a bottle of mineral water, with (without) gas — **une bouteille d'eau minérale gazeuse (plate)** *ewn boo-tehy doh mee-nay-rahl gah-zuhz (plaht)*
- a beer — **une bière** *ewn byehr*

I'd like to order now.	**Je voudrais commander maintenant.** *zhuh voo-dreh koh-mahn-day mant-nahn*
I'd like ____.	**Je voudrais ____.** *zhuh voo-dreh*

(see the listings that follow for individual dishes, and also the regional specialties noted on pages 102–103)

Do you have a house wine?	**Avez-vous du vin ordinaire?** *ah-vay-voo dew van ohr-dee-nehr*
Is it dry (mellow, sweet)?	**Est-ce sec (moelleux, doux)?** *ehss sehk (mwah-luh, doo)*
Please also bring us ____.	**Apportez-nous aussi, s'il vous plaît ____.** *ah-pohr-tay noo oh-ssee seel voo pleh*

- ■ a roll   **un petit pain** *uhn puh-tee pan*
- ■ bread   **du pain** *dew pan*
- ■ butter   **du beurre** *dew buhr*

| Waiter, we need ____. | **Garçon, apportez-nous ____, s'il vous plaît.** *gahr-ssohn ah-pohr-tay noo seel voo pleh* |

- ■ a knife   **un couteau** *uhn koo-toh*
- ■ a fork   **une fourchette** *ewn foor-sheht*
- ■ a spoon   **une cuiller** *ewn kwee-yehr*
- ■ a teaspoon   **une cuiller à café** *ewn kwee-yehr ah kah-fay*
- ■ a glass   **un verre** *uhn vehr*
- ■ a goblet   **un gobelet** *uhn gohb-leh*
- ■ a cup   **une tasse** *ewn tahss*
- ■ a saucer   **une soucoupe** *ewn soo-koop*
- ■ a plate   **une assiette** *ewn ah-ssyeht*
- ■ a napkin   **une serviette** *ewn sehr-vyeht*
- ■ a toothpick   **un cure-dent** *uhn kewr-dahn*

APPETIZERS (STARTERS)

Appetizers can be either hot or cold; if you order both, have the cold one first. The following are among the most common items you'll see on a menu.

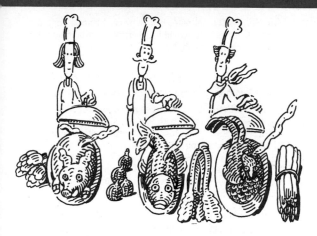

1. ARTICHAUTS À LA VINAIGRETTE   artichokes in a vinaigrette dressing.
2. CRUDITÉS VARIÉES   assorted vegetables—sliced tomatoes, shredded carrots, sliced cooked beets—in a vinaigrette dressing.
3. ESCARGOTS À LA BOURGUIGNONNE   snails cooked and served in the shell, seasoned with a garlic, shallot, and parsley butter.
4. FOIE GRAS   fresh, often uncooked liver of a force-fed goose; sliced and served with toasted French bread slices.
5. PÂTÉ   any of a number of meat loaves, made from puréed liver and usually also with meat—pork, veal, or chicken. **Pâté de foie gras** is made with goose liver; **pâté de campagne** is "of the country" and is a coarser mixed meat paté; **pâté en croute** is a liver pâté encased in pastry.
6. QUICHE LORRAINE   an egg custard tart, sometimes with bacon strips or bits; some versions now also made with Gruyère cheese.
7. QUENELLES   light dumplings, usually made from **brochet** (pike) but also from shellfish; served in a white sauce.
8. RILLETTES   a pork mixture that has been potted, then served as a spread, usually with French bread.

9. TERRINE   A type of pâté, usually served from a deep pot rather than sliced as pâté would be. Terrines can be made from pork, poultry, game, or fish.

SOUPS
Some of those that appear on menus are the following:

1. BISQUE D'ÉCREVISSES   a creamy soup made with crawfish; other bisques are made with lobster, shrimp, or oysters.
2. BOUILLABAISSE   a seafood stew, made with a variety of fish and shellfish depending on the region, seasoned with saffron and fennel or pernod.
3. CONSOMMÉ   a clear broth, made usually from chicken or beef and flavored with herbs; **en gelée** is consommé that has been jelled and sliced; **madrilène** is with tomatoes; **printanier** has a variety of vegetables.
4. CRÈME   A creamy soup, made from any of a number of vegetables and usually enriched with egg yolks. **D'Argenteuil** is cream of asparagus soup; **de volaille** is a creamy chicken soup.
5. PETITE MARMITE   a rich consommé served with the meat and vegetables.
6. POTAGE   a coarser soup, usually made with a purée of vegetables; some varieties of potage are **parmentier** (leeks and potatoes), **au cresson** (watercress), **julienne** (shredded vegetables).
7. SOUPE À L'OIGNON   famous French onion soup, served over French bread and covered with cheese.
8. VELOUTÉ   a creamy soup, most common of which is **de volaille** (cream of chicken) and **de tomate** (tomato).

EGG DISHES
As is true for most of the continent, eggs are not eaten for breakfast but rather are served as a beginning course in a variety of preparations.

1. OEUFS BERCY   eggs baked with sausages in a tomato sauce.
2. OEUFS EN COCOTTE   eggs gently baked in individual cups until softly cooked, sometimes with cream, then eaten with a spoon.

3. OEUFS EN GELÉE   poached eggs that are set into jelled consommé and served chilled as a salad.

4. OMELETTE   a French omelette is puffy and contains a variety of fillings—**aux fines herbes** is with a mixture of parsley, chives, and tarragon.

5. PIPERADE   scrambled eggs mixed with tomatoes, onions, and sweet peppers.

6. SOUFFLÉ   soufflés can be made with almost any ingredients—vegetables, chicken livers, cheese, ham, and so on; they are always light and puffy.

FISH COURSE

The French often eat a fish course preceding meat or poultry. You can also order the fish course as your main selection. Here are some of the names for fish and shellfish you'll find on menus; for the names of preparations, see pages 92–93. When there is no price on the menu, the abbreviation s.g. *(selon grosseur)* refers to a dish that is sold by weight.

les anchois	*lay zahn-shwah*	anchovies
les anguilles	*lay zahn-gee*	eel
le bar	*luh bahr*	bass (hake)
la barbue	*lah bahr-bew*	brill
la baudroie	*lah boh-drwah*	anglerfish, monk-fish
le brochet	*luh broh-sheh*	pike
le cabillaud	*luh kah-bee-yoh*	cod
le calmar	*luh kahl-mahr*	squid
la carpe	*lah kahrp*	carp
le carrelet	*luh kahr-leh*	flounder
le congre	*luh kohn-gruh*	conger eel
les crevettes	*lay kruh-veht*	shrimp
la daurade	*lah doh-rahd*	porgy
les écrevisses	*lay zay-kruh-veess*	crawfish

les escargots	*lay zehss-kahr-goh*	snails
les harengs (fumés)	*lay ah-rahn (few-may)*	herring (smoked)
le homard	*luh oh-mahr*	lobster
les huîtres	*lay zwee-truh*	oysters
la lamproie	*lah lahn-prwah*	lamprey
la langouste	*lah lahn-goosst*	spiny lobster
les langoustines	*lay lahn-goo-ssteen*	large shrimp
la lotte	*lah loht*	monkfish
le loup de mer	*luh loo duh mehr*	sea bass
le maquereau	*luh mah-kroh*	mackerel
le merlan	*luh mehr-lahn*	whiting
la morue	*lah moh-rew*	cod
les moules	*lay mool*	mussels
les palourdes	*lay pah-loord*	clams
la perche	*lah pehrsh*	perch
les poulpes	*lay poolp*	octopus
la rascasse	*lah rahss-kahss*	scorpionfish
les sardines	*lay sahr-deen*	sardines
le saumon	*luh soh-mohn*	salmon
les scampi	*lay skahn-pee*	large shrimp
le thon	*luh tohn*	tuna
la truite	*lah trweet*	trout
le turbot	*luh tewr-boh*	European turbot

POULTRY AND GAME

The French have several names for chicken, depending on its size or age. They also have varying names for duck and some game. Below are some of the more common terms you'll see on menus:

la caille	*lah kahy*	quail
le cerf	*luh sehr*	venison
la canard, cane-ton	*luh kah-nahr, kahn-tohn*	duckling
le chapon	*luh shah-pohn*	capon
le chevreuil	*luh shuh-vruhy*	venison
le cochon de lait	*luh koh-shohn duh leh*	suckling pig
la dinde	*lah dand*	turkey
le faisan	*luh feh-zahn*	pheasant
le lapin	*luh lah-pan*	rabbit
le lièvre	*luh lyeh-vruh*	hare
l'oie *(f.)*	*lwah*	goose
le perdreau, la perdrix	*luh pehr-droh, lah pehr-dree*	partridge
le pigeon, le pigeonneau	*luh pee-zhohn, luh pee-zhoh-noh*	squab
la pintade, le pintadeau	*lah pan-tahd, luh pan-tah-doh*	guinea fowl
la poule	*lah pool*	stewing fowl
le poulet, poussin, la volaille	*luh poo-leh, poo-ssan, lah voh-lahy*	chicken

Suprême de volaille is the fillet from a young chicken breast, usually served with a sauce or garnish.

MEATS
Here are some basic terms for different kinds of meat, followed by a listing of some common cuts of meat and other terms you'll find on a menu:

l'agneau *(m.)*	*lah-nyoh*	lamb
le bœuf	*luh buhf*	beef

la chèvre	*lah sheh-vruh*	goat
le jambon	*luh zhah<u>n</u>-boh<u>n</u>*	ham
le mouton	*luh moo-toh<u>n</u>*	mutton
le porc	*luh pohr*	pork
le veau	*luh voh*	veal
les andouilles	*lay zah<u>n</u>-dooy*	pork sausages
le bifteck	*luh beef-tehk*	steak
le boudin	*luh boo-da<u>n</u>*	blood sausage
le carré d'ag-neau	*luh kah-ray dah-nyoh*	rack of lamb
le cervelas	*luh sehr-vuh-lah*	garlicky pork sausage
la cervelle	*lah sehr-vehl*	brains
la charcuterie	*lah shahr-kew-tree*	assorted sausages, pâtés, and terrines
le chateaubriand	*luh shah-toh-bree-ah<u>n</u>*	porterhouse steak
la côte de boeuf	*lah koht duh buhf*	ribs of beef
les côtelettes	*lay koht-leht*	cutlets
les côtes de porc, de veau	*lay koht duh pohr, duh voh*	chops, pork or veal
les crépinettes	*lay kray-pee-neht*	small sausages
l'entrecôte (f.)	*lah<u>n</u>-truh-koht*	sirloin steak
l'escalope (f.)	*lehss-kah-lohp*	cutlet
le filet de bœuf	*luh fee-leh duh buhf*	fillet of beef
le foie	*luh fwah*	liver
le gigot d'agneau	*luh zhee-goh dah-nyoh*	leg of lamb

la langue	*lah lahng*	tongue
le lard	*luh lahr*	bacon
les médaillons de veau	*lay may-dah-yohn duh voh*	small rounds of veal
les noisettes	*lay nwah-zeht*	small fillets
les pieds de porc	*lay pyay duh pohr*	pig's feet
le ris de veau	*luh ree duh voh*	veal sweetbreads
les rognons d'agneau	*lay roh-nyohn dah-nyoh*	lamb kidneys
le rosbif	*luh rohss-beef*	roast beef
les saucisses	*lay soh-sseess*	sausages
la selle d'agneau	*lah sehl dah-nyoh*	saddle of lamb
le steak	*luh stehk*	steak
le tournedos	*luh toor-nuh-doh*	small fillets of beef
les tripes	*lay treep*	tripe
Is it ___?	**C'est ___?**	*seh*
■ baked	**au four**	*oh foor*
■ boiled	**bouilli(e)**	*boo-yee*
■ braised (stewed)	**braisé(e)**	*breh-zay*
■ broiled (grilled)	**grillé(e)**	*gree-yay*
■ roasted	**rôti(e)**	*roh-tee*
■ poached	**poché(e)**	*poh-shay*
I like the steak ___.	**Je préfère le steak ___.**	*zhuh pray-fehr luh stehk*
■ well-done	**bien cuit(e)**	*byan kwee*
■ medium	**à point**	*ah pwan*
■ rare	**saignant(e)**	*seh-nyahn*
■ tender	**tendre**	*tahn-druh*

PREPARATIONS AND SAUCES

Of necessity, these descriptions are very brief and generalized, but they should give you an impression of what to expect.

1. aioli   mayonnaise heavily flavored with garlic
2. allemande   a light (blond) sauce
3. à la bonne femme   white wine sauce with vegetables
4. alsacienne   with sauerkraut
5. béarnaise   a butter-egg sauce flavored with shallots, wine, and tarragon
6. bercy   basic meat or fish sauce
7. beurre blanc   butter sauce flavored with shallots and wine
8. beurre noir   browned butter sauce
9. blanquette   an egg-enriched cream sauce, usually part of a stewed dish
10. bordelaise   a dish prepared with Bordeaux wine
11. bourguignonne   a dish prepared with Burgundy red wine
12. bretonne   a dish that includes beans
13. caen   a dish made with Calvados (apple brandy)
14. chantilly   a sauce of whipped cream and hollandaise; or as a dessert, sweetened whipped cream
15. chasseur   a sauce made with mushrooms, white wine, shallots, and parsley
16. choron   a béarnaise sauce with tomatoes
17. coquilles   a preparation served in a scallop shell
18. coulibiac   a preparation served in a pastry shell
19. crécy   a dish made with carrots
20. daube   a stew, usually beef, made with red wine, onions, and garlic
21. demi-deuil   when slices of truffles are inserted beneath the skin of a chicken
22. diable   a spicy sauce, usually with chili or cayenne pepper
23. duxelles   a mushroom mixture, usually as a stuffing or sauce base
24. estragon   a dish made with tarragon
25. farcie   a stuffing, or forcemeat filling
26. fenouil   a sauce made with fennel
27. financière   madeira sauce with truffles
28. fines herbes   a dish made with a variety of chopped fresh herbs
29. florentine   a dish that includes spinach

30. <u>forestière</u>   a dish made with wild mushrooms
31. <u>fricassée</u>   a stewed or potted dish, usually chicken
32. <u>gratin</u>   a crusty baked dish, named for the dish in which it is cooked
33. <u>hollandaise</u>   an egg yolk and butter sauce, with vinegar or lemon juice
34. <u>jardinière</u>   a dish with fresh vegetables
35. <u>lyonnaise</u>   a preparation made with onions
36. <u>madère</u>   a dish made with madeira wine
37. <u>maître d'hôtel</u>   a butter sauce with parsley and lemon juice
38. <u>marchand de vin</u>   a sauce with a meat stock and red wine
39. <u>meunière</u>   a simple dish lightly dusted with flour and sauteed, served in a lemon-butter sauce
40. <u>mornay</u>   a simple white sauce with grated cheese, usually gruyère
41. <u>mousseline</u>   a hollandaise sauce with whipped cream
42. <u>moutarde</u>   with mustard
43. <u>nantua</u>   a basic white sauce with cream and shellfish
44. <u>normande</u>   either a fish sauce with oysters or shrimp; or a sauce with apples
45. <u>parmentier</u>   a dish with potatoes
46. <u>périgourdine</u>   with truffles
47. <u>poivrade</u>   a dark sauce, seasoned with pepper
48. <u>provençale</u>   a vegetable garnish, usually with tomatoes, olives, anchovies, and garlic
49. <u>quenelles</u>   light-as-air dumplings made from fish or shellfish
50. <u>ragoût</u>   a thick stew
51. <u>rémoulade</u>   a mayonnaise flavored with mustard and sometimes capers
52. <u>véronique</u>   a dish with grapes
53. <u>verte</u>   a green mayonnaise, flavored with parsley and other herbs
54. <u>vinaigrette</u>   an oil and vinegar dressing for salads
55. <u>vol-au-vent</u>   a puff-pastry shell in which is usually served a creamed meat dish

VEGETABLES

l'artichaut *(m.)*	*lahr-tee-shoh*	artichoke
les asperges	*lay zahss-pehrzh*	asparagus

l'aubergine (f.)	*loh-behr-zheen*	eggplant
la betterave	*lah beh-trahv*	beet
les carottes	*lay kah-roht*	carrots
le céleri	*luh sayl -ree*	celery
le mäis	*luh mah yeess*	corn
le céleri rave	*luh sayl -ree-rahv*	knob celery
les champignons	*lay shahn-pee-nyohn*	mushrooms
le chou	*luh shoo*	cabbage (green)
le chou-fleur	*luh shoo-fluhr*	cauliflower
la courgette	*lah koor-zheht*	zucchini
le cresson	*luh kreh-ssohn*	watercress
les épinards	*lay zay-pee-nahr*	spinach
les flageolets	*lay flah-zhoh-leh*	green shell beans
les haricots verts	*lay ah-ree-koh vehr*	green beans
les oignons	*lay zoh-nyohn*	onions
l'oseille (f.)	*loh-zehy*	sorrel
le piment	*luh pee-mahn*	green pepper
les pois	*lay pwah*	peas
le poireau	*luh pwah-roh*	leek
les pommes de terre	*lay pohm duh tehr*	potatoes
la tomate	*lah toh-maht*	tomato

SEASONINGS

Although French food is most often perfectly seasoned, personal preferences sometimes intercede. Here's how to ask for what you want.

I'd like ____.	**Je voudrais ____.**	*zhuh voo-dreh*
■ butter	**du beurre**	*dew buhr*
■ horseradish	**du raifort**	*dew reh-fohr*
■ ketchup	**du ketchup**	*dew keht-chuhp*
■ margarine	**de la margarine**	*duh lah mahr-gah-reen*
■ mayonnaise	**de la mayonnaise**	*duh lah mah-yoh-nehz*
■ mustard	**de la moutarde**	*duh lah moo-tahrd*
■ olive oil	**de l'huile d'olive**	*duh lweel doh-leev*
■ pepper (black)	**du poivre (noir)**	*dew pwah-vruh (nwahr)*
■ pepper (red)	**du poivre (rouge)**	*dew pwah-vruh (roozh)*
■ saccharine	**de la saccharine**	*duh lah sah-kah-reen*
■ salt	**du sel**	*dew sehl*
■ sugar	**du sucre**	*dew sew-kruh*
■ vinegar	**du vinaigre**	*dew vee-neh-gruh*
■ worcestershire sauce	**de la sauce anglaise**	*du lah sohss ahn-glehz*

CHEESE COURSE

The cheese course is offered after the meat course and before the dessert. Most often, the restaurant will offer a tray of cheeses, from which you select two or three that balance one another. The cheese course is an opportunity to sample some cheeses that never get exported.

What is that cheese?	**Quel est ce fromage?**	*kehl eh suh froh-mahzh*
Is it ____?	**Est-il ____?**	*eh-teel*
■ mild	**maigre**	*meh-gruh*
■ sharp	**piquant**	*pee-kahn*
■ hard	**fermenté**	*fehr-mahn-tay*
■ soft	**à pâte molle**	*ah paht mohl*

Among the more popular cheeses are the following.

1. BANON   Made from sheep's or goat's milk, a soft cheese with a natural rind; a mild cheese with a mild nutty flavor.

2. BLEU D'AUVERGNE   Made from cow's milk, this soft cheese has an internal mold and when cut, the veins are visible. With a very sharp flavor.

3. BOURSIN   A soft cow's milk cheese, with a mild flavor, sometimes enhanced with herbs.

4. BRIE   A variety of cheeses made from cow's milk and with a bloomy rind. Varieties range in flavor from mild to very pronounced, some with a fruity flavor.

5. CAMEMBERT   Less delicate than brie, but also a cow's milk cheese with a bloomy rind. Should be eaten firm.

6. CANTAL   A cow's milk cheese that varies with length of aging. Some varieties are softer and milder, while more aged ones are hard and with a more pronounced flavor.

7. CHÈVRE   Any of an almost infinite variety of goat's milk cheeses, which vary from very soft to quite firm, and from mild and creamy to tart and crumbly. There will always be a few chèvres on the cheese tray.

8. COLOMBIÈRE   This cow's milk cheese is soft and supple, with a mild flavor.

9. MUNSTER   A cow's milk cheese that is soft and spicy, with a tangy flavor. In Alsace, where the cheese comes from, it is eaten young.

10. PONT-L'ÉVÊQUE   A cow's milk cheese that is very smooth and supple, with a pronounced flavor.

11. PORT-SALUT   The brand name for the Saint-Paulin from the monastery of Port-du-Salut.

12. REBLOCHON   A soft cow's milk cheese with a mild and creamy flavor.

13. ROQUEFORT   A sheep's milk cheese that is soft and pungent. The cheese is cured in caves, an ancient process with rigid standards for production. Texture is very buttery.

14. SAINT-PAULIN   Made from cow's milk, this is a velvety smooth cheese with a mild flavor.

15. TOMME DE SAVOIE   A mild cow's milk cheese with a nutty flavor.

Petit Suisse is a fresh, unsalted cheese made from cow's milk and enriched with cream, then molded into heart shapes and sprinkled with sugar; it is a common dessert.

Fromage à la crème is *fromage blanc*, a rich, creamy white cheese made from unskimmed cow's milk. It is eaten topped with cream and sugar for breakfast.

Fondue is a specialty of Switzerland and parts of France that border on Switzerland. It is a large pot of bubbling melted cheese (usually gruyère or emmenthal), into which is dipped cubes of French bread. Fondue is served as a warming lunch or dinner course.

Raclette is a specialty of French-speaking Switzerland. It involves the slow melting of a hard cheese, usually alongside a roaring fire, during which the diners scrape off the cheese as it melts onto slices of French bread.

FRUITS AND NUTS

Here are the names of some common fruits, followed by nuts.

l'abricot	*lah-bree-koh*	apricot
l'ananas	*lah-nah-nah*	pineapple
la banane	*lah bah-nahn*	banana
les cassis	*lay kah-sseess*	black currants
la cerise	*lah suh-reez*	cherry
le citron	*luh see-trohn*	lemon
la datte	*lah daht*	date

la figue	*lah feeg*	fig
les fraises	*lay frehz*	strawberries
les fraises des bois	*lay frehz duh bwah*	wild strawberries
les framboises	*lay frahn-bwahz*	raspberries
les groseilles	*lay groh-sehy*	red currants
la limette	*lah lee-meht*	lime
la mandarine	*lah mahn-dah-reen*	tangerine
le melon	*luh muh-lohn*	melon
les mûres	*lay mewr*	mulberries
les myrtilles	*lay meer-tee*	blueberries
l'orange	*loh-rahnzh*	orange
la noix de coco	*lah nwah duh koh-koh*	coconut
le pample-mousse	*luh pahn-pluh-mooss*	grapefruit
la pêche	*lah pehsh*	peach
la poire	*lah pwahr*	pear
la pomme	*lah pohm*	apple
la prune	*lah prewn*	plum
le pruneau	*luh prew-noh*	prune
le raisin	*luh reh-zan*	grape
l'amande *(f.)*	*lah-mahnd*	almond
le marron	*luh mah-rohn*	chestnut
la noisette	*lah nwah-zeht*	hazelnut
les noix	*lay nwah*	nuts

DESSERTS—SWEETS

Often, a restaurant will display its desserts on a table in the dining room or the waiter will roll the cart to your table so you can make a selection. On the cart will be a variety of tarts, fruits in light syrup, and pastries. Here are some common items you might consider for dessert.

1. BAVAROISE   A bavarian cream; mont-blanc is a bavarian cream made with chestnuts.

2. BEIGNETS   Fritters, often made from fruit such as apple.

3. BOMBE   An ice cream construction, often with different flavors and sometimes also with sherbet.

4. CHARLOTTE   An assemblage of sponge fingers and pudding; usually the sponge cake is used to line the dish and pudding is in the center.

5. CRÈME CARAMEL   An egg custard served with a caramel sauce.

6. CRÊPES   Dessert crêpes, the most famous of which are **Crêpes Suzette,** made with orange flavoring and served flaming with Grand Marnier.

7. GÂTEAU   An elaborate layer cake, made with thin layers of sponge cake and pastry cream, and decorated.

8. MOUSSE AU CHOCOLAT   An airy pudding made with chocolate, cream, eggs, and brandy, garnished with whipped cream.

9. MACÉDOINE DE FRUITS   A fresh fruit salad.

10. OEUFS À LA NEIGE   Soft meringue ovals served floating on a custard sauce.

11. OMELETTE NORVÉGIENNE   Baked Alaska.

12. PÂTISSERIE   Pastry selection of any variety, including éclairs, millefeuilles, savarin, Saint-Honoré (cream puff cake).

13. POIRES HÉLÈNE   A poached pear, served with vanilla ice cream and chocolate sauce.

14. PROFITEROLES   Cream puffs, served with chocolate sauce.

15. SOUFFLÉ   An endless variety of sweet soufflés, the famous one being the Grand Marnier soufflé.

16. TARTE   Open-faced fruit pies, often made with apples or plums.

In addition, ice cream is a French favorite, as is sherbet and granité (fruit ice). Here's how to ask for these:

ice cream	**une glace**	*ewn glahss*
■ chocolate	**au chocolat**	*oh shoh-koh-lah*
■ vanilla	**à la vanille**	*ah lah vah-nee*
■ strawberry	**aux fraises**	*oh frehz*
sundae	**une coupe**	*ewn koop*
sherbet	**un sorbet**	*uhn sohr-beh*
fruit ice	**un granité**	*uhn grah-nee-tay*

SPECIAL CIRCUMSTANCES

Many travelers have special dietary requirements, so here are a few phrases that might help you get what you need or avoid what does you wrong.

I don't want anything fried (salted).	**Je ne veux rien de frit (salé).** *zhuh nuh vuh vuh ryan duh free (sah-lay)*
I cannot eat anything made with ____.	**Je ne peux rien manger de cuisiné au (à la) ____.** *zhuh nuh puh ryan mahn-zhay duh kwee-zee-nay oh (ah lah)*
Do you have any dishes without meats?	**Avez-vous des plats sans viande?** *ah-vay voo day plah sahn vyahnd*

BEVERAGES

See pages 103–107 for information on French apéritifs, wines, and brandies. As for other beverages, we give you the following phrases to help you ask for exactly what you wish.

Waiter, please bring me ____.	**Garçon, apportez-moi ____.** *gahr-ssohn ah-pohr-tay mwah*
coffee	**du café** *dew kah-fay*
■ with milk (morning only)	**du café au lait** *dew kah-fay oh leh*
■ espresso	**du café-express** *dew kah-fay ehkss-prehss*
■ with cream	**du café-crème** *dew kah-fay krehm*

■black coffee	**du café noir**	*dew kah-fay nwahr*
■iced coffee	**du café glacé**	*dew kah-fay glah-ssay*
cider (alcoholic)	**du cidre**	*dew see-druh*
juice	**du jus**	*dew zhew*
lemonade	**de la citronnade**	*duh lah see-troh-nahd*
milk	**du lait**	*dew leh*
■cold	**froid**	*frwah*
■hot	**chaud**	*shoh*
■milk shake	**un frappé**	*uhn frah-pay*
orangeade	**une orangeade**	*ewn oh-rahn-zhahd*
punch	**un punch**	*uhn puhnsh*
soda	**un soda**	*uhn soh-dah*
tea	**un thé**	*uhn tay*
■with milk	**au lait**	*oh leh*
■with lemon	**au citron**	*oh see-trohn*
■with sugar	**sucré**	*sew-kray*
■iced	**glacé**	*glah-ssay*
water	**de l'eau** *(f.)*	*duh loh*
■cold	**de l'eau fraîche**	*duh loh frehsh*
■ice	**de l'eau glacée**	*duh loh glah-ssay*
■mineral	**de l'eau minérale**	*duh loh mee-nay-rahl*
■with gas	**gazeuse**	*gah-zuhz*
■without gas	**plate**	*plaht*

SETTLING UP

The bill normally includes a surcharge for service. In addition, most people leave the small change from the bill as a token of appreciation.

The check, please.	**L'addition, s'il vous plaît.** *lah-dee-ssyohn seel voo pleh*
Separate checks.	**Des notes séparées.** *day noht say-pah-ray*
Is the service (tip) included?	**Le service est compris?** *luh sehr-veess eh kohn-pree*
I haven't ordered this.	**Je n'ai pas commandé ceci.** *zhuh nay pah koh-mahn-day suh-ssee*
I don't think the bill is right.	**Je crois qu'il y a une erreur dans l'addition.** *zhuh krwah keel yah ewn ehr-ruhr dahn lah-dee-ssyohn*
We're in a hurry.	**Nous sommes pressés.** *noo sohm preh-ssay*
Is it ready?	**Est-elle prête?** *eh-tehl preht*
Will it take long?	**Il faudra longtemps?** *eel foh-drah lohn-tahn*
This is for you.	**Ceci est pour vous.** *suh-ssee eh poor voo*

REGIONAL FRENCH SPECIALTIES

French food is noted for its ingredients: wild mushrooms such as **chanterelles, cèpes,** and morels; truffles; fresh **foie gras;** chickens from Bresse; butter and cream from Normandy; cheese from all parts of France. Below we give you some of the notable dishes from some of the provinces of France, most of which are famous for their regional ingredients.

1. ALSACE-LORRAINE This region has a strong German influence in its food and the most famous dish is **choucroute garnie,** a sauerkraut, pork and sausage mixture; also **pâté de foie gras, quiche lorraine,** and **chicken in riesling wine.** The food is hearty, with much emphasis on fish, fruit, and pork.
2. BORDEAUX Food from here is prepared simply, with use of Bordeaux wine, **cèpes,** and **confit d'oie,** a potted goose, preserved in its own fat. This is a noted wine-producing area.

3. BRITTANY **Crêpes** are the best-known food from here, with a variety of sweet and savory fillings. There is also much seafood and sausages. Cider is the popular beverage.

4. BURGUNDY With Lyons in the gastronomic center, this region has some of the best food in France. The chickens from Bresse are world famous, as is the beef; from Burgundy we also get the savory mustards, spiced gingerbread, and black-currant liqueur—cassis. This is also a major wine-producing region.

5. NORMANDY Foods from here are marked by a use of apples or apple **eau de vie.** The omelettes from Mère Poulard are famous; the fish dishes in this region are also noteworthy.

6. PROVENCE This is a southern region that uses much olive oil and garlic in its dishes. Fish and seafood predominate, with a generous use of vegetables and fruits. The most famous dish is **bouillabaisse,** a fish stew; **salade niçoise,** with lettuce, tuna, hard-cooked eggs, olives, and anchovies, and **pissaladière,** a pizza made with anchovies are also popular.

7. PARIS Food from all parts of France influences the dishes that are served in Paris. Those especially Parisian are **boeuf à la mode** (boiled beef with vegetables) and brie cheese.

APÉRITIFS, WINES, AND AFTER-DINNER DRINKS

APÉRITIFS

Most French people prefer to drink an apéritif before a meal rather than a cocktail. An apéritif is an appetite stimulant, and can be a variety of drinks, ranging from a simple vermouth or vermouth mixed with a liqueur (such as cassis), to a distilled drink such as Cynar, made from artichoke hearts. Among the most popular are:

Byrrh **Dubonnet** **Saint-Raphaël** }	wine-and-brandy–based, flavored with herbs and bitters
Pernod **Ricard** }	anise-based, licorice-flavored
Vermouth	fortified wine made from red or white grapes

Cynar	bitter tasting, distilled from artichoke hearts

WINE

The high quality of the soil and the moderate climate have given French vineyards their historically unique position among wine-producing countries. Wine served with meals follows a progression from the light white wines to richer, heartier reds. (One wouldn't drink a Mâcon after a Pommard, or a Bordeaux after a Burgundy.)

White wines and rosés are served very cold (52°F). Beaujolais, although red, should be lightly chilled. Bordeaux is served at room temperature (62°), Burgundy just above room temperature. Sweet wines should be chilled, and Champagne iced. The chart below will help you select a wine to suit your tastes and your food.

wine	**le vin**	*luh van*
■ red wine	**le vin rouge**	*luh van roozh*
■ rosé	**le vin rosé**	*luh van roh-zay*
■ sparkling wine	**le vin mous-seux**	*luh van moo-ssuh*
■ sherry	**un sherry**	*uhn sheh-ree*
■ white wine	**le vin blanc**	*luh van blahn*

AFTER-DINNER DRINKS

Brandy is often enjoyed after a lengthy, especially fine meal. **Cognac,** the finest of brandies, is distilled from grapes grown in the Charente district, the principal city of which is Cognac. It is usually aged for 20 years in barrels made from Limousin oak trees. Four different types that differ in character and taste are Remy-Martin, Martel, Courvoisier, and Hennessy. Ordering these cognacs in France is considerably less expensive than elsewhere.

Armagnac comes from the Basque region. It is often bottled straight, rather than blended as cognac is.

Eaux-de-vie are distilled fruit brandies. Unlike cognac and other brandies, they are aged in crockery, not wood, so their taste is harsher. Some eaux-de-vie are **kirsch** (black cherry), **framboise** (wild raspberries), **poire william** (Swiss William pears), **mirabelle** (yellow plum), **calvados** (apple), and **marc** (from stems, pits, and skins of certain grapes).

Some liqueurs to choose from are:

absinthe	light drink with a pronounced anise aroma.
anisette	clear, sweet aromatic liqueur made from aniseeds and herbs.
Bénédictine	a blend of 150 different herbs and plants.
B & B	a combination of Bénédictine and brandy.
Chambord	raspberry-flavored, combined with honey.
Chartreuse	a combination of 130 herbs, in green and yellow.
Cointreau	made from sweet and bitter tropical orange peels blended with cognac.
Crème de Cassis	made from black currants.
Grand Marnier	an orange-flavored liqueur made from the peel of bitter Curaçao oranges and blended with cognac.

TRAVEL TIP

Every traveler needs to carry a few small items for emergencies. Sealed, pre-wet wash cloths, Band-Aids, a fold-up toothbrush, a small tube of toothpaste, a tiny sewing kit, notebook and pen, and aspirin are musts for the handbag or backpack. Skip Swiss army knives or any object that could be considered a weapon by airport security guards.

WINE	REGION	DESCRIPTION	ORDER WITH
Anjou	Loire	semisweet rosé	fish, meat, game, poultry, esp. ham
Beaujolais	Burgundy	light, young, fruity red wine	meat, poultry, fowl, cheese
Chablis	Burgundy	dry white, flinty bouquet, nutty taste	fish, seafood, esp. lobster
Champagne	Champagne	delicate, sparkling white wine	
		Extra Dry (fruity)—medium dry	aperitif
		Brut—driest	aperitif
		Sec—least dry	dessert
Châteauneuf-du-Pape	Rhône	full-bodied red wine	game, poultry, meat
Côte de Beaune	Burgundy	very delicate light red wine	meat, esp. prime ribs, fowl, poultry
Côte de Bourg	Bordeaux	medium, full-bodied red wine	meat, poultry, fowl, cheese
Côtes du Rhône	Rhône	light, fruity, red wine	meat, poultry, fowl
		full-bodied white wine	fish, fowl, veal
Gewürztraminer	Alsace	light, crisp white wine	fish, poultry, some cheese
Graves (blanc)	Bordeaux	soft white wine	fish, poultry

Graves (rouge)	Bordeaux	robust red wine	meat, fowl, poultry, cheese
Mâconnais (Pouilly-Fuissé)	Burgundy	light, dry, white wine	fish, seafood, egg and cheese dishes
Médoc	Bordeaux	light red wine	meat, poultry, fowl, cheese
Muscadet	Loire	light, dry white wine	fish, seafood, esp. scallops
Muscat	Alsace	sweet white wine (also sparkling)	fish, seafood, desserts
Pinot	Alsace	light, fruity, white wine	fish, shellfish, cold vegetable dishes, egg and cheese dishes
Pomerol	Bordeaux	mellow, full-bodied red wine	meat, fowl, poultry, cheese
Riesling	Alsace	light, fruity, white wine	fish, shellfish, cold vegetable dishes, egg and cheese dishes
Saumur	Loire	dry, white wine	fish, seafood, poultry
Sauternes (Barsac)	Bordeaux	honey-sweet white wine	desserts
St-Emilion	Bordeaux	full-bodied, dark red wine	meat, fowl, poultry, cheese, esp. ham
Vouvray	Loire	white or sparkling white	fish, seafood, meat

GETTING TO KNOW PEOPLE

Remember to shake hands when meeting people. A Frenchman may feel offended if you do not. In general, Europeans don't ask many personal questions at the beginning of an acquaintance. Make contact through a neutral topic like the weather or the traffic.

MEETING PEOPLE

Do you live here?	**Habitez-vous ici?**	*ah-bee-tay voo zee-ssee*
I am ____.	**Je suis ____.**	*zhuh swee*
■ from the United States	**des États-Unis**	*day zay-tah zew-nee*
■ from England	**d'Angleterre**	*dahn-gluh-tehr*
■ from Canada	**du Canada**	*dew kah-nah-dah*
■ from Australia	**de Australie**	*duh ohss-trah-lee*
I like France (Paris) very much.	**La France (Paris) me plaît beaucoup.**	*lah frahnss (pah-ree) muh pleh boh-koo*
I would like to go there.	**Je voudrais y aller.**	*zhuh voo-dreh zee ah-lay*
How long will you be staying?	**Combien de temps resterez-vous ici?**	*kohn-byan duh tahn rehss-tray voo zee-ssee*
I'll stay for a few days (a week).	**Je resterai quelques jours (une semaine).**	*zhuh rehss-tray kehl-kuh zhoor (ewn suh-mehn)*
Where are you living now?	**Où habitez-vous en ce moment?**	*oo ah-bee-tay voo zahn suh moh-mahn*

What hotel are you at?	**À quel hôtel êtes-vous?**	*ah kehl oh-tehl eht voo*
What do you think of ___?	**Que pensez-vous de ___?**	*kuh pahn-ssay voo duh*
I (don't) like it very much.	**Je (ne) l'aime (pas) beaucoup.**	*zhuh (nuh) lehm (pah) boh-koo*
I think its very ___.	**Je pense qu'il (elle) est ___.**	*zhuh pahnss keel (kehl) eh*

- beautiful   **beau (belle)** *boh (behl)*
- interesting   **intéressant(e)** *an-tay-reh-ssahn(t)*
- magnificent   **magnifique** *mah-nyee-feek*
- wonderful   **formidable** *fohr-mee-dah-bluh*

GREETINGS AND INTRODUCTIONS

May I introduce ___.	**Puis-je vous présenter ___.**	*pweezh voo pray-zahn-tay*

- my brother   **mon frère** *mohn frehr*
- my father   **mon père** *mohn pehr*
- my friend   **mon ami(e)** *mohn nah-mee*
- my husband   **mon mari** *mohn mah-ree*
- my mother   **ma mère** *mah mehr*
- my sister   **ma soeur** *mah suhr*
- my sweetheart   **mon(ma) fiancé(e)** *mohn (mah) fee-yahn-ssay*
- my wife   **ma femme** *mah fahm*

How do you do (Glad to meet you).	**Enchanté(e).**	*ahn-shahn-tay*
How do you do (The pleasure is mine).	**Moi de même.**	*mwah duh mehm*

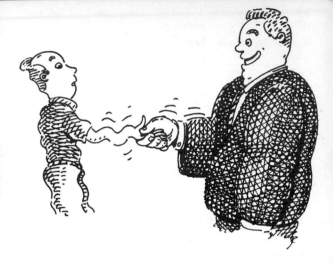

Allow me to intro- duce myself.	**Permettez-moi de me présenter.** *pehr-meh-tay mwah duh muh pray-* *zah<u>n</u>-tay*
My name is _____.	**Je m'appelle _____.** *zhuh mah-* *pehl*
Mine is _____.	**Et moi, je m'appelle _____.** *ay* *mwah zhuh mah-pehl*
I am _____.	**Je suis _____.** *zhuh swee*
■ a teacher	**instituteur (institutrice)** *za<u>n</u>-sstee* *tew-tuhr (za<u>n</u>-sstee-tew-treess)*
■ a doctor	**médecin** *mayd-sa<u>n</u>*
■ a lawyer	**avocat(e)** *zah-voh-kah(t)*
■ a businessperson	**homme (femme) d'affaires** *zohm* *(fahm) dah-fehr*
■ a student	**étudiant(e)** *zay-tew-dyah<u>n</u>(t)*

DATING AND SOCIALIZING

May I have this dance?	**M'accordez-vous cette danse?** *mah-kohr-day voo seht dah<u>n</u>ss*
Yes, all right. With pleasure.	**Oui, d'accord. Avec plaisir.** *wee, dah-kohr. ah-vehk pleh-zeer*
Would you like a cigarette (a drink)?	**Voudriez-vous une cigarette (une boisson)?** *voo-dree-yay voo zewn see-gah-reht (ewn bwah-ssoh<u>n</u>)*
Do you have a light?	**Avez-vous du feu?** *ah-vay voo dew fuh*
Do you mind if I smoke?	**Ça vous dérange si je fume?** *sah voo day-rah<u>n</u>zh see zhuh fewm*
May I take you home?	**Puis-je vous raccompagner chez vous?** *pweezh voo rah-koh<u>n</u>-pah-nyay shay voo*
May I call you?	**Puis-je vous téléphoner?** *pweezh voo tay-lay-foh-nay*
What is your telephone number?	**Quel est votre numéro de téléphone?** *kehl eh voh-truh new-may-roh duh tay-lay fohn*
Here's my telephone number (address).	**Voici mon numéro de téléphone (mon adresse).** *vwah-ssee moh<u>n</u> new-may-roh duh tay-lay fohn (moh<u>n</u> nah-drehss)*
Will you write to me?	**Est-ce que vous m'écrirez?** *ehss kuh voo may-kree-ray*
Are you married?	**Êtes-vous marié(e)?** *eht voo mah-ree-ay*
Are you alone?	**Êtes-vous seul(e)?** *eht voo suhl*
Is your husband (wife) here?	**Êtes-vous ici avec votre mari (femme)?** *eht voo zee-ssee ah-vehk voh-truh mah-ree (fahm)*

I'm here with my family.	**Je suis ici avec ma famille.** *zhuh swee zee-ssee ah-vehk mah fah-mee*
Do you have any children?	**Avez-vous des enfants?** *ah-vay voo day zahn-fahn*
How many?	**Combien en avez-vous?** *kohn-byan-ahn nah-vay voo*
How old are they?	**Quel âge ont-ils?** *kehl ahzh ohn teel*
I'm single.	**Je suis célibataire.** *zhuh swee say-lee-bah-tehr*
You must come to visit us.	**Vous devez venir nous rendre visite.** *voo duh-vay vuh-neer noo rahn-druh vee-zeet*
Would you like me to take a picture (snapshot) of you?	**Voudriez-vous que je vous prenne en photo?** *voo-dree-yay voo kuh zhuh voo prehn ahn foh-toh*
Stand here.	**Restez ici.** *rehss-tay zee-ssee*
Don't move.	**Ne bougez pas.** *nuh boo-zhay pah*
Smile.	**Souriez.** *soo-ryay*
That's it.	**C'est ça.** *seh sah*
Will you take a picture of me (us)?	**Voudriez-vous me (nous) prendre en photo?** *voo-dree-yay voo muh (noo) prahn-druh-ahn foh-toh*
Are you doing anything tomorrow?	**Avez-vous quelque chose à faire demain?** *ah-vay voo kehl-kuh shohz ah fehr duh-man?*
Are you free this evening?	**Êtes-vous libre ce soir?** *eht voo lee-bruh suh swahr*
Would you like to go together?	**Voudriez-vous aller ensemble?** *voo-dree-yay voo zah-lay ahn-sahn-bluh*
I'll wait for you in front of the hotel.	**Je vous attendrai devant l'hôtel.** *zhuh voo zah-tahn-dray duh-vahn loh-tehl*

I'll pick you up at your house (hotel).	**Je viendrai vous prendre chez vous (à votre hôtel).** *zhuh vyan-dray voo prahn-druh shay voo (ah voh-truh oh-tehl*

SAYING GOOD-BYE

Nice to have met you.	**(Je suis) enchanté(e) d'avoir fait votre connaissance.** *(zhuh swee z)ahn-shahn-tay dah-vwahr feh voh-truh koh-neh-ssahnss*
The pleasure is mine.	**Le plaisir est partagé.** *luh pleh-zeer eh pahr-tah-zhay*
Regards to _____.	**Mon meilleur souvenir à _____.** *mohn meh-yuhr soo-vuh-neer ah*

TRAVEL TIP

A T.V.A. (value added tax) of over 18% is levied on all goods except medicine, food and books. A 33% luxury tax is added to such items as jewelry, video and photography equipment. This money may, however, be refunded to you. A *détaxe* desk in most large department stores helps non-European foreigners receive a 13–23% discount on large purchases of luxury items. Spending 1200 francs or more in one store, within a six-month period, entitles the buyer to this rebate. Naturally, it is essential that you save all sales slips for the *détaxe*. They will be stamped by a French custom official upon departure from the country.

SHOPPING

SHOPS AND STORES

It is best to start by shopping in the large department stores so that you may browse without feeling obligated to make a purchase. Most department stores are open Monday through Saturday, from 9:30 AM to 6:30 PM. Many boutiques are open on Sunday; closed on Monday. In Switzerland, however, stores are open from 8 AM to 6:30 PM and on Saturday from 8 AM to 4 PM. Smaller stores have similar hours and many close between noon and 2 PM. Most of the hairdressers are closed on Monday and the fashion boutiques on Monday morning. Sales are usually at the beginning of January and at the end of June and the beginning of July. Most of the stores (even the department stores) remain closed on public holidays. Food stores are open on Sunday morning from 8:00 AM to 12:00 noon.

In Paris the main shopping centers are located in the Palais de Congrès de Paris, the Montparnasse area, and in the Forum des Halles. Sales usually take place the first week in January and the last week of June or July. Couturier sales are in March or July.

Discounts of up to 20% are still given in many shops for purchases made in foreign currency, in the form of a refund mailed to your home address.

GOING SHOPPING

I'd like to go shopping today.	**Je voudrais aller faire des courses aujourd'hui.** *zhuh voo-dreh zah-lay fehr day koorss oh-zhoor-dwee*
Where can I find _____?	**Où pourrais-je trouver _____?** *oo poo-rehzh troo-vay*
■ a bakery	**une boulangerie** *ewn boo-lah<u>n</u>zh-ree*
■ a barber shop	**un coiffeur** *uh<u>n</u> kwah-fuhr*

■ a beauty parlor   **un salon de beauté** *uhn sah-lohn duh boh-tay*

■ a bookstore   **une librairie** *ewn lee-breh-ree*

■ a butcher   **une boucherie** *ewn boosh-ree*

■ a camera shop   **un magasin d'appareils-photo** *uhn mah-gah-zan dah-pah-rehy foh-toh*

■ a candy store   **une confiserie** *ewn kohn-feess-ree*

■ a clothing store   **un magasin de vêtements** *uhn mah-gah-zan duh veht-mahn*

　　for children's clothes   **pour enfants** *poor ahn-fahn*

　　men's store   **pour hommes** *poor ohm*

　　women's boutique   **pour femmes** *poor fahm*

■ a delicatessen   **une charcuterie** *ewn shahr-kew-tree*

■ a department store   **un grand magasin** *uhn grahn mah-gah-zan*

■ a drugstore   **une pharmacie** *ewn fahr-mah-ssee*

■ a dry cleaner's   **une teinturerie** *ewn tan-tew-ruh-ree*

■ a florist   **un fleuriste** *uhn fluh-reesst*

■ a gift (souvenir) shop   **un magasin de souvenirs** *uhn mah-gah-zan duh soov-neer*

■ a grocery store   **une épicerie** *ewn ay-peess-ree*

■ a hardware store   **une quincaillerie** *ewn kahn-kahy-ree*

■ a jewelry store   **une bijouterie** *ewn bee-zhoo-tree*

■ a laundry   **une blanchisserie** *ewn blahn-sheess-ree*

■ a liquor store   **un magasin de vins et spiritueux** *uhn mah-gah-zan duh van ay spee-ree-tew-uh*

■ a newsstand   **un kiosque à journaux** *uhn kee-ohsk ah zhoor-noh*

■ an optician   **un opticien** *uhn nohp-tee-ssyan*

■ a record store   **un magasin de disques** *uhn mah-gah-zan duh deessk*

■ a shoemaker   **un cordonnier** *uhn kohr-doh-nyay*

■ a shoe store   **un magasin de chaussures** *uhn mah-gah-zan duh shoh-ssewr*

■ a supermarket   **un supermarché** *uhn sew-pehr-mahr-shay*

■ a tailor   **un tailleur** *uhn tah-yuhr*

■ a tobacco shop   **un bureau de tabac** *uhn bew-roh duh tah-bah*

■ a toy store   **un magasin de jouets** *uhn mah-gah-zan duh zhoo-eh*

■ a travel agent   **une agence de voyages** *ewn ah-zhahnss duh vwah-yahzh*

■ a watchmaker   **un horlogier** *uhn nohr-lohzh-yay*

■ a wine merchant   **un négociant en vins** *uhn nay-gohss-yahn ahn van*

Sir.   **Monsieur.** *muh-ssyuh*

Young man.   **Jeune homme.** *zhuhn ohm*

Miss.   **Mademoiselle.** *mahd-mwah-zehl*

Can you help me?   **Pouvez-vous m'aider?** *poo-vay voo meh-day*

Where is the Lost and Found Office?   **Où est le Bureau des Objets Trouvés?** *oo eh luh bew-roh dayb-zheh troo-vay*

BOOKS

Where is the best (biggest) bookstore here?	**Où se trouve la meilleure (la plus grande) librairie par ici?** *oo suh troov lah meh-yuhr (lah plew grahnd) lee-breh-ree pahr ee-ssee*
What can I do for you?	**On vous sert?** *ohn voo sehr*
I'm looking for a copy of ____.	**Je cherche un exemplaire de ____.** *zhuh shehrsh uhn nehg-zahn-plehr duh*
The title of the book is ____.	**Le titre du livre est ____.** *luh tee-truh dew lee-vruh eh*
The author of the book is ____.	**L'auteur du livre est ____.** *loh-tuhr dew lee-vruh eh*
I don't know the title (author).	**Je ne sais pas le titre (le nom de l'auteur).** *zhuh nuh seh pah luh tee-truh (le nohn duh loh-tuhr)*
I'm just looking.	**Je regarde tout simplement.** *zhuh ruh-gahrd too san-pluh-mahn*
Do you have books (novels) in English?	**Avez-vous des livres (des romans) en anglais?** *ah-vay voo day lee-vruh (day roh-mahn) ahn nahn-gleh*
I would like ____.	**Je voudrais ____.** *zhuh voo-dreh*
■ a guide book	**un guide touristique** *uhn geed too-reess-teek*
■ a map of this city	**un plan de la ville** *uhn plahn duh lah veel*
■ a pocket dictionary	**un dictionnaire de poche** *uhn deek-ssyoh-nehr duh pohsh*
■ a French-English dictionary	**un dictionnaire français-anglais** *uhn deek-ssyoh- nehr frahn-sseh ahn-gleh*
Where can I find ____?	**Où puis-je trouver ____?** *oo pweezh troo-vay*

■ detective stories	**des romans policiers** *day roh-mahn poh-leess-yay*
■ history books	**des livres d'histoire** *day lee-vruh deess-twahr*
■ short story books	**des contes** *day kohnt*
I'll take these books.	**Je vais prendre ces livres.** *zhuh veh prahn-druh say lee-vruh*
Will you wrap them, please?	**Voulez-vous les emballer, s'il vous plaît?** *voo-lay voo lay zahn-bah-lay seel voo pleh*

CLOTHING

Would you please show me ____?	**Veuillez me montrer ____?** *vuh-yay muh mohn-tray*
■ a belt	**une ceinture** *ewn san-tewr*
■ a blouse	**un chemisier** *uhn shuh-mee-zyay*
■ a bra	**un soutien-gorge** *uhn soo-tyan gohrzh*
■ a dress	**une robe** *ewn rohb*
■ an evening gown	**une robe du soir** *ewn rohb duh swahr*
■ leather (suede) gloves	**des gants en cuir (en daim)** *day gahn ahn kweer (ahn dan)*
■ handkerchiefs	**des mouchoirs** *day moo-shwahr*
■ a hat	**un chapeau** *uhn shah-poh*
■ a jacket	**un veston** *uhn vehss-tohn*
■ an overcoat	**un manteau/pardessus** *uhn mahn-toh/pahr-duh-ssew*
■ panties (women)	**un slip** *uhn sleep*
■ pants	**un pantalon** *uhn pahn-tah-lohn*
■ pantyhose	**des collants** *day koh-lahn*

■ a raincoat	**un imperméable** *uhn nan-pehr-may-ah-bluh*
■ a robe	**une robe de chambre** *ewn rohb duh shahn-bruh*
■ a shirt	**une chemise** *ewn shuh-meez*
■ (a pair of) shoes	**une paire de chaussures** *ewn pehr duh shoh-ssewr*
■ shorts (briefs)	**des caleçons** *day kahl-ssohn*
■ a skirt	**une jupe** *ewn zhewp*
■ a slip	**un jupon** *uhn zhew-pohn*
■ slippers	**des pantoufles** *day pahn-too-fluh*
■ socks	**des chaussettes** *day shoh-sseht*
■ (nylon) stockings	**des bas (nylon)** *day bah (nee-lohn)*
■ a suit	**un complet/un tailleur** *uhn kohn-pleh/uhn tah-yuhr*
■ a sweater	**un chandail** *uhn shahn-dahy*
■ a tie	**une cravate** *ewn krah-vaht*

■ an undershirt (T-shirt)	**un sous-vêtement** *uhn soo veht-mahn*
■ a wallet	**un portefeuille** *uhn pohr-tuh-fuhy*
Is there a special sale today?	**Y a-t-il des soldes aujourd'hui?** *ee ah teel day sohld oh-zhoor-dwee*
I'd like the _____ with short (long) (no) sleeves.	**Je voudrais le/la _____ à manches courtes (longues) (sans manches).** *zhuh voo-dreh luh/lah _____ ah mahnsh koort (lohng) (sahn mahnsh)*
Do you have anything _____?	**Avez-vous quelque chose _____?** *ah-vay voo kehl-kuh shohz*
■ cheaper	**de moins cher** *duh mwan shehr*
■ else	**d'autre** *doh-truh*
■ larger	**de plus grand** *duh plew grahn*
■ more (less) expensive	**de plus (moins) cher** *duh plew (mwan) shehr*
■ longer	**de plus long** *duh plew lohn*
■ of better quality	**de meilleure qualité** *duh meh-yuhr kah-lee-tay*
■ shorter	**de plus court** *duh plew koor*
■ smaller	**de plus petit** *duh plew puh-tee*
I don't like the color.	**Je n'aime pas la couleur.** *zhuh nehm pah lah koo-luhr*
Do you have it in _____?	**L'avez-vous en _____?** *lah-vay voo zahn*
■ black	**noir** *nwahr*
■ blue	**bleu** *bluh*
■ brown	**brun/marron** *bruhn/mah-rohn*
■ gray	**gris** *gree*
■ green	**vert** *vehr*
■ pink	**rose** *rohze*

■ red   **rouge** *roozh*

■ white   **blanc** *blah<u>n</u>*

■ yellow   **jaune** *zhohn*

I want something in _____.   **Je voudrais quelque chose en _____.** *zhuh voo-dreh kehl-kuh shohz ah<u>n</u>*

CHART OF MATERIALS

■ chiffon   **mousseline de soie** *mooss-leen duh swah*

■ corduroy   **velours côtelé** *vuh-loor koht-lay*

■ cotton   **coton** *koh-toh<u>n</u>*

■ denim   **coutil´** *koo-tee*

■ felt   **feutre** *fuh-truh*

■ flannel   **flanelle** *flah-nehl*

■ gabardine   **gabardine** *gah-bahr-deen*

■ lace   **dentelle** *dah<u>n</u>-tehl*

■ leather   **cuir** *kweer*

■ linen   **lin** *la<u>n</u>*

■ nylon   **nylon** *nee-loh<u>n</u>*

■ permanent press   **infroissable** *a<u>n</u>-frwah-ssah-bluh*

■ polyester   **polyester** *poh-lee-ehss-tehr*

■ satin   **satin** *sah-ta<u>n</u>*

■ silk   **soie** *swah*

■ suede   **daim** *da<u>n</u>*

■ terrycloth   **tissu-éponge** *tee-ssew-ay-poh<u>n</u>zh*

■ velvet   **velours** *vuh-loor*

■ wash and wear   **ne pas repasser** *nuh pah ruh-pah-ssay*

■ wool   **laine** *lehn*

Show me something ____.	**Montrez-moi quelque chose** ____. *mohn-tray mwah kehl-kuh shohz*
■ in a solid color	**uni** *ew-nee*
■ with stripes	**à rayures** *ah rah-yewr*
■ with polka dots	**à pois** *ah pwah*
■ in plaid	**en tartan** *ahn tahr-tahn*
■ in herringbone	**à chevrons** *ah shuh-vrohn*
■ checked	**à carreaux** *ah kah-roh*
It doesn't fit me.	**Cela ne me va pas.** *suh-lah nuh muh vah pah*
It fits very well.	**Ça va à la perfection.** *sah vah ah lah pehr-fehk-ssyohn*
I'll take it.	**Je le/la prends.** *zhuh luh/lah prahn*
Will you wrap it?	**Voulez-vous l'emballer, s'il vous plaît?** *voo-lay voo lahn-bah-lay, seel voo pleh*
I'd like to see a pair of shoes (boots).	**Je voudrais voir une paire de chaussures (bottes).** *zhuh voo-dreh vwahr ewn pehr duh shoh-ssewr (boht)*
Show me the pair in the window.	**Montrez-moi la paire en vitrine.** *mohn-tray mwah lah pehr ahn vee-treen*
I take size ____.	**Je chausse du** ____. *zhuh shohss dew*
These shoes are too narrow (wide).	**Ces chaussures sont trop étroites (larges).** *say shoh-ssewr sohn troh pay-trwaht (lahrzh)*
They pinch me.	**Elles me serrent.** *ehl muh sehr*
They fit fine.	**Elles me vont très bien.** *ehl muh vohn treh byan*
I'll take them.	**Je vais les prendre.** *zhuh veh lay prahn-druh*

CONVERSION TABLES FOR CLOTHING SIZES

WOMEN												
SHOES												
American	4	$4\frac{1}{2}$	5	$5\frac{1}{2}$	6	$6\frac{1}{2}$	7	$7\frac{1}{2}$	8	$8\frac{1}{2}$	9	$9\frac{1}{2}$	10
Continental	35	35	36	36	37	37	38	38	39	39	40	40	41

DRESSES, SUITS						
American	8	10	12	14	16	18
Continental	36	38	40	42	44	46

BLOUSES, SWEATERS						
American	32	34	36	38	40	42
Continental	40	42	44	46	48	50

MEN										
SHOES										
American	7	$7\frac{1}{2}$	8	$8\frac{1}{2}$	9	$9\frac{1}{2}$	10	$10\frac{1}{2}$	11	$11\frac{1}{2}$
Continental	39	40	41	42	43	43	44	44	45	45

SUITS, COATS							
American	34	36	38	40	42	44	46	48
Continental	44	46	48	50	52	54	56	58

SHIRTS							
American	14	$14\frac{1}{2}$	15	$15\frac{1}{2}$	16	$16\frac{1}{2}$	17	$17\frac{1}{2}$
Continental	36	37	38	39	40	41	42	43

I also need shoe-laces.	**Il me faut aussi des lacets.** *eel muh foh toh-ssee day lah-sseh*
That's all I want for now.	**C'est tout pour le moment.** *seh too poor luh moh-mahn*
Please take my measurements.	**Veuillez prendre mes mesures.** *vuh-yay prahn-druh may muh-zewr*
I take size (My size is) ____.	**Je porte du (Ma taille est) ____.** *zhuh pohrt dew (mah tahy eh)*
■ small	**petit (petite)** *puh-tee (puh-teet)*
■ medium	**moyen (moyenne)** *mwah-yan (mwah-yehn)*
■ large	**grand (grande)** *grahn (grahnd)*
Can I try it on?	**Puis-je l'essayer?** *pweezh leh-sseh-yay*
Can you alter it?	**Pouvez-vous le/la retoucher?** *poo-vay voo luh/lah ruh-too-shay*
Can you let it out?	**Pouvez-vous l'élargir?** *poo-vay voo lay-lahr-zheer*
Can I return the article?	**Puis-je rendre cet article?** *pweezh rahn-druh seht ahr-tee-kluh*
Do you have something hand-made?	**Avez-vous quelque chose fait à la main?** *ah-vay voo kehl-kuh shohz feh-tah-lah-man*
The zipper doesn't work.	**La fermeture-éclair ne marche pas.** *lah fehr muh-tewr ay-klehr nuh mahrsh pah*

ELECTRICAL APPLIANCES

When buying electrical items, check the voltage, which may not correspond to what you have at home. Or look for appliances with dual voltage.

I want to buy _____.	**Je voudrais acheter _____.** *zhuh voo-dreh zahsh-tay*
■ a battery	**une pile** *ewn peel*
■ a blender	**un mixer** *uhn meek-sehr*
■ an electric shaver	**un rasoir électrique** *uhn rah-zwahr ay-lehk-treek*
■ a hair dryer	**un sèche-cheveux** *uhn sehsh shuh-vuh*
■ a plug	**une fiche** *ewn feesh*
■ a (portable) radio	**une radio (portative)** *ewn rah-dyoh pohr-tah-teev*
■ an (automatic) record player	**un tourne-disques (automatique)** *uhn toorn deessk oh-toh-mah-teek*
■ a cassette player/recorder	**un magnétophone à cassettes** *uhn mah-nyay-toh-fohn ah kah-sseht*
■ a (color) television set	**une télévision (en couleurs)** *ewn tay-lay-vee-zyohn (ahn koo-luhr)*
■ a toaster	**un grille-pain** *uhn gree pan*
It's out of order (broken).	**Il/elle ne marche pas. Il/elle est cassé(e).** *eel/ehl nuh mahrsh pah eel/ehl eh kah-ssay*

FOOD AND HOUSEHOLD ITEMS

Don't forget to bring your basket when you go to the food market. Large paper bags are not given out. The cashier does not load the basket for you; you must do that yourself. The French are more inclined to shop in specialty stores than we are, so you may want to follow their lead, buying bread in the **boulangerie,** pastries in a **patisserie** or candy in a **confiserie.**

I'd like _____.	**Je voudrais _____.** *zhuh voo-dreh*
■ a bar of soap	**une savonnette** *zewn sah-voh-neht*

■ a bottle of juice **une bouteille de jus** *zewn boo-tehy duh zhew*

■ a box of cereal **une boîte de céréale** *zewn bwaht duh say-ray-ahl*

■ a can of tomato sauce **une boîte de sauce-tomate** *zewn bwaht duh sohss toh-maht*

■ a dozen eggs **une douzaine d'oeufs** *zewn doo-zehn duh*

■ a jar of coffee **un bocal de café** *zuhn boh-kal duh kah-fay*

■ a kilo (2.2 lbs.) of potatoes **un kilo de pommes de terre** *zuhn kee-loh duh pohm duh tehr*

■ a half-kilo (1.1 lbs.) of cherries **un demi-kilo de cerises** *zuhn duh-mee kee-loh duh suh-reez*

■ a liter (quart) of milk **un litre de lait** *zuhn lee-truh duh leh*

■ a package of candies **un paquet de bonbons** *zuhn pah-keh duh bohn-bohn*

■ a $\frac{1}{4}$ pound of cheese **cent grammes de fromage** *sahn grahm duh froh-mahzh*

■ a quart of milk **un litre de lait** *uhn lee-truh duh leh*

■ a roll of toilet paper **un rouleau de papier hygiénique** *uhn roo-loh duh pah-pyay ee-zhyay-neek*

Can you give me 2 liters (half a gallon) of milk? **Pouvez-vous me donner deux litres de lait?** *poo-vay voo muh dohnay duh lee-truh duh leh*

I'd like a half liter of beer. **Je voudrais un demi-litre de bière.** *zhuh voo-dreh zuhn duh-mee lee-truh duh byehr*

I'd like ____. **Je voudrais ____.** *zhuh voo-dreh*

■ a kilo of oranges   **un kilo d'oranges** *zuhn kee-loh doh-rahnzh*

METRIC WEIGHTS AND MEASURES			
Solid Measures *(approximate measurements only)*			
OUNCES	GRAMS (GRAMMES)	GRAMS	OUNCES
$\frac{1}{4}$	7	10	$\frac{1}{3}$
$\frac{1}{2}$	14	100	$3\frac{1}{2}$
$\frac{3}{4}$	21	300	$10\frac{1}{2}$
1	28	500	18
POUNDS	KILOGRAMS (KILO)	KILOGRAMS	POUNDS
1	$\frac{1}{2}$	1	$2\frac{1}{4}$
5	$2\frac{1}{4}$	3	$6\frac{1}{2}$
10	$4\frac{1}{2}$	5	11
20	9	10	22
50	23	50	110
100	45	100	220
Liquid Measures *(approximate measurements only)*			
OUNCES	MILLILITERS (MILLILITRES)	MILLILITERS	OUNCES
1	30	10	$\frac{1}{3}$
6	175	50	$1\frac{1}{2}$
12	350	100	$3\frac{1}{2}$
16	475	150	5
GALLONS	LITERS (LITRES)	LITERS	GALLONS
1	$3\frac{3}{4}$	1	$\frac{1}{4}$ (1 quart)
5	19	5	$1\frac{1}{3}$
10	38	10	$2\frac{1}{2}$

Note: Common measurements for purchasing food are a kilo or fractions thereof, 100 (cent), 200 (deux cent), and 500 (cinq cent) grams (grammes). See also NUMBERS, p. 13–17'.

■ a half kilo of butter	**un demi-kilo de beurre**	*zuhn duh-mee kee-loh duh buhr*
■ 200 grams (about $\frac{1}{2}$ pound) of cookies	**deux cents grammes de biscuits**	*duh sahn grahm duh beess-kwee*
■ a hundred grams of bologna.	**cent grammes de mortadelle**	*sahn grahm duh mohr-tah-dehl*
What is this (that)?	**Qu'est-ce que c'est?**	*kehss kuh seh*
Is it fresh?	**Est-ce frais?**	*ehss freh*

THE CHARCUTERIE

A **charcuterie** is a rather special type of French delicatessen where you may buy food to take out, including various sausages and smoked meats. You will often see ordinary butcher's meat being sold in the same case as the sausage. Besides smoked meats you can find simple items like salads or paté. The **Rue de bucherie** in Paris is a street entirely filled with **charcuteries,** where you may go from one to another, selecting the items that appeal to you, for your lunch or for a picnic.

JEWELER

I'd like to see _____.	**Je voudrais voir _____.**	*zhuh voo-dreh vwahr*
■ a bracelet	**un bracelet**	*uhn brahss-leh*
■ a brooch	**une broche**	*ewn brohsh*
■ a chain	**une chaînette**	*ewn sheh-neht*
■ a charm	**un porte-bonheur**	*uhn pohrt boh-nuhr*
■ some earrings	**des boucles d'oreille**	*day boo-kluh doh-rehy*
■ a necklace	**un collier**	*uhn koh-lyay*
■ a pin	**une épingle**	*ewn ay-pan-gluh*

■ a ring   **une bague** *ewn bahg*

   an engagement ring   **une bague de fiançailles** *ewn bahg duh fee-ahn-ssahy*

   a wedding ring   **une alliance** *ewn ah-lee-ahnss*

■ a watch   **une montre** *ewn mohn-truh*

■ a wristwatch (digital)   **une montre-bracelet (digitale)** *ewn mohn-truh brahss-leh (dee-zhee-tahl)*

Is this _____?   **Est-ce _____?** *ehss*

■ gold   **en or** *ahn nohr*

■ platinum   **en platine** *ahn plah-teen*

■ silver   **en argent** *ahn nahr-zhahn*

■ stainless steel   **en acier inoxydable** *ahn nah-ssyay ee-nohk-ssee-dah-bluh*

Is it solid gold or gold-plated?   **C'est en or massif ou en plaqué or?** *seh-tahn-nohr mah-sseef oo ahn plah-kay ohr*

How many carats is it?   **Combien de carats y a-t-il?** *kohn-byan duh kah-rah ee ah teel*

What is that stone?   **Quelle est cette pierre?** *kehl eh seht pyehr*

I would like _____.   **Je voudrais _____.** *zhuh voo-dreh*

■ an amethyst   **une améthyste** *zewn ah-may-teesst*

■ an aquamarine   **une aigue-marine** *zewn ehg mah-reen*

■ a diamond   **un diamant** *zuhn dee-ah-mahn*

■ an emerald   **une émeraude** *zewn aym-rohd*

■ ivory   **un ivoire** *zuhn nee-vwahr*

■ jade   **un jade** *zuhn zhahd*

■ onyx   **un onyx** *zuhn oh-neeks*

■ pearls   **des perles** *day pehrl*

■ a ruby **un rubis** *uhn rew-bee*

■ a sapphire **un saphir** *uhn sah-feer*

■ a topaz **une topaze** *ewn toh-pahz*

■ turquoise **une turquoise** *ewn tewr-kwahz*

I love this ring! **J'adore cette bague.** *zhah-dohr seht bahg*

How much is it? **Cela coûte combien?** *suh-lah koot kohn-byan*

MUSIC, RECORDS AND TAPES

Is there a record shop around here? **Y a-t-il un magasin de disques par ici?** *ee ah teel uhn mah-gah-zan duh deessk pahr ee-ssee*

Do you sell ____? **Vendez-vous ____?** *vahn-day voo*

■ cartridges **des cartouches** *day kahr-toosh*

■ cassettes **des cassettes** *day kah-sseht*

■ needles **des diamants** *day dee-ah-mahn*

■ records **des disques** *day deessk*

■ tapes **des bandes** *day bahnd*

Do you have an album of ____? **Avez-vous un disque de ____?** *ah-vay voo uhn deessk duh*

■ 33 R.P.M. **trente-trois tours** *trahn trwah toor*

■ 45 R.P.M. **quarante-cinq tours** *kah-rahnt sank toor*

Where is the ____ section? **Où est le rayon de/des ____?** *oo eh luh reh-yohn duh/day*

■ American music **la musique américaine** *lah mew-zeek ah-may-ree-kehn*

■ classical music **la musique classique** *lah mew-zeek klah-sseek*

■ folk music — **la musique folklorique** *lah mew-zeek fohl-kloh-reek*

■ latest hits — **derniers succès** *dehr-nyay sewk-sseh*

■ French music — **la musique française** *lah mew-zeek frahn-ssehz*

■ opera — **l'opéra** *loh-pay-rah*

■ pop music — **la musique pop** *lah mew-zeek pohp*

rock music — **la musique rock** *lah mew-zeek ruhk*

NEWSSTAND

Do you carry newspapers (magazines) in English? — **Avez-vous des journaux (magazines) en anglais?** *ah-vay voo day zhoor-noh (mah-gah-zeen) ahn nahn-gleh*

I'd like to buy some (picture) postcards. — **Je voudrais acheter des cartes postales (illustrées).** *zhuh voo-dreh zahsh-tay day kahrt pohss-tahl (ee-lewss-tray)*

Do you have stamps? — **Avez-vous des timbres?** *ah-vay voo day tan-bruh*

How much is it? — **C'est combien?** *seh kohn-byan*

I'd like ____. — **Je voudrais ____.** *zhuh voo-dreh*

■ a daily — **un quotidien** *zuhn koh-tee-dyan*

■ a weekly — **un hebdomadaire** *zuhn ehb-doh-mah-dehr*

■ a monthly — **un mensuel** *zuhn mahn-ssew-ehl*

PHOTOGRAPHIC SUPPLIES

Where is there a camera shop? — **Où y a-t-il un magasin de photos?** *oo ee-ah-teel uhn mah-gah-zan duh foh-toh*

Do you develop film here?	**Développez-vous les films ici?** *Day-vloh-pay voo lay feelm ee-ssee*
How much does it cost to develop a roll?	**Combien coûte le développement d'une pellicule?** *kohn-byan koot luh day-vlohp-mahn dewn peh-lee-kewl*
I have two rolls.	**J'ai deux pellicules.** *zhay duh peh-lee-kewl*
I want ____.	**Je voudrais ____.** *zhuh voo-dreh*
■ a print of each	**une épreuve de chacune** *zewn ay-pruhv duh shah-kewn*
■ an enlargement	**un agrandissement** *zuhn nah-grahn-deess-mahn*
with a glossy finish	**sur papier brillant** *sewr pah-pyay bree-yahn*
with a matte finish	**sur papier mat** *sewr pah-pyay maht*
I want a roll of 20 (36) exposures of color (black and white) film.	**Je voudrais une pellicule de vingt (trente-six) en couleur (noir et blanc).** *zhuh voo-dreh zewn peh-lee-kewl duh van (trahn-seess) ahn koo-luhr (nwahr ay blahn)*
■ for slides	**pour diapositives** *poor dee-ah-poh-zee-teev*
■ a film pack, number . . .	**une cartouche, numéro . . .** *ewn kahr-toosh, new-may-roh*
When can I pick up the pictures?	**Quand puis-je venir chercher les photos?** *kahn pweezh vuh-neer shehr-shay lay foh-toh*
Do you sell cameras?	**Vendez-vous des appareils?** *vahn-day voo day zah-pah-rehy*
I want an expensive (inexpensive) camera.	**Je cherche un appareil cher (pas très cher).** *zhuh shehrsh uhn nah-pah-rehy shehr (pah treh shehr)*

SOUVENIRS

You may want to purchase specialties of certain cities or regions as gifts or as souvenirs.

FRANCE

Alençon	lace products
Aubusson, Beauvais	rugs
Baccarat	crystal
Besançon	watches and clocks
Grasse	perfume (Coty, Fragonard, Lanvin)
Grenoble	gloves
Limoges, Sèvres	fine porcelain
Nancy	crystal
Paris	haute couture, high style fashions at stores like Rive Gauche, Galeries Lafayette, Au Printemps, La Samaritaine

If you are in Paris, you may be able to pick up real bargains at the Flea Market (Marché aux Puces) and, at the small book shops along the Seine, old books, magazines, or comic strips.

Don't forget the famous wines and cheeses, of course!

BELGIUM

Ghent and Kortrijk	linen
Brussels, Brugge	lace
Antwerp	diamonds and jewelry
Val-Saint-Lambert	crystal and glassware
Dinant and Brugge	copperware

Everywhere in the country you can find the renowned Belgian beers, candy, and chocolate.

SWITZERLAND

There are "Swiss-craft" shops throughout the country where you will find a large selection of handmade products from all parts of Switzerland. Typical items include: linen, embroideries, fine handkerchiefs, textiles, wood carvings, ceramics, music boxes, and multi-blade knives. Switzerland is also known for its watches, cuckoo clocks, fondue forks and pots, and, of course, the chocolates and cheese available in all sizes and shapes.

Don't forget the high quality of Swiss-printed books.

GIFT SHOP

I'd like _____.	**Je voudrais _____.** *zhuh voo-dreh*
■ a pretty gift	**un joli cadeau** *zuhn zhoh-lee kah-doh*
■ a small gift	**un petit cadeau** *zuhn puh-tee kah-doh*
■ a souvenir	**un souvenir** *zuhn soov-neer*
It's for . . .	**C'est pour . . .** *seh poor*
Could you suggest something?	**Pourriez-vous me suggérer quelque chose?** *poo-ree-yay voo muh sewg-zhay-ray kehl-kuh shohz*
Would you show me your selection of _____.	**Voudriez-vous me montrer votre choix de _____.** *voo-dree-yay voo muh mohn-tray voh-truh shwah duh*
■ blown glass	**verre soufflé** *vehr soo-flay*
■ carved objects	**objets sculptés** *ohb-zheh skewl-tay*
■ cut crystal	**cristal taillé** *kreess-tahl tah-yay*
■ dolls	**poupées** *poo-pay*
■ earthenware (pottery)	**poterie** *poh-tree*
■ fans	**éventails** *ay-vahn-tahy*
■ jewelry	**bijouterie** *bee-zhoo-tree*

■ lace	**dentelles** *dahn-tehl*
■ leather goods	**objets en cuir** *ohb-zheh ahn kweer*
■ liqueurs	**liqueurs** *lee-kuhr*
■ musical instruments	**instruments de musique** *an-strew-mahn duh mew-zeek*
■ perfumes	**parfums** *pahr-fuhn*
■ pictures	**tableaux** *tah-bloh*
■ posters	**affiches** *ah-feesh*
■ religious articles	**articles religieux** *ahr-tee-kluh ruh-lee-zhuh*

I don't want to spend more than _____ francs.	**Je ne voudrais pas dépenser plus de _____ francs.** *zhuh nuh voo-dreh pah day-pahn-ssay plew duh _____ frahn*

ANTIQUE SHOPPING

French-speaking Europe boasts a large number of antique shops where you can find old books, watches, toys, antiquities, etc.

Haggle as much as you can!

PRINCIPAL SHOPPING AREAS FOR ANTIQUES

FRANCE

Paris

Rue du Bac and Rue des Saints Pères	7ème arrondissement
Marché aux Puces	18ème arrondissement
Quai Voltaire	7ème arrondissement
Rue Jacob and Rue Bonaparte	6ème arrondissement

BELGIUM

Brussels	le Sablon (there is also an open-air market here on Saturday and on Sunday morning)
Antwerp	Near the House of Rubens

What's the price of this old book?	**Quel est le prix de ce vieux livre?** *Kehl eh luh pree duh suh vyuh lee-vruh*
From what century is this item?	**De quel siècle date cet objet?** *Duh kehl see-yeh-kluh daht seht ohb-zheh*
Where does this Roman plate come from?	**Quelle est l'origine de cette assiette romaine?** *Kehl eh loh-ree-zheen duh seht ah-ssyeht roh-mehn*
Does that clock work with a key?	**Cette horloge se remonte-t-elle avec une clé?** *Seht ohr-lohzh suh ruh-mohn-tehl ah-vehk ewn klay*
For what price will you give me the statue?	**A quel prix me laissez-vous la statue?** *Ah kehl pree muh leh-ssay voo lah stah-tew*

STATIONERY

I want to buy _____.	**Je voudrais acheter _____.** *zhuh voo-dreh zahsh-tay*
■ a ball-point pen	**un stylo à bille** *uhn stee-loh ah bee*
■ a deck of cards	**un paquet de cartes** *uhn pah-keh duh kahrt*
■ envelopes	**des enveloppes** *day zahn-vlohp*
■ an eraser	**une gomme** *ewn gohm*
■ glue	**de la colle** *duh lah kohl*
■ a notebook	**un cahier** *uhn kah-yay*
■ pencils	**des crayons** *day kreh-yohn*

- a pencil sharpener **un taille-crayon** *uhn tahy kreh-yohn*
- a ruler **une règle** *ewn reh-gluh*
- Scotch tape **une bande adhésive (du scotch)** *ewn bahnd ahd-ay-zeev (dew skohtsh)*
- some string **de la ficelle** *duh lah fee-ssehl*
- typing paper **du papier pour machine à écrire** *dew pah-pyay poor mah-sheen ah ay-kreer*
- wrapping paper **du papier d'emballage** *dew pah-pyay dahn-bah-lahzh*
- a writing pad **un bloc-note** *uhn blohk-noht*
- writing paper **du papier à lettres** *dew pah-pyay ah leh-truh*

TOBACCO SHOP

Tobacco, cigarettes and cigars may be purchased from a state-licensed tobacconist. Look for the sign with the red cones outside cafés and bars.

Newly promulgated laws have outlawed smoking in many public places and fines are imposed. Be careful to heed the no smoking signs: DÉFENSE DE FUMER.

A pack (carton) of cigarettes, please. **Un paquet (une cartouche) de cigarettes, s'il vous plaît.** *uhn pah-keh (ewn kahr-toosh) duh see-gah-reht, seel voo pleh*

- filtered **avec filtre** *ah-vehk feel-truh*
- unfiltered **sans filtre** *sahn feel-truh*
- menthol **mentholées** *mahn-toh-lay*
- king-size **long format** *lohn fohr-mah*

Are these cigarettes (very) strong (mild)?	**Ces cigarettes sont elles (très) fortes (douces)?** *say see-gah-reht sohn-tehl (treh) fohrt (dooss)*
Do you have American cigarettes?	**Avez-vous des cigarettes américaines?** *ah-vay voo day see-gah-reht ah-may-ree-kehn*
What brands?	**Quelles marques?** *kehl mahrk*
Please give me a pack of matches also.	**Donnez-moi aussi une boîte d'allumettes, s'il vous plaît.** *doh-nay mwah oh-ssee ewn bwaht dah-lew-meht, seel voo pleh*
Do you sell ____?	**Vendez-vous ____?** *vahn-day voo*
■ chewing tobacco	**du tabac à chiquer** *dew tah-bah ah shee-kay*
■ a cigarette holder	**un fume-cigarettes** *uhn fewm see-gah-reht*
■ cigars	**des cigares** *day see-gahr*
■ flints	**des pierres à briquet** *day pyehr ah bree-keh*
■ lighter fluid	**de l'essence à briquet** *duh leh-ssahnss ah bree-keh*
■ lighters	**des briquets** *day bree-keh*
■ pipes	**des pipes** *day peep*
■ pipe tobacco	**du tabac pour pipe** *dew tah-bah poor peep*

TOILETRIES

The new *drugstores* in France resemble small department stores. They sell newspapers, international magazines, books, maps, guides, small gifts, records and have fast-food restaurants for items such as ice cream, sandwiches or drinks. Many of these drugstores even have a counter where prescriptions may be filled. Perfumes and cosmetics may also be purchased at a *parfumerie*.

Do you have ____?	**Avez-vous ____?** *ah-vay voo*
■ bobby pins	**des épingles à cheveux** *day zay-pan-gluh ah shuh-vuh*
■ a brush	**une brosse** *ewn brohss*
■ cleansing cream	**une crème démaquillante** *ewn krehm day-mah-kee-yahnt*
■ a comb	**un peigne** *uhn peh-nyuh*
■ a condom	**un préservatif** *uhn pray-zehr-vah-teef*
■ (disposable) diapers	**des couches disponibles** *day koosh deess-poh-nee-bluh*
■ emery boards	**des limes à ongles** *day leem ah ohn-gluh*
■ eye liner	**du traceur à paupières** *dew trah-ssuhr ah poh-pyehr*
■ eyebrow pencil	**le crayon pour les yeux** *luh kreh-yohn poor lay zyuh*
■ eye shadow	**du fard à paupières** *dew fahr ah poh-pyehr*
■ hair spray	**la laque** *lah lahk*
■ lipstick	**le rouge à lèvres** *luh roozh ah leh-vruh*
■ makeup	**le maquillage** *luh mah-kee-yahzh*
■ mascara	**le cosmétique pour les cils** *luh kohz-may-teek poor lay seel*
■ a mirror	**un miroir** *uhn meer-wahr*
■ mouth wash	**le dentifrice** *luh dahn-tee-freess*
■ nail clippers	**un coupe-ongles** *uhn koop ohn-gluh*
■ a nail file	**une lime à ongles** *ewn leem ah ohn-gluh*

■ nail polish **du vernis à ongles** *dew vehr-nee ah ohn-gluh*

■ nail polish remover **du dissolvant** *dew dee-ssohl-vahn*

■ a prophylactic **un préservatif** *uhn pray-sehr-vah-teef*

■ a razor **un rasoir** *uhn rah-zwahr*

■ razor blades **une lame de rasoir** *ewn lahm duh rah-zwahr*

■ rouge **du fard** *dew fahr*

■ sanitary napkins **des serviettes hygiéniques** *day sehr-vyeht ee-zhyay-neek*

■ (cuticle) scissors **des ciseaux** *day see-zoh*

■ shampoo **le shampooing** *luh shahn-pwan*

■ shaving lotion **la lotion à raser** *lah loh-ssyohn ah rah-zay*

■ soap **du savon** *dew sah-vohn*

■ a sponge **une éponge** *ewn ay-pohnzh*

■ talcum powder **le talc** *luh tahlk*

■ tampons **des tampons périodiques** *day tahn-pohn pay-ree-oh-deek*

■ tissues **des mouchoirs en papier** *day moo-shwahr ahn pah-pyay*

■ toilet paper **du papier hygiénique** *dew pah-pyay ee-zhyay-neek*

■ a toothbrush **un dentifrice** *uhn dahn-tee-freess*

■ toothpaste **de la pâte dentifrice** *duh lah paht dahn-tee-freess*

■ tweezers **une pince à épiler** *ewn panss ah ay-pee-lay*

PERSONAL CARE AND SERVICES

If your hotel doesn't offer these amenities, ask the desk clerk to recommend someone nearby.

AT THE BARBER

Where is there a good barber shop?	**Où y a-t-il un bon coiffeur?** *oo eeah-teel uhn bohn kwah-fuhr*
Do I have to wait long?	**Faut-il attendre longtemps?** *foh teel ah-tahn-druh lohn-tahn*
Whose turn is it?	**C'est à qui le tour?** *seh tah kee luh toor*
I want a shave.	**Je voudrais me faire raser.** *zhuh voo-dreh muh fehr rah-zay*
I want a haircut.	**Je voudrais une coupe de cheveux.** *zhuh voo-dreh zewn koop duh shuh-vuh*
Short in back, long in front.	**Plus courts sur la nuque, plus longs sur le dessus.** *plew koor sewr lah newk plew lohn sewr luh duh-ssew*
Leave it long.	**Laissez-les longs.** *leh-ssay lay lohn*
I want it (very) short.	**Je les veux (très) courts.** *zhuh lay vuh treh koor*
You can cut a little _____.	**Vous pouvez dégager un peu _____.** *voo poo-vay day-gah-zhay uhn puh*
■ in back	**derrière** *deh-ryehr*
■ in front	**devant** *duh-vahn*
■ off the top	**dessus** *duh-ssew*
■ on the sides	**les côtés** *lay koh-tay*

I part my hair _____.	**Je fais la raie** _____. *zhuh feh lah ray*
■ on the left	**à gauche** *ah gohsh*
■ on the right	**à droite** *ah drwaht*
■ in the middle	**au milieu** *oh meel-yuh*
I comb my hair straight back.	**Je me peigne en arrière.** *zhuh muh peh-nyuh ahn nah-ryehr*
Cut a little bit more here.	**Coupez un peu plus ici.** *koo-pay uhn puh plew ee-ssee*
That's enough.	**Ça suffit.** *sah sew-fee*
It's fine that way.	**C'est parfait comme ça.** *seh pahr-feh kohm sah*
I (don't) want _____.	**Je (ne) veux (pas de)** _____. *zhuh (nuh) vuh (pah duh)*
■ shampoo	**un shampooing** *uhn shan-pwan*
■ tonic	**une lotion** *ewn loh-ssyohn*
Use the scissors only.	**Employez seulement les ciseaux.** *ahn-plwah-yay suhl-mahn lay see-zoh*
I would like a razor cut.	**Je voudrais une coupe au rasoir.** *zhuh voo-dreh zewn koop oh rah-zwahr*
You can use the machine.	**Vous pouvez employer la machine.** *voo poo-vay zahn-plwah-yay lah mah-sheen*
Please trim my _____.	**Rafraîchissez moi** _____. *rah-freh-sshee-ssay mwah*
■ beard	**la barbe** *lah bahrb*
■ moustache	**la moustache** *lah mooss-tahsh*
■ sideburns	**les favoris** *lay fah-voh-ree*
Where's the mirror?	**Où est le miroir?** *oo eh luh meer-wahr*

I'd like to look at myself in the mirror.	**Je voudrais me regarder dans le miroir.** *zhuh voo-dreh muh ruh-gahr-day dahn luh meer-wahr*
How much do I owe you?	**Combien vous dois-je?** *kohn-byan voo dwahzh*

AT THE BEAUTY PARLOR

Is there a beauty parlor (hairdresser) near the hotel?	**Y a-t-il un salon de beauté près de l'hôtel?** *ee ah teel uhn sah-lohn duh boh-tay preh duh loh-tehl*
I'd like to make an appointment for this afternoon (tomorrow).	**Je voudrais prendre rendez-vous pour cet après-midi (demain).** *zhuh voo-dreh prahn-druh rahn-day voo poor seht ah-preh mee-dee (duh-man)*
Can you give me _____?	**Pouvez-vous me donner _____?** *poo-vay voo muh doh-nay*
■ a color rinse	**un shampooing colorant** *uhn shahn-pwan koh-loh-rahn*
■ a facial massage	**un massage facial** *uhn mah-ssahzh fah-ssyahl*
■ a haircut	**une coupe de cheveux** *ewn koop duh shuh-vuh*
■ a manicure	**une manucure** *ewn mah-new-kewr*
■ a permanent	**une permanente** *ewn pehr-mah-nahnt*
■ a shampoo	**un shampooing** *uhn shahn-pwan*
■ a tint	**des reflets** *day ruh-fleh*
■ a touch up	**une retouche** *ewn ruh-toosh*
■ a wash and set	**un shampooing et une mise en plis** *uhn shahn-pwan ay ewn meez ahn plee*

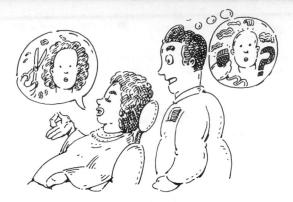

I'd like to see a color chart.	**Je voudrais voir une échelle de teintes.** *zhuh voo-dreh vwahr ewn ay-shehl duh tant*
I want ____.	**Je voudrais ____.** *zhuh voo-dreh*
■ auburn	**auburn** *oh-buhrn*
■ (light) blond	**blond (clair)** *blohn (klehr)*
■ brunette	**brun** *bruhn*
■ a darker color	**une teinte plus foncée** *ewn tant plew fohn-ssay*
■ a lighter color	**une teinte plus claire** *ewn tant plew klehr*
■ the same color	**la même couleur** *lah mehm koo-luhr*
Don't apply any hairspray.	**Ne mettez pas de laque, s'il vous plaît.** *nuh meh-tay pah duh lahk seel voo pleh*
Not too much hairspray.	**Pas trop de laque.** *pah troh duh lahk*

LAUNDRY AND DRY CLEANING

Where is the nearest laundry?	**Où est la blanchisserie la plus proche?** *oo eh lah blah<u>n</u>-sheess-ree lah plew prohsh*
Where is the nearest laundromat?	**Où est la laverie automatique la plus proche?** *oo eh lah lah-vree oh-toh-mah-teek lah plew prohsh*
Where is the nearest dry cleaner's?	**Où est la teinturerie la plus proche?** *oo eh lah tah<u>n</u>-tew-ruh-ree lah plew prohsh*
I have a lot of (dirty) clothes to be _____.	**J'ai beaucoup de vêtements (sales) à faire _____.** *zhay boh-koo duh veht-mah<u>n</u> sahl ah fehr*
■ dry cleaned	**nettoyer à sec** *neh-twah-yay ah sehk*
■ washed	**laver** *lah-vay*
■ mended	**réparer** *ray-pah-ray*
■ ironed	**repasser** *ruh-pah-ssay*
Here's the list: _____.	**Voici la liste: _____.** *vwah-ssee lah leesst.*
■ 3 shirts (men's)	**trois chemises** *trwah shuh-meez*
■ 12 handkerchiefs	**douze mouchoirs** *dooz moo-shwahr*
■ 6 pairs of socks	**six paires de chaussettes** *see pehr duh shoh-sseht*
■ 1 blouse (nylon)	**un chemisier (nylon)** *uh<u>n</u> shuh-mee-zyay (nee-loh<u>n</u>)*
■ 4 panties	**quatre slips** *kah-truh sleep*
■ 2 pyjamas	**deux paires de pyjama** *duh pehr duh pee-zhah-mah*
■ 2 suits	**deux complets** *duh koh<u>n</u>-pleh*

■ 3 ties **trois cravates** *trwah krah-vaht*

■ 2 dresses (cotton) **deux robes (en coton)** *duh rohb ahn koh-tohn*

■ 1 sweater (wool) **un chandail (laine)** *uhn shahn-dahy (lehn)*

■ 1 pair of gloves **une paire de gants** *ewn pehr duh gahn*

I need them for _____. **J'en ai besoin pour _____.** *zhahn nay buh-zwan poor*

■ tonight **ce soir** *suh swahr*

■ tomorrow **demain** *duh-man*

■ next week **la semaine prochaine** *lah suh-mehn proh-shehn*

■ the day after tomorrow **après-demain** *ah-preh duh-man*

■ at the latest **au plus tard** *oh plew tahr*

I'm leaving _____. **Je pars _____.** *zhuh pahr*

■ soon **bientôt** *byan-toh*

■ tomorrow **demain** *duh-man*

When will you bring it back? **Quand est-ce que vous me le rendrez?** *kahn tehss kuh voo muh luh rahn-dray*

When will it be ready? **Quand sera-t-il prêt?** *kahn suh-rah teel preh*

There's a button missing. **Il y a un bouton qui manque.** *eel yah uhn boo-tohn kee mahnk*

Can you sew it back on? **Pouvez-vous le recoudre?** *poo-vay voo luh ruh-koo-druh*

This isn't my laundry. **Ce n'est pas ma lessive.** *suh neh pah mah lay-sseev*

SHOE REPAIRS

Can you fix these shoes (boots)?	**Pouvez-vous réparer ces chaussures (bottes)?** *poo-vay voo ray-pah-ray say shoh-ssewr (boht)*
Put on (half) soles and rubber heels.	**Mettez les (demi-) semelles et les talons en caoutchouc.** *meh-tay lay duh-mee suh-mehl ay lay tah-lohn ahn kah-oo-tshoo*
I'd like to have my shoes shined (too).	**Je voudrais un cirage (aussi).** *zhuh voo-dreh zuhn see-rahzh (oh-ssee)*
	Je voudrais me faire cirer les chaussures. *zhuh voo-dreh muh fehr see-ray lay shoh-ssewr*
When will they be ready?	**Quand seront-elles prêtes?** *kahn suh-rohn tehl preht*
I need them by Saturday (without fail).	**Il me les faut samedi (sans faute).** *eel muh lay foh sahm-dee (sahn foht)*

WATCH REPAIRS

Can you fix this watch (alarm clock) for me?	**Pouvez-vous me réparer cette montre (ce réveil)?** *poo-vay voo muh ray-pah-ray seht mohn-truh (suh ray-vehy)*
I need ____.	**Il me faut ____.** *eel muh foh*
■ a crystal, glass	**un verre** *tuhn vehr*
■ an hour hand	**une petite aiguille** *tewn puh-teet ay-gwee*
■ a minute hand	**une aiguille des minutes** *tewn y-ay-gwee day mee-newt*
■ a screw	**une vis** *tewn veess*
■ a second hand	**une aiguille des secondes** *tewn ay-gwee day suh-gohnd*

When will it be ready?	**Quand sera-t-elle prête?** *kahn suh-rah tehl preht?*
May I have a receipt?	**Puis-je avoir un reçu?** *pweezh ah-vwahr uhn ruh-ssew?*
Can you look at it?	**Pouvez-vous l'examiner?** *poo-vay voo lehg-zah-mee-nay*
Can you clean it?	**Pouvez-vous la nettoyer?** *poo-vay voo lah neh-twah-yay*
I dropped it.	**Je l'ai laissé tomber.** *zhuh lay leh-ssay tohn-bay*
It doesn't run well.	**Elle ne marche pas bien.** *ehl nuh mahrsh pah byan*
It's fast (slow).	**Cette montre avance (retarde).** *seht mohn-truh ah-vahnss (ruh-tahrd)*
It's stopped.	**Elle s'est arrêtée.** *ehl seh tah-reh-tay*
I wind it every day.	**Je la remonte tous les jours.** *zhuh lah ruh-mohnt too lay zhoor*

CAMERA REPAIRS

Can you fix this camera?	**Pouvez-vous réparer cet appareil?** *poo-vay voo ray-pah-ray seht ah-pah-rehy*
It doesn't work well.	**Il ne fonctionne pas bien.** *eel nuh fohnk-ssyohn pah byan*
How much will the repair cost?	**Combien coûtera la réparation?** *kohn-byan koo-trah lah ray-pah-rah-ssyohn*
When can I come and get it?	**Quand puis-je venir le chercher?** *kahn pweezh vuh-neer luh shehr-shay*
I need it as soon as possible.	**Il me le faut aussitôt que possible.** *Eel muh luh foh toh-see-toh kuh poh-ssee-bluh*

MEDICAL CARE

AT THE PHARMACY

A green cross indicates a pharmacy, where you buy over-the-counter or prescription drugs. If the pharmacy is closed there will be a sign on the door to indicate which pharmacies are open in the neighborhood.

Where is the nearest (all-night) pharmacy?	**Où se trouve la pharmacie de garde (de nuit) la plus proche?** *oo suh troov lah fahr-mah-ssee duh gahrd (duh nwee) lah plew prohsh*
At what time does the pharmacy open (close)?	**À quelle heure ouvre (ferme) la pharmacie?** *ah kehl uhr oo-vruh (fehrm) lah fahr-mah-ssee*
I need something for ____.	**Il me faut quelque chose pour ____.** *eel muh foh kehl-kuh shohz poor*
■ a cold	**un rhume** *uhn rewm*
■ constipation	**la constipation** *lah kohn-sstee-pah-ssyohn*
■ a cough	**une toux** *ewn too*
■ diarrhea	**la diarrhée** *lah dee-ah-ray*
■ a fever	**une fièvre** *ewn fyeh-vruh*
■ hay fever	**le rhume des foins** *luh rewm day fwan*
■ a headache	**un mal de tête** *uhn mahl duh teht*
■ insomnia	**l'insomnie** *lan-sohm-nee*
■ nausea	**la nausée** *lah noh-zay*
■ sunburn	**les coups de soleil** *lay koo duh soh-lehy*
■ a toothache	**un mal de dents** *uhn mahl duh dahn*

■ an upset stomach	**les indigestions** *lay-zan-dee-zhehss-tyohn*
Is a prescription needed for the medicine?	**Faut-il avoir une ordonnance pour ce médicament?** *foh-teel ah-vwahr ewn ohr-doh-nahnss poor suh may-dee-kah-mahn*
Can you fill this prescription for me now?	**Pourriez-vous me préparer cette ordonnance maintenant?** *poo-ree-yay voo muh pray-pah-ray seht ohr-doh-nahnss mant-nahn*
It's an emergency.	**C'est urgent.** *seh-tewr-zhahn*
Can I wait for it?	**Puis-je l'attendre?** *pweezh lah-tahn-druh*
How long will it take?	**Ça prendra combien de temps?** *sah prahn-drah kohn-byan duh tahn*
When can I come for it?	**Quand puis-je venir la chercher?** *kahn pweezh vuh-neer lah shehr-shay*
When can I come back?	**Quand puis-je revenir?** *kahn pweezh ruh-vuh-neer*
I would like _____.	**Je voudrais _____.** *zhuh voo-dreh*
■ adhesive tape	**une bande adhésive** *zewn bahnd ahd-ay-zeev*
■ alcohol	**l'alcool** *lahl-kohl*
■ an antacid	**un anti-acide** *zuhn nahn-tee ah-sseed*
■ an antiseptic	**un antiseptique** *zuhn nahn-tee-ssehp-teek*
■ aspirins	**des aspirines** *day-zahss-pee-reen*
■ bandages	**des bandes** *day bahnd*
■ Band-Aids	**des bandages** *day bahn-dazh*
■ corn plasters	**des emplâtres pour les cors** *day zahn-plah-truh poor lay kohr*
■ (absorbent) cotton	**du coton** *dew koh-tohn*

■ cough drops	**des pastilles contre la toux** *day pahss-tee kohn-truh lah too*
■ cough syrup	**le sirop contre la toux** *luh see-roh kohn-truh lah too*
■ ear drops	**les gouttes pour les oreilles** *lay goot poor lay zoh-rehy*
■ eye drops	**les gouttes pour les yeux** *lay goot poor lay zyuh*
■ iodine	**de la teinture d'iode** *duh lah tan-tewr dyohd*
■ a (mild) laxative	**un laxatif (léger)** *zuhn lahk-ssah-teef (lay-zhay)*
■ milk of magnesia	**le lait de magnésie** *luh leh duh mah-nyay-zee*
■ suppositories	**les suppositoires** *lay sew-poh-zee-twahr*
■ a thermometer	**un thermomètre** *uhn tehr-moh-meh-truh*
■ tranquilizers	**des tranquillisants** *day trahn-kee-lee-zahn*
■ vitamins	**des vitamines** *day vee-tah-meen*

DOCTORS

You never know when you may need a doctor while on vacation. In Paris the U.S. Embassy (tel: (1) 42 96 12 02) has a list of English-speaking doctors. There is also an American Hospital where most of the doctors speak English (tel: (1) 47 47 53 00) and the Hertford British Hospital (tel: (1) 47 58 13 12). In other areas and situations, the following phrases will help you:

I don't feel well	**Je ne me sens pas bien.** *zhuh nuh muh sahn pah byan*
I feel sick.	**Je me sens mal.** *zhuh muh sahn mahl*

I need a doctor.	**Il me faut un docteur.**	*eel muh foh tuhn dohk-tuhr*
Do you know a doctor who speaks English?	**Connaissez-vous un docteur qui parle anglais?**	*koh-neh-ssay voo uhn dohk-tuhr kee pahrl ahn-gleh*
Where is his office?	**Où se trouve son cabinet?**	*oo suh troov sohn kah-bee-neh*
I'm dizzy.	**J'ai des vertiges.**	*zhay day vehr-teezh*
I feel weak.	**Je me sens faible.**	*zhuh muh sahn feh-bluh*
I want to sit down for a while.	**Je voudrais m'asseoir un moment.**	*zhuh voo-dreh mah-sswahr uhn moh-mahn*
My temperature is normal (37°C).	**Ma température est normale (trente-sept degrés).**	*mah tahn-pay-rah-tewr eh nohr-mahl (trahnt seht duh-gray)*

PARTS OF THE BODY

head	**la tête**	*lah teht*
face	**la figure**	*lah fee-gewr*
ear	**l'oreille**	*loh-rehy*
eye	**l'oeil**	*luhy*
nose	**le nez**	*luh nay*
mouth	**la bouche**	*lah boosh*
tooth	**la dent**	*lah dahn*
throat	**la gorge**	*lah gohrzh*
neck	**le cou**	*luh koo*
shoulder	**l'épaule**	*lay-pohl*
chest	**la poitrine**	*lah pwah-treen*

heart	**le coeur**	*luh kuhr*
arm	**le bras**	*luh brah*
elbow	**le coude**	*luh kood*
wrist	**le poignet**	*luh pwah-nyeh*
hand	**la main**	*lah man*
appendix	**l'appendice**	*lah-pan-deess*
hip	**la hanche**	*lah ahnsh*
leg	**la jambe**	*lah zhahnb*
knee	**le genou**	*luh zhuh-noo*
ankle	**la cheville**	*lah shuh-vee*
foot	**le pied**	*luh-pyay*
skin	**la peau**	*lah poh*

TELLING THE DOCTOR

I have _____. **J'ai** _____. *zhay*

■ an abscess **un abcès** *uhn nahb-sseh*

■ a broken bone **une fracture** *ewn frahk-tewr*

■ a bruise **une contusion** *ewn kohn-tew-zyohn*

■ a burn **une brûlure** *ewn brew-lewr*

■ something in my eye **quelque chose dans l'oeil** *kehl-kuh shohz dahn luhy*

■ the chills **des frissons** *day free-ssohn*

■ a cold **un rhume** *uhn rewm*

    a chest cold **une bronchite** *ewn brohn-sheet*

    a head cold **un rhume de cerveau** *uhn rewm duh sehr-voh*

■ cramps **des crampes** *day krahnp*

■ a cut	**une coupure** *ewn koo-pewr*
■ diarrhea	**la diarrhée** *lah dee-ah-ray*
■ dysentery	**la dysenterie** *lah dee-ssahn-tree*
■ a fever	**de la fièvre** *duh lah fyeh-vruh*
■ a fracture	**une fracture** *ewn frahk-tewr*
■ a headache	**mal à la tête** *mahl ah lah teht*
■ an infection	**une infection** *ewn an-fehk-ssyohn*
■ a lump	**une grosseur** *ewn groh-ssuhr*
■ a sore throat	**mal à la gorge** *mahl ah lah gohrzh*
■ a stomach ache	**mal à l'estomac** *mahl ah lehss-toh-mah*
■ swelling	**une enflure** *ewn ahn-flewr*
■ a wound	**une blessure** *ewn bleh-ssewr*
I am constipated.	**Je suis constipé(e).** *zhuh swee kohn-sstee-pay*
It hurts me here.	**J'ai mal ici.** *zhay mahl ee-ssee*
My whole body hurts.	**Tout mon corps me fait mal.** *too mohn kohr muh feh mahl*
My _____ hurts.	**J'ai mal _____.** *zhay mahl*
■ ankle	**à la cheville** *ah lah shuh-vee*
■ arm	**au bras** *oh brah*
■ back	**au dos** *oh doh*
■ cheek	**à la joue** *ah lah zhoo*
■ ear	**à l'oreille** *ah loh-rehy*
■ eye	**aux yeux** *oh zyuh*
■ face	**à la figure** *ah lah fee-gewr*
■ finger	**au doigt** *oh dwah*
■ foot	**au pied** *oh pyay*

- glands   **aux ganglions**   *oh gah<u>n</u>-glee-yoh<u>n</u>*
- head   **à la tête**   *ah lah teht*
- hand   **à la main**   *ah lah ma<u>n</u>*
- hip   **à la hanche**   *ah lah ah<u>n</u>sh*
- leg   **à la jambe**   *ah lah zhah<u>n</u>b*
- lip   **à la lèvre**   *ah lah leh-vruh*
- neck   **au cou**   *oh koo*
- nose   **au nez**   *oh nay*
- shoulder   **à l'épaule**   *ah lay-pohl*
- throat   **à la gorge**   *ah lah gohrzh*
- thumb   **au pouce**   *oh pooss*
- toe   **à l'orteil**   *ah lohr-tehy*
- wrist   **au poignet**   *oh pwah-nyeh*

I've had this pain since yesterday.

J'ai cette douleur depuis hier. *zhay seht doo-luhr duh-pwee yehr*

There's a (no) history of asthma (diabetes) in my family.

Il y a (Il n'y a pas) d'asthme (de diabète) dans ma famille. *eel yah (eel nyah pah) dahss-muh (duh dee-ah-beht) dah<u>n</u> mah fah-mee*

I'm (not) allergic to antibiotics (penicillin).	**Je (ne) suis (pas) allergique aux antibiotiques.** *zhuh (nuh) swee (pah) zah-lehr-zheek oh zahn-tee-bee-oh-teek*
I have a pain in my chest around my heart.	**J'ai une douleur à la poitrine près du coeur.** *zhay ewn doo-luhr ah lah pwah-treen preh dew kuhr*
I had a heart attack ____ year(s) ago.	**J'ai eu une crise cardiaque il y a ____ ans.** *zhay ew ewn kreez kahr-dyahk eel yah ____ ahn*
I'm taking this medicine.	**Je prends ce médicament.** *zhuh prahn suh may-dee-kah-mahn*
I'm pregnant.	**J'attends un enfant.** *zah-tahn zuhn nahn-fahn*
I feel faint.	**Je vais m'évanouir.** *zhuh veh may-vah-nweer*
I feel all right now.	**Je vais bien maintenant.** *zhuh veh byan mant-nahn*
I feel better.	**Je vais mieux.** *zhuh veh myuh*
I feel worse.	**Je me sens moins bien.** *zhuh muh sahn mwan byan*
Do I have ____?	**Est-ce que j'ai ____?** *ehss kuh zhay*
■ appendicitis	**l'appendicite** *lah-pahn-dee-sseet*
■ the flu	**la grippe** *lah greep*
■ tonsilitis	**une amygdalite** *ewn nah-meeg-dah-leet*
Is it serious (contagious)?	**C'est grave? (contagieux)?** *seh grahv (kohn-tah-zhyuh)*
Do I have to go to the hospital?	**Dois-je aller à l'hôpital?** *dwahzh ah-lay ah loh-pee-tahl*
When can I continue my trip?	**Quand pourrai-je poursuivre mon voyage?** *kahn poo-rayzh poor-swee-vruh mohn vwah-yahzh*

DOCTOR'S INSTRUCTIONS

Open your mouth.	**Ouvrez la bouche.** *oo-vray lah boosh*
Stick out your tongue.	**Tirez la langue.** *tee-ray lah lah<u>ng</u>*
Cough.	**Toussez.** *too-ssay*
Breathe deeply.	**Respirez profondément.** *rehss-pee-ray proh-foh<u>n</u>-day-mah<u>n</u>*
Take off your clothing (to the waist).	**Déshabillez-vous (jusqu'à la ceinture).** *day-zah-bee-yay voo (zhewss-kah lah sa<u>n</u>-tewr)*
Lie down.	**Étendez-vous.** *ay-tah<u>n</u>-day voo*
Stand up.	**Levez-vous.** *luh-vay voo*
Get dressed.	**Habillez-vous.** *ah-bee-yay voo*

PATIENT

Are you going to give me a prescription?	**Allez-vous me donner une ordonnance?** *ah-lay voo muh doh-nay ewn ohr-doh-nah<u>n</u>ss*
How often must I take this medicine (these pills)?	**Combien de fois par jour dois-je prendre ce médicament (ces pilules)?** *koh<u>n</u>-bya<u>n</u> duh fwah pahr zhoor dwahzh prah<u>n</u>-druh suh may-dee-kah-mah<u>n</u> (seh pee-lewl)*
(How long) do I have to stay in bed?	**(Combien de temps) dois-je garder le lit?** *(koh<u>n</u>-bya<u>n</u> duh tah<u>n</u>) dwahzh gahr-day luh lee*
Thank you (for everything), doctor.	**Merci bien (pour tout), docteur.** *mehr-ssee bya<u>n</u> (poor too), dohk-tuhr*
What is your fee?	**Quels sont vos honoraires?** *kehl soh<u>n</u> voh zoh-noh-rehr*
I have medical insurance.	**J'ai une assurance médicale.** *zhay ewn ah-ssew-rah<u>n</u>ss may-dee-kahl*

IN THE HOSPITAL (ACCIDENTS)

Help!	**Au secours!** *oh suh-koor*
Help me, somebody!	**Que quelqu'un m'aide, je vous en prie!** *kuh kehl-kuhn mehd zhuh voo zahn pree*
Get a doctor, quick!	**Vite, appelez un docteur!** *veet, ah-play uhn dohk-tuhr*
Call an ambulance!	**Faites venir une ambulance!** *feht vuh-neer ewn ahn-bew-lahnss*
Take me (him, her) to the hospital.	**Emmenez-moi (le, la) à l'hôpital.** *ahn-muh-nay mwah (luh, lah) ah loh-pee-tahl*
I need first aid.	**J'ai besoin de premiers soins.** *zhay buh-zwan duh pruh-myay swan*
I've fallen.	**Je suis tombé(e).** *zhuh swee tohn-bay*
I was knocked down (run over).	**On m'a renversé(e).** *ohn mah rahn-vehr-ssay*
I've had a heart attack.	**J'ai eu une crise cardiaque.** *zhay ew ewn kreez kahr-dyahk*
I burned myself.	**Je me suis brûlé(e).** *zhuh muh swee brew-lay*
I cut myself.	**Je me suis coupé(e).** *zhuh muh swee koo-pay*
I'm bleeding.	**Je saigne.** *zhuh seh-nyuh*
I've (He's) lost a lot of blood.	**J'ai (Il a) perdu beaucoup de sang.** *zhay (eel ah) pehr-dew boh-koo duh sahn*
I think the bone is broken (dislocated).	**Je crois que l'os est fracturé (déboîté).** *zhuh krwah kuh lohss eh frahk-tew-ray (day-bwah-tay)*
The leg is swollen.	**La jambe est enflée.** *lah zhahnb eh tahn-flay*

The wrist (ankle) is sprained (twisted).	**Le poignet (la cheville) est démis (démise) (tordu(e)).** *luh pwah-nyeh (lah shuh-vee) eh day-mee (day-meez) (tohr-dew)*
I can't move my elbow (knee).	**Je ne peux pas remuer le coude (le genou).** *zhuh nuh puh pah ruh-mew-ay luh kood (luh zhuh-noo)*

EMERGENCY PHONE NUMBERS IN PARIS

These lines are open twenty-four hours a day.

Ambulance	(1) 45 67 50 50
Anti-Poison Squad	(1) 42 05 63 29; (1) 40 37 04 04
Dentist	(1) 47 07 33 68; (1) 47 07 44 44
Drugs	707 85 05
Police	17
Fire Department	18
SAMU (emergency ambulance)	(1) 45 67 50 50

AT THE DENTIST

I have to go to the dentist.	**Il me faut aller chez le dentiste.** *eel muh foh tah-lay shay luh dahn-teesst*
Can you recommend a dentist?	**Pouvez-vous me recommander un dentiste?** *poo-vay voo muh ruh-koh-mahn-day uhn dahn-teesst*
I have a toothache that's driving me crazy.	**J'ai un mal de dents à tout casser. (J'ai une rage de dents.)** *zhay uhn mahl duh dahn ah too kah-ssay (zhay ewn rahzh duh dahn)*
I have a rotten tooth that's giving me a lot of pain.	**J'ai une dent cariée qui me fait très mal.** *zhay ewn dahn kah-ree-yay kee muh feh treh mahl*

I've lost a filling.	**J'ai perdu un plombage.**	*zhay pehr-dew uhn plohn-bahzh*
I've broken a tooth.	**Je me suis cassé une dent.**	*zhuh muh swee kah-ssay ewn dahn*
I can't chew.	**Je ne peux pas mâcher.**	*zhuh nuh puh pah mah-shay*
My gums hurt me.	**Les gencives me font mal.**	*lay zhahn-sseev muh fohn mahl*
Is there an infection?	**Y a-t-il une infection?**	*ee ah-teel ewn an-fehk-ssyohn*
Will you have to extract the tooth?	**Faut-il extraire la dent?**	*foh teel ehkss-trehr lah dahn*
Can you fill it ____?	**Pouvez-vous l'obturer ____?**	*poo-vay voo lohb-tew-ray*
■ with amalgam	**avec une amalgame**	*ah-vehk ewn ah-mahl-gahm*
■ with gold	**avec de l'or**	*ah-vehk duh lohr*
■ with silver	**avec de l'argent**	*ah-vehk duh lahr-zhahn*
■ for now	**pour le moment**	*poor luh moh-mahn*
■ temporarily	**provisoirement**	*proh-vee-zwahr-mahn*
Can you fix ____?	**Pouvez-vous réparer ____?**	*poo-vay voo ray-pah-ray*
■ this bridge	**ce bridge**	*suh breedzh*
■ this crown	**cette couronne**	*seht koo-rohn*
■ this denture	**ce dentier**	*suh dahn-tyay*
■ these false teeth	**ces fausses dents**	*say fohss dahn*
When should I come back?	**Quand devrais-je revenir?**	*kahn duh-vrehzh ruh-vuh-neer*

What is your fee?	**Combien vous dois-je?** *kohn-byan voo dwahzh*
. . . are your fees?	

WITH THE OPTICIAN

Can you repair these glasses (for me)?	**Pouvez-vous (me) réparer ces lunettes?** *poo-vay voo (muh) ray-pah-ray say lew-neht*
I've broken a lens (the frame).	**J'ai cassé un verre (la monture).** *zhay kah-ssay uhn vehr (lah mohn-tewr)*
Can you put in a new lens?	**Pouvez-vous mettre un nouveau verre?** *poo-vay voo meh-truh uhn noo-voh vehr*
Can you tighten the screw?	**Pouvez-vous resserrer la vis?** *poo-vay voo ruh-sseh-ray lah veess*
I need the glasses as soon as possible.	**Il me faut ces lunettes aussitôt que possible.** *eel muh foh say lew-neht oh-ssee-toh kuh poh-ssee-bluh*
I don't have any others.	**Je n'ai pas d'autre paire.** *zhuh nay pah doh-truh pehr*
Do you sell contact lenses?	**Vendez-vous des verres de contact?** *vahn-day voo day vehr duh kohn-tahkt*
I've lost a lens.	**J'ai perdu un verre.** *zhay pehr-dew uhn vehr*
Can you replace it right away?	**Pouvez-vous le remplacer tout de suite?** *poo-vay voo luh rahn-plah-ssay toot sweet*
Do you sell sun glasses?	**Vendez-vous des lunettes de soleil?** *vahn-day voo day lew-neht duh soh-lehy*

COMMUNICATIONS

POST OFFICE

The letters P.T. (**Postes et Télécommunications**—for letters and telephones) identify the post offices. They are open from 8 AM–7 PM, with a two hour break for lunch in many instances and on Saturdays from 8:00 AM to noon. The main Paris post office never closes. Purchase stamps at post offices, at cafétabacs, or at your hotel. Look for the yellow mail box.

I want to mail a letter.	**Je voudrais mettre cette lettre à la poste.** *zhuh voo-dreh meh-truh seht leh-truh ah lah pohsst*
Where's the post office?	**Où se trouve le bureau de poste?** *oo suh troov luh bew-roh duh pohsst*
Where's a letterbox?	**Où se trouve la boîte aux lettres?** *oo suh troov lah bwaht oh leh-truh*
What is the postage on _____ to the United States?	**Quel est l'affranchissement _____ pour les États-Unis?** *kehl eh lah-frahn-sheess-mahn poor lay zay-tah zew-nee*
■ a letter	**d'une lettre** *dewn leh-truh*
■ an air-mail letter	**pour une lettre envoyée par avion** *poor ewn leh-truh ahn-vwah-yay pahr ah-vyohn*
■ an insured letter	**pour une lettre recommandée** *poor ewn leh-truh ruh-koh-mahn-day*
■ a registered letter	**pour une lettre recommandée** *poor ewn leh-truh ruh-koh-mahn-day*
■ a special delivery letter	**pour une lettre par exprès** *poor ewn leh-truh pahr ehkss-preh*
■ a package	**un colis** *zuhn koh-lee*
■ a post card	**une carte postale** *zewn kahrt pohss-tahl*

When will it arrive?	**Quand arrivera-t-il (elle)?** *kahn tah-ree-vrah teel? (tehl)*
Which is the ____ window?	**Quel est le guichet ____?** *kehl eh luh gee-sheh*
■ general delivery	**pour la poste restante** *poor lah pohsst rehss-tahnt*
■ money order	**pour les mandats-poste** *poor lay mahn-dah pohsst*
■ stamp	**pour les timbres-poste** *poor lay tan-bruh pohsst*
■ wholesale	**en gros** *ahn groh*
■ retail	**en détail** *ahn day-tahy*
Are there any letters for me?	**Y a-t-il des lettres pour moi?** *ee ah-teel day leh-truh poor mwah*
My name is ____.	**Je m'appelle ____.** *zhuh mah-pehl*
I'd like ____.	**Je voudrais ____.** *zhuh voo-dreh*
■ 10 post cards	**dix cartes postales** *dee kahrt pohss-tahl*
■ 5 (air mail) stamps	**cinq timbres (courrier aérien)** *sank tahn-bruh (koo-ryay ah-ay-ryan)*

TELEGRAMS

Where's the telegraph window?	**Où est le guichet pour les télégrammes?** *oo eh luh gee-sheh poor lay tay-lay-grahm*
How late is it open?	**Jusqu'à quelle heure est-il ouvert?** *zhewss-kah kehl uhr eh teel oo-vehr*
I'd like to send a telegram (night letter) to ____.	**Je voudrais envoyer un télégramme (une lettre-télégramme) à ____.** *zhuh voo-dreh zahn-vwah-yay uhn tay-lay-grahm (ewn leh-truh' tay-lay-grahm) ah*

How much is it per word?	**Quel est le tarif par mot?** *kehl eh luh tah-reef pahr moh*
Where are the forms?	**Où sont les formulaires (imprimés)?** *oo sohn lay fohr-mew-lehr (an-pree-may)*
May I please have a form?	**Puis-je avoir un formulaire (un imprimé) s'il vous plaît?** *pweezh ah-vwahr uhn fohr-mew-lehr (uhn an-pree-may) seel voo pleh*
I want to send it collect.	**Je voudrais l'envoyer en P.C.V.** *zhuh voo-dreh lahn-vwah-yay ahn pay say vay*
When will it arrive?	**Quand arrivera-t-il?** *kahn tah-ree-vrah teel*

TELEPHONES

Virtually the entire French telephone system is now automatic and is hooked up to the international dialing system. Public pay phone booths can be found at the post office, in cafés and on the streets of larger cities.

To place a local call from the older phones, you must purchase a slug (**un jeton**) at the café or post office. Long distance calls must be made from the post office or from your hotel. Do the following to complete a call:

1. Put your "jeton" in the slot.
2. Lift the receiver.
3. Wait for the dial tone.
4. Dial the number.
5. When you hear someone answer (NOT BEFORE), push the button on the front of the phone.

If there is no answer, if the line is busy, or if the phone isn't working, hang up the receiver and the jeton will be returned to you.

The more modern phones accept coins and, unlike the old phones, you may place international and long distance calls from them. Do the following to complete a call:

1. Lift the receiver.
2. Insert the coin.
3. Wait for the dial tone.
4. Dial the number.

Telephone numbers in France consist of 8 digits and are given in pairs. Phones in Paris have the area code (1) and 8 digits.

To dial direct to the U.S. from a new public pay phone, dial: 19 + 1 + area code + number.

Where is ____?	**Où y a-t-il ____?** *oo ee ah-teel*
■ a public telephone	**un téléphone public** *uhn tay-lay-fohn pew-bleek*
■ a telephone booth	**une cabine téléphonique** *ewn kah-been tay-lay-foh-neek*
■ a telephone directory	**un annuaire téléphonique** *uhn nah-new-ehr tay-lay-foh-neek*
May I use your phone?	**Puis-je me servir de votre téléphone?** *pweezh muh sehr-veer duh voh-truh tay-lay-fohn*
I want to make a ____ to	**Je voudrais téléphoner ____** *zhuh voo-dreh tay-lay-foh-nay*
■ local call	**en ville** *ahn veel*
■ long distance call	**à l'extérieur** *ah lehkss-tay-ryuhr*
■ person to person call	**avec préavis** *ah-vehk pray-ah-vee*
Can I call direct?	**Puis-je téléphoner en direct?** *pweezh tay-lay-foh-nay ahn dee-rehkt*
Do I need tokens for the phone?	**Faut-il des jetons pour le téléphone?** *foh teel day zhuh-tohn poor luh tay-lay-fohn*
Can you give me a token, please?	**Pourriez-vous me donner un jeton, s'il vous plaît?** *poo-ree-yay voo muh doh-nay uhn zhuh-tohn seel voo pleh*

How do I get the ____.	**Que fait-on pour ____?** *kuh feh-tohn poor*
■ Operator?	**parler à la téléphoniste?** *pahr-lay ah lah tay-lay-foh-neesst*
■ area code	**obtenir le code régional** *ohp-tuh-neer luh kohd ray-zhyohn-nahl*
Operator, can you get me number 23.34.56?	**Mademoiselle, pourriez vous me donner le vingt-trois, trente-quatre, cinquante-six?** *mahd-mwah-zehl poo-ree-yay voo muh doh-nay luh van-trwah trahnt kah-truh san-kahnt seess*
My number is ____.	**Mon numéro est ____.** *mohn new-may-roh eh*
May I speak to ____?	**Est-ce que je pourrais parler à ____?** *ehss kuh zhuh poo-reh pahr-lay ah*

I'd like to speak to ____.	**Je voudrais parler à ____.** *zhuh voo-dreh pahr-lay ah*
Is Mr. ____ in?	**Monsieur ____, est-il là?** *Muh-ssyuh ____ eh-teel lah*
Speaking.	**C'est ____ à l'appareil.** *seh ____ ah lah-pah-rehy*
Hello.	**Allô.** *ah-loh*
Who is calling?	**Qui est à l'appareil?** *kee eh tah lah-pah-rehy*
I can't hear.	**Je ne peux pas vous entendre.** *zhuh nuh puh pah voo zahn-tahn-druh*
Speak louder.	**Parlez plus fort.** *pahr-lay plew fohr*
Don't hang up.	**Ne quittez pas.** *nuh kee-tay pah*
This is ____.	**Ici ____.** *ee-ssee*
Operator, there's no answer (They don't answer).	**Mademoiselle, ça ne répond pas.** *mahd-mwah-zehl, sah nuh ray-pohn pah*
The line is busy.	**La ligne est occupée.** *lah lee-nyuh eh toh-kew-pay*
You gave me (that was) a wrong number.	**Vous m'avez donné le mauvais numéro.** *voo mah-vay doh-nay luh moh-veh new-may-roh*
I was cut off.	**J'ai été coupé.** *zhay ay-tay koo-pay*
Please dial it again.	**Veuillez recomposez le numéro.** *vuh-yay ruh-kohn-poh-zay luh new-may-roh*
I want to leave a message.	**Je voudrais laisser un message.** *zhuh voo-dreh leh-ssay uhn meh-ssahzh*

DRIVING A CAR

ROAD SYSTEM

You may choose to drive on one of the following kinds of roads:

Autoroute
a high-speed super freeway for long distance trips. These are toll roads.

Route nationale
a main highway used by cars going from one small town to another.

Route départementale
minor highway

Chemin communal
a local road

Chemin rural
a scenic country road

A good idea would be to purchase a French **Code de la Route** which explains driving rules and regulations. The French Government Tourist Office issues free road maps. Speed limits are high and it will take some time getting used to the French way of driving. Remember to buckle up.

PARKING

During the day you may park at parking meters located in metropolitan areas, or you may find a spot in a "Blue Zone." To park there you must use a special parking disk (**disque**) which can be obtained free of charge at auto clubs, garages, gas stations, hotels, police stations or tourist offices. You must set the time of your arrival, and departure time will show automatically on the disk. The disk should be displayed on your windshield. Be careful; if you are caught cheating, you risk a fine. Parking at night is usually free.

SIGNS

Familiarize yourself with the traffic signs listed below:

Accotement non stabilisé
Soft shoulder

Allumez vos phares
Put on headlights

Arrêt interdit	No stopping
Attention	Caution
Céder le passage	Yield
Chaussée déformée	Poor roadway
Chute de pierres	Falling rocks
Circulation interdite	No thoroughfare
Descente (Pente) dangereuse	Steep slope (hill)
Déviation	Detour
Douane	Customs
École	School
Entrée interdite	No entrance
Fin d'interdiction de _____	End of _____ zone
Interdiction de doubler	No Passing
Interdiction de stationner	No Parking
Interdit aux piétons	No Pedestrians
Piste réservée aux transports publics	Lane for Public Transportation
Ralentir (Ralentissez)	Slow
Réservé aux piétons	Pedestrians only
Sens interdit	Wrong way
Sens unique	One Way
Serrez à gauche (à droite)	Keep left (right)
Sortie d'autoroute	Freeway (throughway) Exit
Sortie de véhicules	Vehicle Exit

Guarded railroad crossing

Yield

Stop

Right of way

Dangerous intersection ahead

Gasoline (petrol) ahead

Parking

No vehicles allowed

Dangerous curve

Pedestrian crossing

Oncoming traffic has right of way

No bicycles allowed

No parking allowed

No entry

No left turn

No U-turn

No passing

Border crossing

Traffic signal ahead

Speed limit

Traffic circle (roundabout) ahead

Minimum speed limit

All traffic turns left

End of no passing zone

One-way street

Detour

Danger ahead

Entrance to expressway

Expressway ends

Stationnement autorisé	Parking Permitted
Stationnement interdit	No Parking
Tenez la droite (gauche)	Keep to the right (left)
Verglas	Icy Road
Virage dangereux	Dangerous Curve
Voie de dégagement	Private Entrance
Zone Bleue	Blue Zone (parking)

CAR RENTALS

To drive in France you may use your driver's license. Cars may be rented or leased at airports or major railway stations. This can be quite costly since the price of gasoline abroad is prohibitive. The most economical method of renting a car is to reserve it with one of the rental agencies before you leave home.

Where can I rent a car?	**Où puis-je louer une voiture?** *oo pweezh loo-ay ewn vwah-tewr*
■ a motorcycle	**une motocyclette** *ewn moh-toh-see-kleht*
■ a bicycle	**une bicyclette** *ewn bee-ssee-kleht*
■ a scooter	**un scooter** *uhn skoo-tehr*
■ a moped	**un mobylette** *ewn moh-bee-leht*
I want a _____.	**Je voudrais _____.** *zhuh voo-dreh*
■ a small car	**une petite voiture** *zewn puh-teet vwah-tewr*
■ large car	**une grande voiture** *zewn grahnd vwah-tewr*
■ sports car	**une voiture de sport** *zewn vwah-tewr duh spohr*
I prefer automatic transmission.	**Je préfère la transmission automatique.** *zhuh pray-fehr lah trahnz-mee-ssyohn oh-toh-mah-teek*

How much does it cost ____?	**Quel est le tarif ____?** *kehl eh luh tah-reef*
■ per day	**à la journée** *ah lah zhoor-nay*
■ per week	**à la semaine** *ah lah suh-mehn*
■ per kilometer	**au kilomètre** *oh kee-loh-meh-truh*
How much is the insurance?	**Quel est le montant de l'assurance?** *kehl eh luh mohn-tahn duh lah-ssew-rahnss*
Is the gas included?	**Est-ce que l'essence est comprise?** *ehss kuh leh-ssahnss eh kohn-preez*
Do you accept credit cards? Which ones?	**Acceptez vous des cartes de crédit? Lesquelles?** *ahk-ssehp-tay voo day kahrt duh kray-dee? Lay-kehl*
Here's my driver's license.	**Voici mon permis de conduire.** *vwah-ssee mohn pehr-mee duh kohn-dweer*
Do I have to leave a deposit?	**Dois-je verser des arrhes?** *dwahzh vehr-ssay day zahr*
Is there a drop-off charge?	**Faut-il payer plus en cas de non-retour ici?** *foh-teel peh-yay plews ahn kah duh nohn-ruh-toor ee-ssee*
I want to rent the car here and leave it in ____ (name of city).	**Je veux louer la voiture ici et la laisser à ____.** *zhuh vuh loo-ay lah vwah-tewr ee-ssee ay lah leh-ssay ah*
What kind of gas does it take?	**Quelle essence emploie-t-elle?** *kehl eh-ssahnss ahn-plwah-tehl*

ON THE ROAD

Excuse me.	**Excusez-moi.** *ehkss-kew-zay mwah* **Pardon** *pahr-dohn*
Can you tell me ____?	**Pouvez-vous me dire ____?** *poo-vay voo muh deer*

Which way is it to ____?	**Comment aller à ____?** *koh-mahn ah-lay ah*
How do I get to ____?	**Comment puis-je aller à ____?** *koh-mahn pweezh ah-lay ah*
I think we're lost.	**Je crois que nous nous sommes égarés.** *zhuh krwah kuh noo noo sohm zay-gah-ray*
	Nous sommes sur la mauvaise route. *noo sohm sewr lah moh-vehz root*
Which is the road to ____?	**Quelle est la route pour ____?** *kehl eh lah root poor*
Is this the road (way) to ____?	**Est-ce la route de ____?** *ehss lah root duh*
Where does this road go?	**Où mène cette route?** *oo mehn seht root*
How far is it from here to the next town?	**À quelle distance sommes-nous du prochain village?** *ah kehl deess-tahnss sohm noo dew proh-shan vee-lahzh*
How far away is ____?	**À quelle distance est ____?** *ah kehl deess-tahnss eh*
Is the next town far?	**Le prochain village, est-il loin?** *luh proh-shan vee-lahzh eh-teel lwan*
What's the next town called?	**Comment s'appelle le prochain village?** *koh-mahn sah-pehl luh proh-shan vee-lahzh*
Do you have a road map?	**Avez-vous une carte routière?** *Ah-vay voo zewn kahrt roo-tyehr*
Can you show it to me on the map?	**Pourriez-vous me l'indiquer sur la carte?** *poo-ree-yay voo muh lan-dee-kay sewr lah kahrt*
Is the road in good condition?	**Est-ce que la route est en bon état?** *ehss kuh lah root eh tahn bohn nay-tah*

Is this the shortest way?	**Est-ce le chemin le plus court?** *ehss luh shuh-ma̱n luh plew koor*
Are there any detours?	**Y a-t-il des déviations?** *ee ah-teel day day-vee-ah-ssyoẖn*
Do I go straight?	**Est-ce que je vais tout droit?** *ehss kuh zhuh veh too drwah*
Do I turn to the right (to the left)?	**Est-ce que je tourne à droite (à gauche)?** *ehss kuh zhuh toorn ah drwaht (ah gohsh)*

AT THE SERVICE STATION

Gasoline is sold by the liter in Europe, and for the traveler accustomed to gallons, it may seem confusing, especially if you want to calculate your mileage per gallon (kilometer per liter). Here are some tips on making those conversions.

LIQUID MEASURES (APPROXIMATE)		
LITERS	U.S. GALLONS	IMPERIAL GALLONS
30	8	$6\frac{1}{2}$
40	$10\frac{1}{2}$	$8\frac{3}{4}$
50	$13\frac{1}{2}$	11
60	$15\frac{3}{4}$	13
70	$18\frac{1}{2}$	$15\frac{1}{2}$
80	21	$17\frac{1}{2}$

DISTANCE MEASURES (APPROXIMATE)	
KILOMETERS	MILES
1	.62
5	3
10	6
20	12
50	31
100	62

Where is there a gas station?	**Où y a-t-il une station-service?** *oo ee ah-teel ewn stah-ssyohn sehr-veess*
I need gas.	**J'ai besoin d'essence.** *zhay buh-zwan deh-ssahnss*
Fill'er up with ____.	**Faites-le plein, s'il vous plaît ____.** *feht-luh plan seel-voo pleh*
■ diesel	**du gas-oil** *dew gahz-wahl*
■ regular	**de l'ordinaire** *duh lohr-dee-nehr*
■ super	**du super** *dew sew-pehr*
Give me ____ liters.	**Donnez m'en ____ litres, s'il vous plaît.** *doh-nay mahn ____ lee-truh, seel voo pleh*
I need 60 liters of gas.	**Je voudrais 60 (soixante) litres d'essence.** *zhuh voo-dreh swah-ssahnt lee-truh deh-ssahnss*
Please check ____.	**Veuillez vérifier ____.** *vuh-yay vay-ree-fyay*
■ the battery	**la batterie** *lah bah-tree*
■ the brakes	**les freins** *lay fran*
■ the carburetor	**le carburateur** *luh kahr-bew-rah-tuhr*
■ the oil	**le niveau de l'huile** *luh nee-voh duh lweel*
■ the spark plugs	**les bougies** *lay boo-zhee*
■ the tires	**les pneus** *lay pnuh*
■ the tire pressure	**la pression des pneus** *lah preh-ssyohn day pnuh*
■ the water	**le niveau de l'eau** *luh nee-voh duh loh*
Change the oil.	**Changez l'huile, s'il vous plaît.** *shahn-zhay lweel seel voo pleh*

Grease the car.	**Faites un graissage complet de la voiture, s'il vous plaît.** *feht zuhn greh-ssahzh kohn-pleh duh lah vwah-tewr seel voo pleh*
Charge the battery.	**Rechargez la batterie, s'il vous plaît.** *ruh-shahr-zhay lah bah-tree, seel voo pleh*
Change this tire.	**Changez ce pneu.** *shahn-zhay suh pnuh*
Wash the car.	**Lavez la voiture.** *Lah-vay lah vwah-tewr*
Where are the rest rooms?	**Où sont les toilettes?** *oo sohn lay twah-leht*

TIRE PRESSURE	
LB./SQ. IN.	KG./CM.^{2}
17	1.2
18	1.3
20	1.4
21	1.5
23	1.6
24	1.7
26	1.8
27	1.9
28	2.0
30	2.1
31	2.2
33	2.3
34	2.4
36	2.5
37	2.6
38	2.7
40	2.8

ACCIDENTS, REPAIRS

It overheats.	**Elle chauffe.** *ehl shohf*
It doesn't start.	**Elle ne démarre pas.** *ehl nuh day-mahr pah*
It doesn't go.	**Elle ne marche pas.** *ehl nuh mahrsh pah*
I have a flat tire.	**J'ai un pneu crevé.** *zhay-uhn pnuh kruh-vay*
My car has broken down.	**Ma voiture est en panne.** *mah vwah-tewr eh tahn pahn*
The radiator is leaking.	**Le radiateur coule.** *luh rah-dee-ah-tuhr kool*
The battery is dead.	**La batterie ne fonctionne plus.** *lah bah-tree nuh fohnk-ssyohn plew*
The keys are locked inside the car.	**Les clés sont enfermées à l'intérieur de la voiture.** *lay klay sohn tahn-fehr-may ah lan-tay-ree-yuhr duh lah vwah-tewr*
Is there a garage near here?	**Y a-t-il un garage par ici?** *ee ah-teel uhn gah-rahzh pahr ee-ssee*
I need a mechanic (tow truck).	**Il me faut un mécanicien (une dépanneuse).** *eel muh foh tuhn may-kah-nee-ssyan (ewn day-pah-nuhz)*
Can you _____?	**Pouvez-vous _____?** *poo-vay voo*
■ give me a hand	me donner un coup de main *muh doh-nay uhn koo duh man*
■ help me	m'aider *meh-day*
■ push me	me pousser *muh poo-ssay*
■ tow me	me remorquer *muh ruh-mohr-kay*
I don't have any tools.	**Je n'ai pas d'outils.** *zhuh nay pas doo-tee*

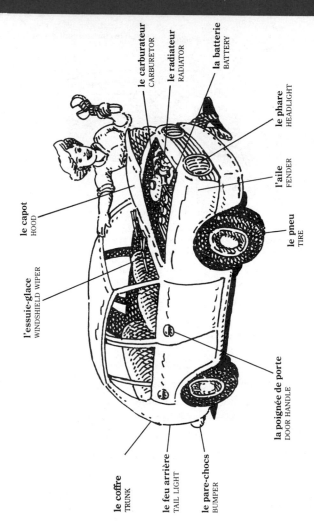

le carburateur CARBURETOR
le radiateur RADIATOR
la batterie BATTERY
le phare HEADLIGHT
l'aile FENDER
le pneu TIRE
le capot HOOD
l'essuie-glace WINDSHIELD WIPER
la poignée de porte DOOR HANDLE
le coffre TRUNK
le feu arrière TAIL LIGHT
le pare-chocs BUMPER

le volant
STEERING WHEEL

le changement de vitesse
GEAR SHIFT

le clignotant
DIRECTIONAL SIGNAL

la radio
RADIO

le frein à main
PARKING BRAKE
HAND BRAKE

la pédale d'embrayage
CLUTCH PEDAL

la pédale de frein
BRAKE PEDAL

la pédale d'accélérateur (l'accélérateur)
GAS PEDAL

Can you lend me _____?	**Pouvez-vous me prêter _____?** *poo-vay voo muh preh-tay*
■ a flashlight	**une lampe de poche** *ewn lahnp duh pohsh*
■ a hammer	**un marteau** *uhn mahr-toh*
■ a jack	**un cric** *uhn kree*
■ a monkey wrench	**une clé anglaise** *ewn klay ahn-glehz*
■ pliers	**des pinces** *day panss*
■ a screwdriver	**un tournevis** *uhn toorn-veess*
I need _____.	**J'ai besoin _____.** *zhay buh-zwan*
■ a bolt	**d'un boulon** *duhn boo-lohn*
■ a bulb	**d'une ampoule** *dewn ahn-pool*
■ a filter	**d'un filtre** *duhn feel-truh*
■ a nut	**d'un écrou** *duhn nay-kroo*
Can you fix the car?	**Pouvez-vous réparer la voiture?** *Poo-vay voo ray-pah-ray lah vwah-tewr*

Can you repair it temporarily?	**Pouvez-vous la réparer provisoirement?** *poo-vay voo lah ray-pah-ray proh-vee-zwahr-mahn*
Do you have the part?	**Avez-vous la pièce de rechange?** *ah-vay voo lah pyehss duh ruh-shahnzh*
I think there's something wrong with ____.	**Je crois que ____ ne fonctionne pas.** *zhuh krwah kuh ____ nuh fohnk-ssyohn pas.*

- the directional signal — **le clignotant** *luh klee-nyoh-tahn*
- the door handle — **la poignée** *lah pwah-nyay*
- the electrical system — **l'installation électrique** *lan-stah-lah-ssyohn ay-lehk-treek*
- the fan — **le ventilateur** *luh vahn-tee-lah-tuhr*
- the fan belt — **la courroie de ventilateur** *lah koor-wah duh vahn-tee-lah-tuhr*
- the fuel pump — **la pompe à essence** *lah pohnp ah eh-ssahnss*
- the gears — **l'engrenage** *lahn-gruh-nahzh*
- the gear shift — **le changement de vitesses** *luh shahnzh-mahn duh vee-tehss*
- the headlight — **le phare** *luh fahr*
- the horn — **le klaxon** *luh klahk-ssohn*
- the ignition — **l'allumage** *lah-lew-mahzh*
- the radio — **la radio** *lah rah-dyoh*
- the starter — **le démarreur** *luh day-mah-ruhr*
- the steering wheel — **le volant** *luh voh-lahn*
- the tail light — **le feu arrière** *luh fuh ah-ryehr*
- the transmission — **la transmission** *lah trahnz-mee-ssyohn*

■ the water pump	**la pompe à eau** *lah pohnp ah oh*
■ the windshield wipers	**les essuie-glaces** *lay zeh-sswee glahss*
Can you take a look at (check out) ___?	**Pouvez-vous regarder ___?** *poo-vay voo ruh-gahr-day*
■ the brakes	**les freins** *lay fran*
■ the bumper	**le pare-choc** *luh pahr-shohk*
■ the exhaust	**l'échappement** *lay-shahp-mahn*
■ the fender	**l'aile** *lehl*
■ the gas tank	**le réservoir à essence** *luh ray-zehr-vwahr ah eh-ssahnss*
■ the hood	**le capot** *luh kah-poh*
■ the trunk	**le coffre** *luh koh-fruh*
What's the matter?	**Qu'est-ce qui ne va pas?** *kehss kee nuh vah pah*
Is it possible to (Can you) fix it today?	**Pouvez-vous la réparer aujourd'hui?** *poo-vay-voo lah ray-pah-ray oh-zhoor-dwee*
How long will it take?	**Combien de temps faudra-t-il?** *kohn-byan duh tahn foh-drah-teel*
Is everything O.K. now?	**Tout est arrangé (réparé) maintenant?** *too teh tah-rahn-zhay (ray-pah-ray) mant-nahn*
How much do I owe you?	**Combien vous dois-je?** *kohn-byan voo dwahzh*

TRAVEL TIP

Hotels often levy a service charge for calls made from a guest room. To avoid paying too much, make all calls from a telephone booth and use a telephone company calling card for long distance.

GENERAL INFORMATION

TELLING TIME

What time is it?	**Quelle heure est-il?**	*kehl uhr eh teel*
It is ____.	**Il est ____.**	*eel eh*
■ noon	**midi**	*mee-dee*
■ 1:05	**une heure cinq**	*ewn-uhr sank*
■ 2:10	**deux heures dix**	*duh-zuhr deess*
■ 3:15	**trois heures et quart**	*trwah-zuhr ay kahr*
■ 4:20	**quatre heures vingt**	*kahtruh-uhr van*
■ 5:25	**cinq heures vingt-cinq**	*sank-uhr van sank*
■ 6:30	**six heures et demie**	*seez-uhr ay duh-mee*
■ 7:35	**sept heures trente-cinq**	*seht-uhr trahnt-sank*
■ 8:40	**neuf heures moins vingt**	*nuhv-uhr mwan van*
■ 9:45	**dix heures moins le quart**	*deez-uhr mwan luh kahr*
■ 10:50	**onze heures moins dix**	*ohnz uhr mwan deess*
■ 11:55	**midi moins cinq**	*mee-dee mwan sank*
■ 8:00	**huit heures**	*weet-uhr*
■ 2:30	**deux heures et demie**	*duhz-uhr ay duh-mee*
■ 7:15	**sept heures et quart**	*seht-uhr ay kahr*

EXPRESSIONS OF TIME

At what time ____?	À quelle heure ____?	*ah kehl-uhr____?*
When?	**Quand?**	*kahn?*
at ____ o'clock	**à ____ heures**	*ah ____ uhr*
at exactly noon	**à midi précis**	*ah mee-dee pray-ssee*
at exactly 5 o'clock	**à cinq heures précises**	*ah sank uhr pray-sseez*
in an hour	**dans une heure**	*dahn zewn-uhr*
in 2 hours	**dans deux heures**	*dahn duhz-uhr*
not before 2 a.m.	**pas avant deux heures du matin**	*pah zah-vahn duhz-uhr dew mah-tan*
after 3 p.m.	**après trois heures de l'après-midi**	*ah-preh trwah-zuhr duh lah-preh mee-dee*
at about 9 p.m.	**vers neuf heures du soir**	*vehr nuhv-uhr dew swahr*
between 8 and 9 o'clock	**entre huit et neuf heures**	*ahn-truh weet ay nuhv-uhr*
until 5 o'clock	**jusqu'à cinq heures**	*zhewss-kah sank uhr*
since what time ____?	**depuis quelle heure ____?**	*duh-pwee kehl uhr*
since 7 o'clock	**depuis sept heures**	*duh-pwee seht uhr*

per hour	**par heure**	*pahr uhr*
three hours ago	**il y a trois heures**	*eel yah trwah-zuhr*
early	**tôt**	*toh*
	de bonne heure	*duh bohn-uhr*
late	**tard**	*tahr*
late (in arriving)	**en retard**	*ah<u>n</u> ruh-tahr*
on, in time	**à l'heure**	*ah luhr*
noon	**midi**	*mee-dee*
midnight	**minuit**	*mee-nwee*
in the morning	**le matin**	*luh mah-ta<u>n</u>*
in the afternoon	**l'après-midi**	*lah-preh mee-dee*
in the evening	**le soir**	*luh swahr*
at night	**la nuit**	*lah nwee*
second	**une seconde**	*ewn suh-goh<u>n</u>d*
minute	**une minute**	*ewn mee-newt*
hour	**une heure**	*ewn uhr*
a quarter of an hour	**un quart d'heure**	*uh<u>n</u> kahr duhr*
a half hour	**une demi-heure**	*ewn duh-mee uhr*

Official time is based on the 24-hour clock. You will find train schedules and other such times expressed in terms of a point within the 24-hour sequence.

The train leaves at 15:30.	**Le train part à 15:30.** *luh tran pahr ah kanz-uhr trahnt*
The time is now 21:15.	**Il est maintenant 21 heures 15.** *eel eh mant-nahn van-tay-ewn uhr kanz*

DAYS OF THE WEEK

What day is today?	**Quel jour est-ce aujourd'hui?** *kehl zhoor ess oh-zhoor-dwee*
	Quel jour sommes-nous aujourd'hui? *kehl zhoor sohm noo oh-zhoor-dwee*
Today is ____.	**C'est aujourd'hui ____.** *seh toh-zhoor-dwee*
	Nous sommes ____ *noo sohm*
Monday	**lundi** *luhn-dee*
Tuesday	**mardi** *mahr-dee*
Wednesday	**mercredi** *mehr-kruh-dee*
Thursday	**jeudi** *zhuh-dee*
Friday	**vendredi** *vahn-druh-dee*
Saturday	**samedi** *sahm-dee*
Sunday	**dimanche** *dee-mahnsh*

NOTE: In French, the names of the days and the months and seasons are written in small letters.

last Monday	**lundi dernier**	*luhn-dee dehr-nyay*
the day before	**la veille**	*lah vehy*

the day before yesterday	**avant-hier**	*ah-vah<u>n</u>-tyehr*
yesterday	**hier**	*yehr*
today	**aujourd'hui**	*oh-zhoor-dwee*
tomorrow	**demain**	*duh-ma<u>n</u>*
the day after tomorrow	**après-demain**	*ah-preh-duh-ma<u>n</u>*
the next day	**le lendemain**	*luh lah<u>n</u>-duh-ma<u>n</u>*
next Monday	**lundi prochain**	*luh<u>n</u>-dee proh-sha<u>n</u>*
the day	**le jour**	*luh zhoor*
2 days ago	**il y a deux jours**	*eel-yah duh zhoor*
in 2 days	**dans deux jours**	*dah<u>n</u> duh zhoor*
every day	**tous les jours**	*too lay zhoor*
day off	**(le) jour de congé**	*(luh) zhoor duh kohn-zhay*
holiday	**(le) jour de fête**	*(luh) zhoor duh feht*
birthday	**l'anniversaire**	*lah-nee-vehr-ssehr*
per day	**par jour**	*pahr zhoor*
during the day	**pendant la journée**	*pahn-dah<u>n</u> lah zhoor-nay*
from this day on	**dès aujourd'hui**	*deh zoh-zhoor-dwee*
the week	**la semaine**	*lah suh-mehn*
a week day	**un jour de semaine**	*uh<u>n</u> zhoor duh suh-mehn*
the week end	**le week-end**	*luh week-ehnd*
last week	**la semaine passée**	*lah suh-mehn pah-ssay*
this week	**cette semaine**	*seht suh-mehn*
next week	**la semaine prochaine**	*lah suh-mehn proh-shehn*

a week from today	**dans une se-maine**	*dahn-zewn suh-mehn*
2 weeks from to-morrow	**de demain en quinze**	*duh duh-man ahn kanz*
during the week	**pendant la se-maine**	*pahn-dahn lah suh-mehn*

MONTHS OF THE YEAR

January	**janvier**	*zhan-vee-yay*
February	**février**	*fay-vree-yay*
March	**mars**	*mahrss*
April	**avril**	*ah-vreel*
May	**mai**	*meh*
June	**juin**	*zhwan*
July	**juillet**	*zhwee-yeh*
August	**août**	*oo or oot*
September	**septembre**	*sehp-tahn-bruh*
October	**octobre**	*ohk-toh-bruh*
November	**novembre**	*noh-vahn-bruh*
December	**décembre**	*day-ssahn-bruh*
the month	**le mois**	*luh mwah*
2 months ago	**il y a deux mois**	*eel yah duh mwah*
last month	**le mois dernier**	*luh mwah dehr-nyay*
this month	**ce mois**	*suh mwah*
next month	**le mois prochain**	*luh mwah proh-shan*
during the month of	**pendant le mois de**	*pahn-dahn luh mwah duh*

since the month of	**depuis le mois de**	*duh-pwee luh mwah duh*
for the month of	**pour le mois de**	*poor luh mwah duh*
every month	**tous les mois**	*too lay mwah*
per month	**par mois**	*pahr mwah*
What is today's date?	**Quelle est la date d'aujourd'hui?** *kehl ay lah daht doh-zhoor-dwee?*	
Today is ____.	**C'est aujourd'hui ____.** *seht oh-zhoor-dwee*	
Monday, May 1	**lundi, le premier mai** *luhn-dee luh pruh-myay meh*	
Tuesday, June 2	**mardi, le deux juin** *mahr-dee luh duh zhwan*	

NOTE: Use the ordinal number only for the first of the month.

the year	**l'an/l'année**	*lahn/lah-nay*
per year	**par an**	*pahr ahn*
all year	**toute l'année**	*toot lah-nay*
every year	**chaque année**	*shahk ah-nay*
during the year	**pendant l'année**	*pahn-dahn lah-nay*

THE FOUR SEASONS

spring	**le printemps**	*luh pran-tahn*
summer	**l'été**	*lay-tay*
autumn	**l'automne**	*loh-tohn*
winter	**l'hiver**	*lee-vehr*
in the spring	**au printemps**	*oh pran-tahn*
in the summer	**en été**	*ahn-nay-tay*
in the autumn	**en automne**	*ahn-noh-tohn*
in the winter	**en hiver**	*ahn nee-vehr*

WEATHER

What is the weather like?	**Quel temps fait-il?** *kehl tah<u>n</u> feh-teel*
It is beautiful.	**Il fait beau.** *eel feh boh*
It is hot.	**Il fait chaud.** *eel feh shoh*
It is sunny.	**Il fait du soleil.** *eel feh dew soh-lehy*
It is bad.	**Il fait mauvais.** *eel feh moh-veh*
It is cold.	**Il fait froid.** *eel feh frwah*
It is cool.	**Il fait frais.** *eel feh freh*
It is windy.	**Il fait du vent.** *eel feh dew vah<u>n</u>*
It is foggy.	**Il fait du brouillard.** *eel feh dew broo-yahr*
It is snowing.	**Il neige.** *eel nehzh*
It is raining.	**Il pleut.** *eel pluh*

TEMPERATURE

The average annual daily temperatures in Paris in Fahrenheit and Centigrade are:

MONTH	°F	°C
January	42°	5°
February	45°	7°
March	54°	12°
April	61°	16°
May	68°	20°
June	73°	23°
July	77°	25°
August	75°	23°
September	70°	21°
October	61°	16°
November	50°	10°
December	44°	6°

| What heat! | **Quelle chaleur!** *kehl shah-luhr* |
| What cold! | **Quel froid!** *kehl frwah* |

RELIGIOUS SERVICES

France has many cathedrals and churches that you may wish to visit. There are churches and synagogues in major cities that do conduct some services in English. For more information, speak to the concierge at your hotel.

Is there a ____ near here?	**Y a-t-il ____ près d'ici?** *ee ah teel ____ preh dee-ssee*
■ Catholic church	**une église catholique** *ewn ay-gleez kah-toh-leek*
■ Protestant church	**un temple** *uhn tahn-pluh*
■ synagogue	**une synagogue** *ewn see-nah-gohg*
■ mosque	**une mosquée** *ewn mohss-kay*
At what time is the service (mass)?	**À quelle heure commence le service/la messe?** *ah kehl uhr koh-mahnss luh sehr-veess/lah mehss*
I would like to speak to a ____.	**Je voudrais parler à un ____.** *zhuh voo-dreh pahr-lay ah uhn*
■ priest	**prêtre** *preh-truh*
■ minister	**pasteur** *pahss-tuhr*
■ rabbi	**rabbin** *rah-ban*

PUBLIC HOLIDAYS AND CELEBRATIONS

| Jan. 1 | Le Jour de l'An
Le Nouvel An | New Year's Day |
| May 1 | La Fête du Travail | Labor Day |

July 14	La Fête Nationale	Bastille Day
Aug. 15	L'Assomption	Assumption Day
Nov. 1	La Toussaint	All Saints' Day
Nov. 2	Le Jour des Morts	All Souls' Day
Nov. 11	L'Armistice	Armistice Day
Dec. 25	Noël	Christmas
February	Le Carnaval	Carnival
Last day of carnival	Le Mardi gras	Mardi-Gras
Mar/Apr	Les Rameaux	Palm Sunday
Mar/Apr	Le Vendredi-Saint	Good Friday
Mar/Apr	Pâques	Easter
Mar/Apr	Le Dimanche de Quasimodo	1st Sunday after Easter
40 days after Easter	L'Ascension	Ascension Thursday
7 Mondays after Easter	Lundi de la Pentecôte	Whit Monday
May	La Fête de Jeanne d'Arc	Feast of Joan of Arc

COUNTRIES AND NATIONALITIES

Where are you from? **D'où êtes-vous?** *doo eht voo*

I am from _____. **Je suis de _____.** *zhuh swee duh*

I am _____. **Je suis _____.** *zhuh swee*

NOTE: The feminine form of the adjective is indicated after the masculine form. For this form remember to pronounce the last consonant.

	COUNTRY	NATIONALITY
*Africa	**l'Afrique** *lah-freek*	**africain/e** *ah-free-kan/kehn*
Asia	**l'Asie** *lah-zee*	**asiatique** *ah-zyah-teek*
Australia	**l'Australie** *lah-strah-lee*	**australien/ne** *oh-strah-lyan/lyehn*
Europe	**L'Europe** *lew-rohp*	**européen/ne** *ew-roh-pay-an/ehn*
N. America	**L'Amérique du Nord** *lah-may-reek dew nohr*	**américain/e** *ah-may-ree-kan/ehn*
S. America	**L'Amérique du Sud** *lah-may-reek dew sewd*	**sud-américain/e** *sewd-ah-may-ree-kan/ ehn*
Austria	**L'Autriche** *loh-treesh*	**autrichien/ne** *oh-tree-shyan/shyehn*
Belgium	**La Belgique** *lah behl-zheek*	**belge** *behlzh*
Canada	**Le Canada** *luh kah-nah-dah*	**canadien/ne** *kah-nah-dyan/dyehn*
China	**La Chine** *lah sheen*	**chinois/e** *shee-nwah/nwahz*
Denmark	**Le Danemark** *luh dahn-mahrk*	**danois/e** *dah-nwah/nwahz*
England	**L'Angleterre** *lahn-gluh-tehr*	**anglais/e** *ahn-gleh/glehz*
Finland	**la Finlande** *lah feen-lahnd*	**finlandais/e** *feen-lahn-deh/dehz*

NOTE: When nationality refers to a person (noun) it is capitalized, i.e., **Un(e) Africain(e) parle français.** When the nationality is used as an adjective it begins with a lower case letter, i.e., **C'est un pays africains.**

	COUNTRY	NATIONALITY
France	**la France** *lah Frah<u>n</u>ss*	**français/e** *frahn-sseh/sehz*
Germany	**Allemagne** *ahl-mah-nyuh*	**allemand/e** *ahl-mah<u>n</u>/mah<u>n</u>d*
Greece	**la Grèce** *lah grehss*	**grec/que** *grehk*
Haiti	**Haïti** *ahy-ee-tee*	**haïtien/ne** *ahy-ee-ssya<u>n</u>/ssyehn*
India	**l'Inde** *f. la<u>n</u>d*	**indien/ne** *a<u>n</u>-dya<u>n</u>/dyehn*
Ireland	**l'Irlande** *f. leer-lah<u>n</u>d*	**irlandais/e** *eer-lah<u>n</u>-deh/dehz*
Israel	**Israël** *m. eez-rah-ehl*	**israélite** *eez-rah-ay-leet*
Italy	**l'Italie** *f. lee-tah-lee*	**italien/ne** *ee-tah-lya<u>n</u>/lyehn*
Japan	**le Japon** *luh zhah-poh<u>n</u>*	**japonais/e** *zhah-poh-neh/nehz*
Luxembourg	**le Luxembourg** *luh lewkss-ah<u>n</u>-boor*	**luxembourgeois/e** *lewkss-ah<u>n</u>-boor-zhwah/zhwahz*
Morocco	**le Maroc** *luh mah-rohk*	**marocain/e** *mah-roh-ka<u>n</u>/kehn*
Norway	**la Norvège** *lah nohr-vehzh*	**norvégien/ne** *nohr-vay-zhya<u>n</u>/zhyehn*
Portugal	**le Portugal** *luh pohr-tew-gahl*	**portugais/e** *pohr-tew-geh/gehz*
Russia	**Russie** *roo-see*	**russe** *r<u>oo</u>ss*
Scotland	**l'Ecosse** *lay-kohs*	**écossais/e** *ay-koh-sseh/ssehz*

	COUNTRY	NATIONALITY
Senegal	**le Sénégal** *luh say-nay-gahl*	**sénégalais/e** *say-nay-gah-leh/lehz*
Spain	**l'Espagne** *f. lehss-pah-nyuh*	**espagnol/e** *ehss-pah-nyohl*
Sweden	**la Suède** *lah swehd*	**suédois/e** *sway-dwah/dwahz*
Switzer-land	**la Suisse** *lah sweess*	**suisse** *sweess*
Tunisia	**la Tunisie** *lah tew-nee-zee*	**tunisien/ne** *tew-nee-zyan/zyehn*
U.S.	**les États-Unis** *layz ay-tah-zew-nee*	**américain/e** *ah-may-ree-kan/kehn*
Wales	**le pays de Galles** *luh pay-ee duh gahl*	**gallois/e** *gahl-wah/wahz*

DIRECTIONS

the north	**le nord**	*luh nohr*
the south	**le sud**	*luh sewd*
the east	**l'est**	*lehsst*
the west	**l'ouest**	*lwehsst*

IMPORTANT SIGNS

À louer	*ah loo-ay*	For rent, hire
Ascenseur	*ah-sahn-ssuhr*	Elevator
Attention	*ah-tahn-ssyohn*	Careful
À vendre	*ah vahn-druh*	For sale

Dames	*dahm*	Ladies
Danger	*dah<u>n</u>-zhay*	Danger
Danger de mort	*dah<u>n</u>-zhay duh mohr*	Danger of death
Défense de	*day-fah<u>n</u>ss duh*	Do not _____
Défense d'entrer	*day-fah<u>n</u>ss dah<u>n</u>-tray*	Do not enter
Défense de cracher	*day-fah<u>n</u>ss duh krah-shay*	No spitting
Défense de fumer	*day-fah<u>n</u>ss duh few-may*	No smoking
Défense de marcher sur l'herbe	*day-fah<u>n</u>ss duh mahr-shay sewr lehrb*	Keep off the grass
Eau non potable	*oh noh<u>n</u> poh-tah-bluh*	Don't drink the water
École	*ay-kohl*	School
Entrée	*ah<u>n</u>-tray*	Entrance
Entrée interdite	*ah<u>n</u>-tray a<u>n</u>-tehr-deet*	No Entrance
Entrée libre	*ah<u>n</u>-tray lee-bruh*	Free Admission
Fermé	*fehr-may*	Closed
Fumeurs	*few-muhr*	Smokers
Hommes	*ohm*	Men
Hôpital	*oh-pee-tahl*	Hospital
Horaire	*oh-rehr*	Schedule
Toilettes	*twah-leht*	Washroom
Libre	*lee-bruh*	Free, Unoccupied
Messieurs	*meh-ssyuh*	Gentlemen
Ne pas toucher	*nuh pah too-shay*	Don't touch

Non fumeurs	*nohn few-muhr*	Non smokers
Occupé	*oh-kew-pay*	Occupied
Ouvert	*òo-vehr*	Open
Passage souterrain	*pah-ssahzh soo-teh-ran*	Underground passage
Poussez	*poo-ssay*	Push
Privé	*pree-vay*	Private
Quai/Voie	*kay/vwah*	Track, Platform
Renseignements	*rahn-sseh-nyuh-mahn*	Information
Réservé	*ray-zehr-vay*	Reserved
Salle d'attente	*sahl dah-tahnt*	Waiting room
Soldes	*sohld*	Sales
Sonnez	*soh-nay*	Ring
Sortie	*sohr-tee*	Exit
Sortie de secours	*sohr-tee duh suh-koor*	Emergency exit
Stationnement interdit	*stah-ssyohn-mahn an-tehr-dee*	No parking
Tirez	*tee-ray*	Pull
Toilettes	*twah-leht*	Toilets

COMMON ABBREVIATIONS

ACF	**Automobile Club de France**	Automobile Club of France
apr. J.-C.	**après Jésus-Christ**	A.D.
av. J.-C.	**avant Jésus-Christ**	B.C.

bd.	**boulevard**	boulevard
c.-à-d.	**c'est-à-dire**	that is to say, i.e.
CEE	**Communauté économique européenne (Marché commun)**	European Economic Community (Common Market)
CGT	**Compagnie générale transatlantique**	French Line
Cie.	**compagnie**	Company
EU	**États-Unis**	United States
h.	**heure(s)**	hour, o'clock
M.	**Monsieur**	Mr.
Mlle	**Mademoiselle**	Miss
MM	**Messieurs**	Gentlemen
Mme	**Madame**	Mrs.
ONU	**Organisation des Nations Unies**	United Nations
p.	**page**	page
p. ex.	**par exemple**	for example
P et T.	**Postes et Télécommunications**	Post Office and Telecommunications
RATP	**Régie Autonome des Transports Parisiens**	Paris Transport Authority
RD	**Route Départementale**	local road
RN	**Route Nationale**	national road
SA	**Société anonyme**	Ltd., Inc.
SI	**Syndicat d'initiative**	Tourist Information Office
SNCF	**Société Nationale des Chemins de Fer Français**	French National Railways
s.v.p.	**s'il vous plaît**	please

CENTIMETERS/INCHES

It is usually unnecessary to make exact conversions from your customary inches to the metric system used in France, but to give you an approximate idea of how they compare, we give you the following guide.

Centimètres

Pouces

To convert centimeters into inches, multiply by .39.
To convert inches into centimeters, multiply by 2.54.

METERS/FEET

1 meter (**mètre**) = 39.37 inches	1 foot = 0.3 meters
3.28 feet	1 yard = 0.9 meters
1.09 yards	

How tall are you in meters? See for yourself.

FEET, INCHES		METERS + CENTIMETERS
5		1.52
5	1	1.54
5	2	1.57
5	3	1.59
5	4	1.62

FEET, INCHES		METERS + CENTIMETERS
5	5	1.64
5	6	1.68
5	7	1.70
5	8	1.73
5	9	1.75
5	10	1.78
5	11	1.80
6		1.83
6	1	1.85

WHEN YOU WEIGH YOURSELF

1 kilogram (kilo) = 2.2 pounds
1 pound = 0.45 kilograms

KILOGRAMS	POUNDS
40	88
45	99
50	110
55	121
60	132
65	143
70	154
75	165
80	176
85	187
90	198
95	209
100	220

LIQUID MEASUREMENTS

1 liter = 1.06 quarts
4 liters = 1.06 gallons

For quick, approximate conversions multiply the number of gallons by 4 to get liters (**litres**). Divide the number of liters by 4 to get gallons.

USEFUL TELEPHONE NUMBERS

Time	36 99
Weather	
In Paris and suburbs	36 65 02 02
In Ile-de-France and	
Normandy	36 65 00 00
In all of France	36 65 01 01
Road Conditions and Traffic	48 99 33 33
Railroads	45 82 08 41
Post Office	42 80 67 89

A MINI-DICTIONARY FOR BUSINESS TRAVELERS

amount	le montant	*luh mohn-tahn*
appraise	évaluer	*ay-vah-lew-ay*
authorize	autoriser	*oh-toh-ree-zay*
authorized edi- tion	l'édition autorisée (f)	*lay-dee-ssyohn oh- toh-ree-zay*
bill (noun)	la facture	*lah fahk-tewr*
bill of exchange	la lettre de change	*lah leh-truh duh shahnzh*

bill of lading	le connaissement	*luh koh-nehss-mahn*
bill of sale	la lettre de vente	*lah leh-truh duh vahnt*
business opera-tion	■ l'affaire (f)	*lah-fehr*
	■ le commerce	*luh koh-mehrss*
cash (noun)	l'argent (m.)	*lahr-zhahn*
to buy for cash	payer comptant	*peh-yay kohn-tahn*
to sell for cash	vendre au comp-tant	*vahn-druh oh kohn-tahn*
to cash a check	toucher un chèque	*too-shay uhn shehk*
certified check	le chèque assuré	*luh shehk ah-ssew-ray*
chamber of com-merce	la chambre de commerce	*lah shahn-bruh duh koh-mehrss*
compensation for damage	le dédommagement	*luh day-doh-mahzh-mahn*
competition	la concurrence	*lah kohn-kew-rahnss*
competitive price	le prix de concur-rence	*luh pree duh kohn-kew-rahnss*
contract	le contrat	*luk kohn-trah*
contractual obli-gations	les obligations du contrat	*lay-zoh-blee-gah-ssyohn dew kohn-trah*
controlling inter-est	le droit d'autorité	*luh drwah doh-toh-ree-tay*
co-owner	le co-propriétaire	*luh koh-proh-pree-ay-tehr*
co-partner	le co-associé	*luh koh-ah-ssoh-ssyay*

down payment	■ l'acompte (m) ■ payer en compte	*lah kohnt* *peh-yay ahn-kohnt*
due	■ échu ■ arrivé à l'échéance	*ay-shew* *ah-ree-vay ah lay-shay-ahnss*
enterprise	l'entreprise (f)	*lahn-truh-preez*
expedite delivery (of letters)	expédier la livraison	*ehkss-pay-dee-ay lah lee-vreh-zohn*
expedite delivery (of goods)	expédier la distribution	*ehkss-pay-dee-ay lah deess-tree-bew-ssyohn*
expenses	les frais (m. pl.)	*lay freh*
goods	■ les produits ■ les biens (m. pl.)	*lay proh-dwee* *lay byan*
infringement of patent rights	l'infraction de brevet d'invention	*lan-frahk-ssyohn duh bruh-veh dan-vahn-ssyohn*
insurance against all risks	l'assurance contre tous risques	*lah-ssew-rahnss kohn-truh too reessk*
international law	le droit international	*luh drwah an-tehr-nah-ssyohn-nahl*
lawful possession	la possession légitime	*lah poh-sseh-ssyohn lay-zhee-teem*
lawsuit	le procès	*luh proh-sseh*
lawyer	l'avocat	*lah-voh-kah*
letter of credit	la lettre de crédit	*lah leh-truh duh kreh-dee*
mail-order business	l'établissement de vente par correspondance (m.)	*lay-tah-bleess-mahn duh vahnt pahr koh-rehss-pohn-dahnss*

market-value	le cours du marché	*luh koor dew mahr-shay*
manager	le gérant	*luh zhay-rah<u>n</u>*
payment	le versement	*luh vehrss-mah<u>n</u>*
partial payment	l'acompte (m)	*lah-koh<u>nt</u>*
past due	■ arriéré	*ahr-yay-ray*
	■ en retard	*ah<u>n</u> ruh-tahr*
post office box	la boîte postale	*lah bwaht pohss-tahl*
property	■ la propriété	*lah proh-pree-ay-tay*
	■ les biens	*lay bya<u>n</u>*
purchasing agent	l'acquéreur	*lah-kay-ruhr*
to put on the American market	mettre au marché américain	*meh-truh oh mahr-shay ah-may-ree-ka<u>n</u>*
sale	la vente	*lah vah<u>nt</u>*
to sell	vendre	*vah<u>n</u>-druh*
to send	envoyer	*ah<u>n</u>-vwah-yay*
to send back	renvoyer	*rah<u>n</u>-vwah-yay*
to send C.O.D.	envoyer payable à l'arrivée	*ah<u>n</u>-vwah-yay peh-yah-bluh ah lah-ree-vay*
shipment	l'expédition (f.)	*lehkss-pay-dee-ssyoh<u>n</u>*
tax	l'impôt (m)	*la<u>n</u>-poh*
tax-exempt	exempt d'impôts	*ehg-zah<u>n</u> da<u>n</u>-poh*
sales tax	la taxe de luxe	*lah tahkss duh lewkss*

value added tax	la taxe sur la valeur ajoutée	*lah tahkss sewr lah vah-luhr ah-zhoo-tay*
trade	le commerce	*luh koh-mehrss*
transact business	faire des affaires	*fehr day-zah-fehr*
transfer	transférer	*trahnss-fay-ray*
transportation charges	les frais de transport	*lay freh duh trahnss-pohr*
via	par	*pahr*
yield a profit	rendre un bénéfice	*rahn-druh uhn bay-nay-feess*

TRAVEL TIP

There was a time when buying an airline ticket was simple. Since the airline industry was deregulated, however, travelers must shop and compare prices, buy charter or discount tickets far in advance and join frequent flier clubs to become eligible for free tickets. Read the fine print in ads and ask questions when making reservations. Often, discount fare tickets cannot be exchanged for cash or another ticket if travel plans must be changed. If you must change plans en route, talk to an airline ticket agent. Sometimes they have soft hearts!

QUICK GRAMMAR GUIDE

NOUNS

1. All nouns in French have a gender (masculine or feminine) and a number (singular or plural).
2. There is no easy way to determine gender, so a noun must be learned with its identifying article and its gender memorized.
3. To change a singular noun to the plural, an unpronounced *S* is usually added. Add nothing if the noun ends in *S, X,* or *Z*.

ARTICLES

Articles agree in gender and number with the nouns they modify.

DEFINITE ARTICLES (THE)			
	MASC.		FEM.
SING.	LE	**le livre** the book	LA	**la carte** the map
PLUR.	LES	**les livres** the books	LES	**les cartes** the maps

NOTE: LE and LA become L' before a noun beginning with a vowel or an H: **l'avion, l'homme**

INDEFINITE ARTICLES (A, AN, SOME)			
	MASC.		FEM.
SING.	UN	**un restaurant** a restaurant	UNE	**une voiture** a car
PLUR.	DES	**des restaurants** some restaurants	DES	**des voitures** some cars

THE PARTITIVE (SOME, ANY)		
SINGULAR		
DU (de + le) + masc. sing. noun with consonant	**du pain**	some bread
DE LA + fem. sing. noun with consonant	**de la glace**	some ice cream
DE L' + masc. or fem. sing. noun with vowel or "H"	**de l'eau**	some water
PLURAL		
DES (de + les) + all plural nouns	**des glaces**	some ice creams
NEGATIVE		
DE is used in negative sentences	**Je n'ai pas d'argent.**	I don't have any money.
	Elle n'a pas de cartes.	She doesn't have any maps.

NOTE: DE becomes D' before a vowel or an H.

ADJECTIVES

1. Adjectives agree in number and gender with the nouns they modify.
2. To form the feminine of most adjectives, add E to the masculine form. If the masculine form ends in E, add nothing to get the feminine form.
3. To form the plural of most adjectives, add S to the singular form. If the singular form ends in S, add nothing to get the plural form.

un livre intéressant   **une femme intéressant<u>e</u>**
des livres intéressant<u>s</u>   **des femmes intéressant<u>es</u>**

4. Adjectives usually follow the nouns they modify. A few common exceptions that precede the noun are: **bon/bonne** good; **grand/grande** big; **jeune** young; **joli/jolie** pretty; **petit/petite** small.

un grand appartement

POSSESSIVE ADJECTIVES

Possessive adjectives agree in number and gender with the object possessed, not with the possessor. They precede the noun.

ENGLISH	MASC. SING. OR FEM. SING. WITH VOWEL	FEM. SING. WITH CONS.	ALL PLURALS
my	mon	ma	mes
your	ton	ta	tes
his/her/its	son	sa	ses
our	notre	notre	nos
your	votre	votre	vos
their	leur	leur	leurs

EXAMPLES:

mon ami(e)	my friend	*ami(e) starts with vowel
ma chemise	my shirt	*chemise is fem. sing. with cons.
mes chemises	my shirts	
ton gant	your glove	*gant is masc. sing.
tes gants	your gloves	

NOTE: **sa valise** can mean his or her valise
son argent can mean his or her money
ses parents can mean his or her parents.

Another way to show possession is by using the preposition DE (OF) or any of its forms:

SINGULAR	PLURAL
DU masculine noun with consonant DE LA feminine noun with consonant DE L' masculine or feminine noun with vowel DE proper noun (name)	DES all nouns

EXAMPLES:

la valise de Paul	Paul's valise
l'argent de la femme	the woman's money
la soupe du garçon	the boy's soup
la chemise de l'homme	the man's shirt
les cartes des touristes	the tourists' maps

DEMONSTRATIVE ADJECTIVES
(THIS/THAT; THESE/THOSE)

SINGULAR	
CE masc. noun with consonant	THIS/THAT
CET masc. noun with vowel or H	THIS/THAT
CETTE fem. noun	THIS/THAT
PLURAL	
CES all nouns	THESE/THOSE

EXAMPLES:

ce livre	this/that book
cet hôtel	this/that hotel
cette fille	this/that girl
cette eau	this/that water *eau is fem.
ces arbres	these/those trees

PRONOUNS

Subject pronouns come at the beginning of the sentence before the verb.

| **Je parle** | I speak |
| **Nous sommes** | We are |

Direct object pronouns come before the verb except in an affirmative command* when they come after the verb.

| **Il la voit.** | He sees it. |
| **Prenez-les!*** | Take them! |

Indirect object pronouns come before the verb except in an affirmative command* when they come after the verb.

| **Elle lui parle.** | She speaks to him (to her). |
| **Écrivez-leur!*** | Write to them. |

Object of a preposition is a pronoun that comes after a preposition.

| **Après vous.** | After you. |
| **Avec eux.** | With them |

SUBJECT	DIRECT OBJECT	INDIRECT OBJECT	OBJECT OF A PREPOSITION
Je I	**me** me	**me** to me	**moi** me
Tu You*	**te** you	**te** to you	**toi** you
Il He	**le** him	**lui** to him	**lui** him
Elle She	**la** her	**lui** to her	**elle** her
Nous We	**nous** us	**nous** to us	**nous** us
Vous You*	**vous** you	**vous** to you	**vous** you
Ils They m.	**les** them	**leur** to them	**eux** them
Elles They f.	**les** them	**leur** to them	**elles** them
On One			

*NOTE: Use **tu** for familiar conversation with a relative, a young child or a friend. **tu** is a singular subject pronoun only.

Use **vous** to be polite and to show respect when speaking to people with whom you are not intimate. **Vous** is a singular or plural subject or object pronoun and is used when addressing a group of people.

REGULAR VERBS

Regular verbs follow a specific pattern of conjugation (changing the verb to agree with the subject pronoun) depending upon the infinitive ending.

PRESENT TENSE			
	–ER ENDING	–IR ENDING	–RE ENDING
SUBJECT	PARLER	FINIR	VENDRE
	to speak	to finish	to sell
Je	parle	finis	vends
Tu	parles	finis	vends
Il/Elle	parle	finit	vend
Nous	parlons	finissons	vendons
Vous	parlez	finissez	vendez
Ils/Elles	parlent	finissent	vendent
COMMANDS	Parlez!	Finissez!	Vendez!

In order to conjugate a verb, the infinitive ending (-ER, -IR, -RE) must be removed and replaced by the appropriate ending found in the above table.

EXAMPLES:

désirer to desire, want	I desire	**Je désire**
choisir to choose	We choose	**Nous choisissons**
attendre to wait for	You wait for	**Vous attendez**

COMMON VERBS IN THE –ER FAMILY

admirer to admire	**donner** to give
aider to help	**écouter** to listen to
aimer to like, to love	**entrer** to enter
chercher to look for	**fermer** to close
coûter to cost	**fumer** to smoke
déjeuner to eat lunch	**marcher** to walk
demander to ask	**montrer** to show
dépenser to spend money	**penser** to think
désirer to wish, to desire	**regarder** to look at
dîner to eat dinner	**tourner** to turn
	trouver to find

COMMON VERBS IN THE –IR FAMILY

choisir	to choose
grossir	to become fat
maigrir	to become thin

COMMON VERBS IN THE –RE FAMILY

attendre	to wait for
descendre	to descend, to go down
entendre	to hear
répondre (à)	to answer

NOTE: Je + verb beginning with a vowel = J'

Je + écoute = J'écoute

HELPING VERBS

The auxiliary verbs **avoir** (to have) and **être** (to be) must be memorized. They are used by themselves in the present or with other verbs to form compound tenses.

AVOIR—to have	
J'ai I have	**Nous avons** We have
Tu as you have	**Vous avez** You have
Il a he has	**Ils ont** They have
Elle a she has	**Elles ont** They have

ÊTRE—to be	
Je suis I am	**Nous sommes** We are
Tu es You are	**Vous êtes** You are
Il est He is	**Ils sont** They are
Elle est She is	**Elles sont** They are

IRREGULAR VERBS

Irregular verbs must be memorized. Here are some common irregular verbs that you will find helpful.

PRESENT TENSE			
SUBJECT	ALLER to go	FAIRE to make, do	POUVOIR can, be able to
Je	vais	fais	peux
Tu	vas	fais	peux
Il/Elle	va	fait	peut
Nous	allons	faisons	pouvons
Vous	allez	faites	pouvez
Ils/Elles	vont	font	peuvent
COMMAND	Allez!	Faites!	

PRESENT TENSE	
VOIR to see	VOULOIR to wish, want
vois	veux
vois	veux
voit	veut
voyons	voulons
voyez	voulez
voient	veulent
Voyez!	

The following verbs will also be helpful to you in a more limited sense.

SUBJECT	BOIRE to drink	DIRE to say	ÉCRIRE to write
Je	bois	dis	écris
Vous	buvez	dites	écrivez
COMMAND	Buvez!	Dites!	Écrivez!

SUBJECT	METTRE to put (on)	OUVRIR to open	RECEVOIR to receive
Je	mets	ouvre	reçois
Vous	mettez	ouvrez	recevez
COMMAND	Mettez!	Ouvrez!	Recevez!

REFLEXIVE VERBS

Reflexive verbs show that the subject is acting upon itself. Reflexive verbs consist of a reflexive pronoun and a conjugated verb. Reflexive pronouns agree with their subjects.

JE	ME	NOUS	NOUS
TU	TE	VOUS	VOUS

IL SE	ILS SE
ELLE SE	ELLES SE

NOTE: ME, TE, and SE become M', T', and S' before a vowel or an H.

Verbs that are reflexive in French are not necessarily reflexive in English. Common reflexive verbs are:

s'appeler	to call oneself, to be called
s'asseoir	to sit down
se coucher	to go to bed
se dépêcher	to hurry up
s'habiller	to get dressed
se laver	to wash oneself
se lever	to get up
se peigner	to comb one's hair
se promener	to go for a walk
se raser	to shave oneself
se réveiller	to wake up

Follow this formula:

SUBJECT	REFLEXIVE PRONOUN	VERB
Je	m'	**appelle** My name is (I call myself)
Nous	nous	**réveillons** We wake up
Tu NE	te	**rases PAS** You don't shave

NOTE: A verb is reflexive only if the subject is acting upon itself. If the subject is acting upon another person or thing, the verb is NOT reflexive.

EXAMPLE:

Je me lave.	I wash myself.
Je lave l'enfant.	I wash the child.
Je lave la voiture.	I wash the car.

The infinitive of a reflexive verb is always preceded by the pronoun SE.

NEGATIVES

Form the negative by putting NE before the conjugated verb, and PAS (not) after the verb.

OTHER NEGATIVE CONSTRUCTIONS

NE . . . RIEN nothing

NE . . . JAMAIS never

NE . . . PERSONNE nobody

NE . . . PLUS no longer

NOTE: NE becomes N' before a vowel or H.

Il parle anglais.	**Il ne parle pas anglais.**
He speaks English.	He doesn't speak English.
Je veux manger.	**Je ne veux plus manger.**
I want to eat.	I don't want to eat any more.
Elle écoute.	**Elle n'écoute rien.**
She listens.	She doesn't listen to anything.

QUESTIONS

The two most common ways to ask a question are:

1. Putting EST-CE QUE *ehss-kuh* in front of a phrase.

Vous parlez anglais.	**Est-ce que vous parlez anglais?**

2. Invert the order of the subject pronoun (ONLY) and the verb.

Vous parlez anglais.   Parlez-vous anglais?

NOTE: a) Do NOT invert with the pronoun JE. Use EST-CE QUE.
b) If the verb ends in a vowel and the pronoun begins with a vowel (**il** or **elle**) then **-t-** must separate the two vowels.

Il parle anglais.   Parle-t-il anglais?

Elle a une voiture.   A-t-elle une voiture?

PREPOSITIONS

Study the list of the following prepositions. The prepositions **à** (to, at) and **de** (of, from) have contracted forms.

a + le = au	**de + le = du**
à + les = aux	**de + les = des**
à la (no change)	**de la** (no change)
à l' (no change)	**de l'** (no change)

EXAMPLES:
to the movies	**au cinéma**
to the museums	**aux musées**
to the kitchen	**à la cuisine**
of the boy	**du garçon**
of the children	**des enfants**
of the year	**de l'année**

COMMON PREPOSITIONS

about	**de**	*duh*
according to	**selon**	*suh-lohn*
across	**à travers**	*ah trah-vehr*
after	**après**	*ah-preh*

among	**parmi**	*pahr-mee*
around	**autour de**	*oh-toor duh*
at	**à**	*ah*
at the house of	**chez**	*shay*
before	**avant**	*ah-vah<u>n</u>*
behind	**derrière**	*deh-ryehr*
between	**entre**	*ah<u>n</u>-truh*
by	**par**	*pahr*
down/downstairs	**en bas**	*ah<u>n</u> bah*
during	**pendant**	*pah<u>n</u>-dah<u>n</u>*
except	**sauf**	*sohf*
for	**pour**	*poor*
from	**de**	*duh*
in	**dans, en**	*dah<u>n</u>, ah<u>n</u>*
in front of	**devant**	*duh-vah<u>n</u>*
in order to	**pour**	*poor*
inside	**dedans**	*duh-dah<u>n</u>*
on	**sur**	*sewr*
opposite	**en face de**	*ah<u>n</u> fahss duh*
outside	**dehors**	*duh-ohr*
through	**à travers**	*ah trah-vehr*
to	**à**	*ah*
towards	**vers**	*vehr*
under	**sous**	*soo*
until	**jusqu'à**	*zhewss-kah*
up/upstairs	**en haut**	*ah<u>n</u> oh*
with	**avec**	*ah-vehk*
without	**sans**	*sah<u>n</u>*

ENGLISH-FRENCH DICTIONARY*

A

a, an un (m.) *uhn*, une (f.) *ewn*

able: to be able pouvoir *poo-vwahr*

about à peu près *ah-puh-preh*; environ *ahn-vee-rohn*

above dessus *duh-ssew*

abroad à l'étranger *ah lay-trahn-zhay*

according to selon *suh-lohn*

ache (noun) le mal *luh mahl*; **(head)** mal de tête *mahl duh teht*; **(stomach)** mal d'estomac *mahl dehss-toh-mah*; **(tooth)** mal de dents *mahl duh dahn*

acquaintance: make the . . . of faire la connaissance de *fehr lah koh-neh-ssahnss duh*

across à travers *ah trah-vehr*

add ajouter *ah-zhoo-tay*

address une adresse *ewn ah-drehss*

adjust arranger *ah-rahn-zhay*

advertisement une réclame *ewn ray-klahm*; une annonce *ewn ah-nohnss*

advice l'avis (m.) *lah-vee*; le conseil *luh kohn-ssehy*

afraid: to be afraid of avoir peur de *ah-vwahr puhr duh*

after après *ah-preh*

afternoon l'après-midi (m.) *lah-preh mee-dee*

again encore une fois *ahn-kohr ewn fwah*

against contre *kohn-truh*

agency une agence *ewn ah-zhahnss*; **(travel)** une agence de voyage *ewn ah-zhahnss duh vwah-yahzh*

ago il y a + time *eel yah*

agree être d'accord *eh-truh dah-kohr*

air conditioner le climatiseur *luh klee-mah-tee-zuhr*

air mail par avion *pahr ah-vyohn*

airplane un avion *uhn nah-vyohn*

airport un aéroport *uhn nahy-roh-pohr*

alcohol l'alcool (m.) *lahl-kol*

all tout (m.), toute (f.) *too, toot*

alley la ruelle *lah rew-ehl*

almond une amande *ewn ah-mahnd*

almost presque *prehss-kuh*

alone seul(e) *suhl*

already déjà *day-zhah*

also aussi *oh-ssee*

always toujours *too-zhoor*

ambulance une ambulance *ewn ahn-bew-lahnss*

among parmi *pahr-mee*

and et *ay*

ankle la cheville *lah shuh-vee*

annoy gêner *zheh-nay*; ennuyer *ahn-nwee-yay*

answer (noun) la réponse *lah ray-pohnss*; **(verb)** répondre *ray-pohn-druh*

antiseptic un antiseptique *uhn nahn-tee-ssehp-teek*

any ne . . . aucun(e) *nuh . . . oh-kuhn, oh-kewn*

*Underscored letters indicate nasals.

appendicitis l'appendicite
  lah-pahn-dee-sseet

apple la pomme *lah pohm*

apricot un abricot *uhn nah-bree-koh*

argument la dispute *lah deess-pewt*

arm le bras *luh brah*

around autour de *oh-toor duh*

arrival l'arrivée (f.) *lah-ree-vay*

artichoke l'artichaut
  lahr -tee-shoh

ashtray le cendrier *luh
  ssahn-dree-yay*

ask demander *duh-mahn-day*

asparagus l'asperge (f.)
  lahss-pehrzh

at à *ah*

August août *oo*

author l'auteur (m.) *loh-tuhr*

avoid éviter *ay-vee-tay*

awaken réveiller *ray-veh-yay*

B

back (noun) le dos *luh doh*; **in
  back of** derrière *deh-ryehr*

backward en arrière *ahn nah-ryehr*

bacon le lard *luh lahr*

bad mauvais(e) *moh-veh(z)*

badly mal *mahl*

bag le sac *luh sahk*

baggage room la consigne *lah
  kohn-ssee-nyuh*

baked au four *oh foor*

baked Alaska l'omelette
  norvégienne *lohm-leht
  nohr-vay-zhyehn*

bakery la boulangerie *lah
  boo-lahn-zhree*

balcony le balcon *luh bahl-kohn*

ballet le ballet *luh bah-leh*

banana la banane *lah bah-nahn*

bandage (noun) la bande *lah
  bahnd*

bank la banque *lah bahnk*

bank [branch] la succursale *lah
  sew-kewr-ssahl*

bar le bistro *luh beess-troh*

barber le coiffeur *luh kwah-fuhr*

bargain (noun) l'occasion
  loh-kah-zyohn

basket le panier *luh pah-nyay*

bath le bain *luh ban*

bathe se baigner *suh beh-nyay*

bathing suit le maillot de bain *luh
  mah-yoh duh ban*

bathrobe la robe de chambre *lah
  rohb duh shahn-bruh*

bathroom la salle de bains *lah sahl
  duh ban*

battery la batterie *lah bah-tree*

be être *eh-truh*

beach la plage *lah plahzh*

bean le haricot *luh ah-ree-koh*

beautiful beau (m.) *boh*, belle (f.)
  behl

beauty parlor le salon de beauté
  luh sah-lohn duh boh-tay

because parce que *pahrss kuh*

become devenir *duh-vuh-neer*

bed le lit *luh lee*

bedroom la chambre à coucher *lah
  shahn-bruh ah koo-shay*

beef (noun) le boeuf *luh buhf*

beer la bière *la byehr*

beet la betterave *lah beht-rahv*

before avant *ah-vahn*

begin commencer (à)
  koh-mahn-ssay ah

behind en arrière *ahn nah-ryehr*;
  derrière *deh-ryehr*

believe croire *krwahr*

bell la cloche *lah klohsh*

bellboy le chasseur *luh shah-ssuhr*

belong appartenir *ah-pahr-tuh-neer*

belt la ceinture *lah san-tewr*; **seat belt** la ceinture de sécurité *lah san-tewr duh say-kew-ree-tay*

bench le banc *luh bahn*

beneath dessous *duh-ssoo*

berth la couchette *lah koo-sheht*

beside à côté de *ah koh-tay duh*

better (adj.) meilleur(e) *meh-yuhr*

better (adv.) mieux *myuh*

between entre *ahn-truh*

big grand(e) *grahn(d)*

bill la facture *lah fahk-tewr*; la note *lah noht*

birthday l'anniversaire (m.) *lah-nee-vehr-ssehr*

bitter amer(ère) *ah-mehr*

black noir(e) *nwahr*

blanket la couverture *lah koo-vehr-tewr*

blood le sang *luh sahn*

blouse la blouse *lah blooz*

blue bleu *bluh*

boat le bateau *luh bah-toh*

body le corps *luh kohr*

boiled bouilli(e) *boo-yee*

bone l'os (m.) *lohss*

book le livre *luh lee-vruh*

bookstore la librairie *lah lee-breh-ree*

border la frontière *lah frohn-tyehr*

borrow emprunter *ahn-pruhn-tay*

boss le patron *luh pah-trohn*; le propriétaire *luh proh-pree-ay-tehr*

bother gêner *geh-nay*; ennuyer *ahn-nwee-yay*

bottle la bouteille *lah boo-tehy*

box la boîte *lah bwaht*

box office le bureau de location *luh bew-roh duh loh-kah-ssyohn*

boy le garçon *luh gahr-ssohn*

bra le soutien-gorge *luh soo-tyan gohrzh*

braised braisé *breh-zay*

brakes les freins (m. pl.) *lay fran*

brand la marque *lah mahrk*

bread le pain *luh pan*; **French** la baguette *lah bah-geht*; **pumpernickel** le pain bis *luh pan bee*; **rye** le pain de seigle *luh pan duh seh-gluh*; **white** le pain blanc *luh pan blahn*; **whole wheat** le pain de froment *luh pan duh froh-mahn*

break briser *bree-zay*; casser *kah-ssay*

breakdown (auto) la panne *lah pahn*; **broken down** en panne *ahn pahn*

breakfast le petit déjeuner *luh puh-tee day-zhuh-nay*

bridge le pont *luh pohn*

bring apporter *ah-pohr-tay*

broiled grillé *gree-yay*

brother le frère *luh frehr*

brown brun(e) *bruhn, brewn*; marron *mah-rohn*

bruise (noun) la contusion *lah kohn-tew-zyohn*

brush (noun) la brosse *lah brohss*; **(verb)** brosser *broh-ssay*; **toothbrush** la brosse à dents *lah brohss ah dahn*

Brussel sprouts les choux (m. pl.) de Bruxelles *lay shoo duh brew-ssehl*

building le bâtiment *luh bah-tee-mahn*

bulb (electric) l'ampoule (f.) *lahn-pool*

bun (roll) la brioche *lah bree-ohsh*

burn (noun) la brûlure *lah brew-lewr*; **(verb)** brûler *brew-lay*

bus l' autobus *loh-toh-bewss*; **bus station** la gare routière *lah gahr roo-tyehr*; **bus stop** l'arrêt de bus (m.) *lah-reh duh bewss*

busy occupé(e) *oh-kew-pay*

but mais *meh*

butcher shop la boucherie *lah boosh-ree*

butter le beurre *luh buhr*

button le bouton *luh boo-tohn*

buy acheter *ahsh-tay*

by par *pahr*; en *ahn*

C

cabbage le chou *luh shoo*

cake le gâteau *luh gah-toh*

call (verb) appeler *ah-play*

camera l'appareil photographique *lah-pah-rehy foh-toh-grah-feek*

can (verb) pouvoir *poo-vwahr*

candle la bougie *lah boo-zhee*

candy store la confiserie *lah kohn-feess-ree*

car la voiture *lah vwah-tewr*

carburetor le carburateur *luh kahr-bew-rah-tuhr*

card la carte *lah kahrt*; **credit card** la carte de crédit *lah kahrt duh kray-dee*; **identification card** la carte d'identité *lah kahrt dee-dahn-tee-tay*

care le soin *luh swan*

carefully avec soin *ah-vehk swan*

carefulness la prudence *lah prew-dahnss*

carrot la carotte *lah kah-roht*

carry porter *pohr-tay*; **carry away** emporter *ahn-pohr-tay*

cashier le caissier *luh kehss-yay*

cash register la caisse *lah kehss*

castle le château *luh shah-toh*

cat le chat *luh shah*

catch attraper *ah-trah-pay*

caution attention *ah-tahn-ssyohn*

ceiling le plafond *luh plah-fohn*

cellar la cave *lah kahv*

cemetery le cimetière *luh seem-tyehr*

chain (jewelry) la chaînette *lah sheh-neht*

chair la chaise *lah shehz*

chambermaid la femme de chambre *lah fahm duh shahn-bruh*

change (noun) le changement *luh shahnzh-mahn*; **money** la monnaie *lah moh-nay*

change (verb) changer *shahn-zhay*: **change plane or train** faire la correspondance *fehr lah koh-rehss-pohn-dahnss*

charge (noun) les frais (m. pl.) *lay freh*

charge (verb) charger *shahr-zhay*

charm (noun) le porte-bonheur *luh pohrt boh-nuhr*

cheap bon marché *bohn mahr-shay*; **cheaper** meilleur marché *meh-yuhr mahr-shay*

check (noun) (restaurant) l'addition (f.) *lah-dee-ssyohn*; **(money)** le chèque *luh shehk*; **traveller's check** le chèque de voyage *luh shehk duh vwah-yahzh*; **cash a check** toucher un chèque *too-shay uhn shehk*

check (verb) vérifier *vay-ree-fyay*; **check bags** enregistrer *ahn-ruh-zheess-tray*

checked (material) à carreaux *ah kah-roh*

cheek la joue *lah zhoo*

cheese le fromage *luh froh-mahzh*

cherry la cerise *lah suh-reez*

chest la poitrine *lah pwah-treen*

chicken le poulet *luh poo-leh*

chick-peas les pois (m. pl.) chiches *lay pwah sheesh*

chiffon la mousseline de soie *lah mooss-leen duh swah*

child l'enfant (m./f.) *lahn-fahn*

chin le menton *luh mahn-tohn*

choose choisir *shwah-zeer*

chop (noun) la côtelette *lah koht-leht*

church l'église (f.) *lay-gleez*; le temple (Prot.) *luh tahn-pluh*

cigar le cigare *luh see-gahr*

cigarette la cigarette *lah see-gah-reht*

cigarette lighter le briquet *luh bree-keh*

city la ville *la veel*

clam la palourde *lah pah-loord*

clean (verb) nettoyer *neh-twah-yay*

clean (adj.) propre *proh-pruh*; **dry cleaner's** la teinturerie *lah tan-tew-ruh-ree*

clock la pendule *lah pahn-dewl*; l'horloge (f.) *lohr-lohzh*; **alarm clock** le réveil *luh ray-vehy*

close (verb) fermer *fehr-may*

closet l'armoire (f.) *lahr-mwahr*

clothes les habits (m. pl.) *lay zah-bee*; les vêtements (m. pl.) *lay veht-mahn*

coast la côte *lah koht*

coat le manteau *luh mahn-toh*; **coat check** le vestiaire *luh vehss-tyehr*

coconut la noix de coco *lah nwah duh koh-koh*

coffee le café *luh kah-fay*; **black** le café noir *luh kah-fay nwahr*; **with cream** le café crème *luh kah-fay krehm*; **iced** le café glacé *luh kah-fay glah-ssay*; **with milk** le café au lait *luh kah-fay oh leh*; **espresso** le café express *luh kah-fay ehkss-prehss*

cold (noun) (weather) le froid *luh frwah*; (verb) **to be cold (weather)** faire froid *fehr frwah*; **to be cold (person)** avoir froid *ah-vwahr frwah*

cold (noun) (respiratory) le rhume *luh rewm*; **chest cold** le rhume de poitrine *luh rewm duh pwah-treen*; **head cold** le rhume de cerveau *luh rewm duh sehr-voh*

cold cuts la charcuterie *lah shahr-kew-tree*

collar le col *luh kohl*

color la couleur *lah koo-luhr*

comb le peigne *luh peh-nyuh*

come venir *vuh-neer*; **come back** revenir *ruh-vuh-neer*

company la compagnie *lah kohn-pah-nyee*

complaint la plainte *lah plant*

concert le concert *luh kohn-ssehr*; **concert hall** la salle de concert *lah sahl duh kohn-ssehr*

condom le préservatif *luh pray-zehr-vah-teef*

conductor le contrôleur *luh kohn-troh-luhr*

congratulations félicitations *fay-lee-ssee-tah-ssoyhn*

connect relier *ruh-lee-yay*

contact lense le verre de contact *luh vehr duh kohn-tahkt*

contagious contagieux(ieuse) *kohn-tah-zhuh(z)*

contain contenir *kohn-tuh-neer*

contents le contenu *luh kohnt-new*

cook (noun) le cuisinier *luh kwee-zee-nyay*

cooked cuit(e) *kwee(t)*

cookie le biscuit *luh beess-kwee*

cooking la cuisine *lah kwee-zeen*

corduroy le velours côtelé *luh vuh-loor koht-lay*

corkscrew le tire-bouchon *luh teer boo-shohn*

corn le maïs *luh mah-eess*

corner le coin *luh kwan*

cost coûter *koo-tay*

costly coûteux(euse) *koo-tuh(z)*

cotton le coton *luh koh-tohn*;
  absorbent cotton l'ouate (f.)
  lwaht
cough (noun) la toux *lah too*;
  cough drops les pastilles
  contre la toux *lay pahss-teey
  kohn-truh lah too*; **cough syrup**
  le sirop contre la toux *luh see-roh
  kohn-truh lah too*
cough (verb) tousser *too-ssay*
count (verb) compter *kohn-tay*
country (nation) le pays *luh
  pay-ee*; la campagne *lah
  kahn-pah-nyuh*
countryside le paysage *luh
  pay-ee-zhahzh*
courtyard la cour *lah koor*
cover (verb) couvrir *koo-vreer*
cover charge le couvert *luh
  koo-vehr*
crab le crabe *luh krahb*
cramp la crampe *lah krahnp*
cream la crème *lah krehm*;
  whipped cream la crème
  fouettée *lah krehm foo-eh-tay*
cross (verb) traverser
  trah-vehr-ssay
crust la croûte *lah kroot*
cry pleurer *pluh-ray*
cucumber le concombre *luh
  kohn-kohn-bruh*
cup la tasse *lah tahss*
custard le flan *luh flahn*
customer le client *luh klee-ahn*
customs la douane *lah dwahn*
customs official le douanier *luh
  dwah-nyay*
cut couper *koo-pay*

D

daily quotidien(ne) *koh-tee-dyan
  (yehn)*
dance (noun) la danse *lah dahnss*

dance (verb) danser *dahn-ssay*
dark (color) foncé(e) *fohn-ssay*
date la date *lah daht*
date (fruit) la datte *lah daht*
daughter la fille *lah fee*
day le jour *luh zhoor*; **day before
  yesterday** avant-hier *ah-vahn-
  tyehr*; **day after tomorrow**
  après-demain *ah-preh-duh-man*
dear cher, chère *shehr*
deceive tromper *trohn-pay*
decide décider *day-ssee-day*
declare déclarer *day-klah-ray*
delay le retard *luh ruh-tahr*
delicatessen la charcuterie *lah
  shahr-kew-tree*
deliver livrer *lee-vray*
denim le coutil *luh koo-tee*
deodorant le déodorant *luh
  day-oh-doh-rahn*
department (in store) le rayon
  luh ray-ohn
deserve mériter *may-ree-tay*
desire désirer *day-zee-ray*
detective story le roman policier
  luh roh-mahn poh-lee-ssyay
diaper la couche *lah koosh*
dictionary le dictionnaire *luh
  deek-ssyoh-nehr*
different différent(e) *dee-fay-rahn(t)*
difficult difficile *dee-fee-sseel*
diminish diminuer *dee-mee-new-ay*
dine dîner *dee-nay*
dining car le wagon-restaurant *luh
  vah-gohn rehss-toh-rahn*
dining room la salle à manger *lah
  sahl ah mahn-zhay*
dirty sale *sahl*
disappointed déçu(e) *day-ssew*
discotheque la disco(thèque) *lah
  deess-koh(tehk)*
dish (of food) le plat *luh plah*;
  plate l'assiette *lah-ssyeht*

distance le trajet *luh trah-zheh*

district le quartier *luh kahr-tyay*

do faire *fehr*

doctor le docteur *luh dohk-tuhr*; le médecin *luh mayd-ssan*

dog le chien *luh shyan*

door la porte *lah pohrt*

down: to go down descendre *day-ssahn-druh*

downstairs en bas *ahn bah*

dozen la douzaine *lah doo-zehn*

dress (noun) la robe *lah rohb*

dress (verb) s'habiller *sah-bee-yay*

drink (noun) la boisson *lah bwah-ssohn*; la consommation *lah kohn-ssoh-mah-ssyohn*; **soft drink** la boisson non-alcoolisée *lah bwah-ssohn nohn nahl-koh-lee-zay*

drink (verb) boire *bwahr*

drinkable potable *poh-tab-bluh*; **undrinkable** non potable *nohn poh-tah-bluhdrive*

drive conduire *kohn-dweer*

drunk ivre *ee-vruh*; soûl(e) *soo*

dry (adj.) sec, sèche *sehk, sehsh*

dry (verb) sécher *say-shay*

duck le canard *luh kah-nahr*

during pendant *pahn-dahn*

E

each chaque *shahk*

each one chacun(e) *shah-kuhn (kewn)*

ear l'oreille (f.) *loh-rehy*

early tôt *toh*; de bonne heure *duh bohn-uhr*

earn gagner *gah-nyay*

earring la boucle d'oreille *lah boo-kluh doh-rehy*

east l'est *lehsst*

easy facile *fah-sseel*

eat manger *mahn-zhay*

egg l'oeuf *luhf*; **eggs** les oeufs *lay zuhf*; **fried** au plat *oh plah*; **hard-boiled** durs *dewr*; **soft-boiled** mollets *moh-leh*; **sunny-side up** poêlés *pwah-lay*; **scrambled** brouillés *broo-yay*

eggplant l'aubergine (f.) *loh-behr-zheen*

eight huit *weet*

eighteen dix-huit *deez weet*

eighty quatre-vingts *kah-truh van*

elbow le coude *luh kood*

elevator l'ascenseur (m.) *lah-ssahn-ssuhr*

eleven onze *ohnz*

elsewhere ailleurs *ah-yuhr*

emergency le cas urgent *luh kah zewr-zhahn*; **in case of emergency** en cas d'urgence *ahn kah dewr-zhahnss*

empty vide *veed*

end (noun) la fin *lah fan*

end (verb) finir *fee-neer*

endorse endosser *ahn-doh-ssay*

English anglais (m.) *ahn-gleh*

enough assez (de) *ah-ssay duh*

enter entrer *ahn-tray*

entire entier(ière) *ahn-tyay (yehr)*

entrance l'entrée (f.) *lahn-tray*

envelope l'enveloppe (f.) *lahn-vlohp*

eraser la gomme *lah gohm*

especially surtout *sewr-too*

evening la soirée *lah swah-ray*

evening gown la robe de soir *lah rohb duh swahr*

every tout(e) *too(t)*; chaque *shahk*; **everybody** tout le monde *too luh mohnd*; **every day** tous les jours *too lay zhoor*; **everywhere** partout *pahr-too*

example l'exemple (m.)
lehg-zahn-pluh; **for example**
par exemple *pahr ehg-zahn-pluh*

excellent excellent(e)
ehkss-eh-lahn(t)

exchange échanger *ay-shahn-zhay*;
exchange office le bureau de
change *luh bew-roh duh shahnzh*;
exchange rate le cours de
change *luh koor duh shahnzh*

excursion l'excursion (f.)
lehkss-kewr-zyohn

excuse (verb) pardonner
pahr-doh-nay; **excuse me**
pardon *pahr-dohn*; excusez-moi
ehkss-kew-zay mwah

exhausted épuisé(e) *ay-pwee-zay*

exit la sortie *lah sohr-tee*

expense les frais (m. pl.) *lay freh*

expensive cher, chère *shehr*

express express *ehkss-prehss*

eye l'oeil (m.) *luhy*; **eyes** les
yeux (m. pl.) *lay zyuh*

eyebrow le sourcil *luh soor-ssee*

eyeglasses les lunettes (f. pl.) *lay
lew-neht*

eyelash le cil *luh seel*

eyelid la paupière *lah poh-pyehr*

F

face (noun) la figure *lah fee-gewr*;
le visage *luh vee-zazh*

facing en face de *ahn fahss duh*

factory l'usine (f.) *lew-zeen*

fall tomber *tohn-bay*; **fall sick**
tomber malade *tohn-bay mah-lahd*

fair (market) la foire *lah fwahr*

false faux, fausse *foh, fohss*

family la famille *lah fah-meey*

fan le ventilateur *luh
vahn-tee-lah-tuhr*

far (from) loin de *lwan duh*

farm la ferme *lah fehrm*

fat gros(se) *groh(ss)*

faucet le robinet *luh roh-bee-neh*

fast rapide *rah-peed*; vite *veet*

father le père *luh pehr*

fear la peur *lah puhr*; **to be afraid**
avoir peur *ah-vwahr puhr*

February février *fay-vree-yay*

feel (se) sentir *(suh) sahn-teer*

felt le feutre *luh fuh-truh*

festival la fête *lah feht*

fever la fièvre *lah fyeh-vruh*; **hay
fever** le rhume des foins *luh
rewm day fwan*

few peu de *puh duh*; **a few**
quelques *kehl-kuh*

field le champ *luh shahn*

fifteen quinze *kanz*

fifty cinquante *san-kahnt*

fig la figue *lah feeg*

figure (body) la taille *lah tahy*

fill (out) remplir *rahn-pleer*

film le film *luh feelm*; la pellicule
lah peh-lee-kewl

finger le doigt *luh dwah*

finish finir *fee-neer*; terminer
tehr-mee-nay

fire le feu *luh fuh*; l'incendie (m.)
lan-ssahn-dee

first premier(ière) *pruh-myay
(yehr)*; **at first** d'abord
dah-bohr; **first aid** le premier
secours *luh pruh-myay suh-koor*

fish (noun) le poisson *luh
pwah-ssohn*

fish (verb) pêcher *peh-shay*

five cinq *sank*

flannel la flanelle *lah flah-nehl*

flashlight la lampe de poche *lah
lahnp duh pohsh*

flat plat(te) *plah(t)*

flavor le parfum *luh pahr-fuhn*

flight le vol *luh vohl*

floor le plancher *luh plahn-shay;* **(story)** l'étage (m.) *lay-tahzh*

florist le fleuriste *luh fluh-reesst*

flounder la sole *lah sohl*

flower la fleur *lah fluhr*

fly (verb) voler *voh-lay*

follow suivre *swee-vruh;* **following** suivant(e) *swee-vahn(t)*

food les aliments (m. pl.) *lay zah-lee-mahn;* la nourriture *lah noo-ree-tewr*

foot le pied *luh pyay*

for pour *poor*

forbid interdire *an-tehr-deer;* défendre *day-fahn-druh;* **forbidden** interdit(e) *an-tehr-dee(t);* défendu(e) *day-fahn-dew;* **it is forbidden to** défense de *day-fahnss duh*

forehead le front *luh frohn*

foreign étranger(ère) *ay-trahn-zhay (zhehr)*

forest la forêt *lah foh-reh*

forget oublier *oo-blee-yay*

fork la fourchette *lah foor-sheht*

form (noun) la fiche *lah feesh;* la formule *lah fohr-mewl*

former ancien(ne) *ahn-ssyan(n)*

forty quarante *kah-rahnt*

forward (adv.) en avant *ahn nah-vahn*

fountain la fontaine *lah fohn-tehn*

four quatre *kah-truh*

fourteen quatorze *kah-tohrz*

free libre *lee-bruh;* **for free** gratuit(e) *grah-twee(t);* **free of charge (adv.)** gratuitement *grah-tweet-mahn*

French le français (m.) *luh frahn-sseh*

fresh frais, fraîche *freh, frehsh*

Friday vendredi *vahn-druh-dee*

fried frit(e) *free(t)*

friend ami(e) *ah-mee*

frog's legs les cuisses (f. pl.) de grenouille *lay kweess duh gruh-nuhy*

front: in front of devant *duh-vahn*

fruit le fruit *luh frwee*

fruit salad la macédoine de fruits *lah mah-ssay-dwahn duh frwee*

function (verb) fonctionner *fohnk-ssyoh-nay*

furnished meublé(e) *muh-blay*

G

gabardine la gabardine *lah gah-bahr-deen*

game le jeu *luh zhuh;* la partie *lah pahr-tee*

game (meat) le gibier *luh zhee-byay*

garden le jardin *luh zhahr-dan*

garlic l'ail (m.) *lahy*

gas l'essence (f.) *leh-ssahnss*

gas station le poste d'essence *luh pohsst deh-ssahnss;* la station-service *lah stah-ssyohn sehr-veess*

gas tank le réservoir à essence *luh ray-zehr-vwahr ah eh-ssahnss*

get up se lever *suh luh-vay*

gift le cadeau *luh kah-doh*

girl la fille *lah fee*

give donner *doh-nay*

gladly volontiers *voh-lohn-tyay*

glass le verre *luh vehr*

glove le gant *luh gahn*

glue la colle *lah kohl*

go aller *ah-lay;* **go down** descendre *day-ssahn-druh;* **go home** rentrer *rahn-tray;* **go in** entrer *ahn-tray;* **go out** sortir *sohr-teer;* **go shopping** faire des emplettes *fehr day zahn-pleht;* **go to bed** se coucher *suh koo-shay;* **go up** monter *mohn-tay*

gold l'or (m.) *lohr*

good bon(ne) *bohn, bohn*

goose l'oie (f.) *lwah*

grape le raisin *luh reh-zan*

grapefruit le pamplemousse *luh pahn-pluh-mooss*

grass l'herbe (f.) *lehrb*

grave (adj.) sérieux(ieuse) *say-ree-uh(z)*; grave *grahv*

gray gris(e) *gree(z)*

green vert(e) *vehr(t)*

greet saluer *sah-lew-ay*

grilled grillé(e) *gree-yay*

grocery store l'épicerie (f.) *lay-peess-ree*

ground le terrain *luh teh-ran*; la terre *lah tehr*; **camp ground** le terrain de camping *luh teh-ran duh kahn-peeng*; **golf course** le terrain de golf *luh teh-ran duh gohlf*; **playing field** le terrain de sport *luh teh-ran duh spohr*; **on the ground** par terre *pahr tehr*

ground floor le rez-de-chaussée *luh rayd shoh-ssay*

guava la goyave *lah goh-yahv*

guide le guide *luh geed*; **tourist guide** le guide touristique *luh geed too-reess-teek*

gums (mouth) les gencives (f.) *lay zhahn-sseev*

H

hair les cheveux (m. pl.) *lay shuh-vuh*

haircut la coupe de cheveux *lah koop duh shuh-vuh*

hair dryer le sèche-cheveux *luh sehsh shuh-vuh*

hair spray la laque *lah lahk*

half (noun) la moitié *lah mwah-tyay*

half (adj.) demi(e) *duh-mee*

ham le jambon *luh zhahn-bohn*

hamburger le hamburger *luh ahn-boor-gehr*

hand la main *lah man*

handkerchief le mouchoir *luh moo-shwahr*

handmade fait à la main *feh Tah lah man*

handsome beau (m.), belle (f.) *boh, behl*

hanger le cintre *luh san-truh*

hang up accrocher *ah-kroh-sshay*

happy heureux(euse) *uh-ruh(z)*

hardware store la quincaillerie *lah kahn-kahy-ree*

have avoir *ah-vwahr*; **have just** venir de *vuh-neer duh*; **have to** avoir à *ah-vwahr ah*; devoir *duh-vwahr*

he il *eel*

head la tête *lah teht*

headlight le phare *luh fahr*

health la santé *lah sahn-tay*

hear entendre *ahn-tahn-druh*

heart le coeur *luh kuhr*

heat (noun) la chaleur *lah|shah-luhr*

heat (verb) chauffer *shoh-fay*

heating le chauffage *luh shoh-fahzh*

heel le talon *luh tah-lohn*

height la hauteur (f.) *lah oh-tuhr*

hello bonjour *bohn-zhoor*

help (noun) le secours *luh suh-koor*; **help!** au secours! *oh suh-koor*

help (verb) aider *eh-day*

here ici *ee-ssee*

here is, are voici *vwah-ssee*

herring les harengs (m. pl.) *lay ah-rahn*; **smoked herring** les harengs fumés *lay ah-rahn few-may*

high haut(e) *oh(t)*

high school le lycée *luh lee-ssay*

highway l'autoroute (f.) *loh-toh-root*

hip la hanche *lah ahnsh*

hire louer *loo-ay*

hit frapper *frah-pay*

hold tenir *tuh-neer*

hole le trou *luh troo*

holiday la fête *lah feht*

hope (verb) espérer *ehss-pay-ray*

horn le klaxon *luh klahk-ssohn*

horse le cheval *luh shuh-vahl*; les chevaux (pl.) *lay shuh-voh*

horseradish le raifort *luh reh-fohr*

hospital l'hôpital (m.) *loh-pee-tahl*

host l'hôte (m.) *loht*

hostel (youth) l'auberge (f.) de jeunesse *loh-behrzh duh zhuh-nehss*

hostess l'hôtesse (f.) *loh-tehss*

hot chaud *shoh*; **be hot (person)** avoir chaud *ah-vwahr shoh*; **be hot (weather)** faire chaud *fehr shoh*

hotel l'hôtel (m.) *loh-tehl*

hour l'heure (f.) *luhr*

house la maison *lah meh-zohn*; **at the house of** chez *shay*; **boardinghouse** la pension *lah pahn-ssyohn*

house porter le concierge *luh kohn-ssyehrzh*

how comment *koh-mahn*; **how far** à quelle distance *ah kehl deess-tahnss*; **how long** depuis quand *duh-pwee kahn*

how many, much combien *kohn-byan*

hundred cent *sahn*

hunger la faim *lah fan*; **to be hungry** avoir faim *ah-vwahr fan*

hurry se dépêcher *suh day-peh-shay*; **be in a hurry** être pressé *eh-truh preh-ssay*

husband le mari *luh mah-ree*

I

I je *zhuh*

ice la glace *lah glahss*; **ice cream** la glace *lah glahss*; **ice cubes** les glaçons (m. pl.) *lay glah-ssohn*; **ice water** l'eau (f.) glacée *loh glah-ssay*

if si *see*

ill malade *mah-lahd*

illness la maladie *lah mah-lah-dee*

immediately immédiatement *ee-may-dyaht-mahn*

important important(e) *an-pohr-tahn(t)*

impossible impossible *an-poh-ssee-bluh*

improbable invraisemblable *an-vreh-sahn-blah-bluh*

in dans *dahn*; en *ahn*

incapable incapable *an-kah-pah-bluh*

included compris(e) *kohn-pree(z)*

indefinite imprécis(e) *an-pray-ssee(z)*

infection l'infection (f.) *lan-fehk-ssyohn*

information les renseignements *lay rahn-seh-nyuh-mahn*

inn l'auberge (f.) *loh-behrzh*

inside dedans *duh-dahn*

insomnia l'insomnie (f.) *lan-ssohm-nee*

in spite of malgré *mahl-gray*

instead of au lieu de *oh lyuh duh*

insufficient insuffisant(e) *an-ssew-fee-zahn(t)*

insurance l'assurance (f.) *lah-ssew-rahnss*

insure assurer *ah-ssew-ray*

intelligent intelligent(e) *an-teh-lee-zhahn(t)*

interesting intéressant(e)
a<u>n</u>-tay-reh-ssah<u>n</u>(t)

interpret interpréter
a<u>n</u>-tehr-pray-tay

interpreter l'interprète (m.)
a<u>n</u>-tehr-preht

intersection le croisement *luh
krwahz-mah<u>n</u>*

introduce présenter *pray-zah<u>n</u>-tay*

invite inviter *a<u>n</u>-vee-tay*

invoice la facture *lah fahk-tewr*

iron (noun) le fer *luh fehr*

iron (verb) repasser *ruh-pah-ssay*

island l'île (f.) *leel*

itinerary l'itinéraire *lee-tee-nay-rehr*

J

jack (auto) le cric *luh kree*

jacket le veston *luh vehss-toh<u>n</u>*

jam (marmalade) la confiture *lah
koh<u>n</u>-fee-tewr*

January janvier *zhah<u>n</u>-vyay*

jar la jarre *lah zhahr*

jaw la mâchoire *lah mah-shwahr*

jewel le bijou *luh bee-zhoo*

jeweler le bijoutier *luh
bee-zhoo-tyay*

jewelry shop la bijouterie *lah
bee-zhoo-tree*

joke la plaisanterie *lah
pleh-zah<u>n</u>-tree*

journey le voyage *luh vwah-yahzh*;
le trajet *luh trah-zheh*

judge (noun) le juge *luh zhewzh*

judge (verb) juger *zhew-zhay*

juice le jus *luh zhew*

July juillet *zhwee-yeh*

June juin *zhwa<u>n</u>*

just: have just venir de *vuh-neer
duh*

K

keep garder *gahr-day*

ketchup le ketchup *luh keht-shuhp*

key la clef *lah klay*

kiss embrasser *ah<u>n</u>-brah-ssay*

kitchen la cuisine *lah kwee-zeen*

knee le genou *luh zhuh-noo*

knife le couteau *luh koo-toh*

knock frapper *frah-pay*

know (facts) savoir *sah-vwahr*;
(people) connaître *koh-neh-truh*

L

label l'étiquette (f.) *lay-tee-keht*

lace la dentelle *lah dah<u>n</u>-tehl*

lack (noun) le manque *luh mah<u>n</u>k*

lack (verb) manquer *mah<u>n</u>-kay*

lake le lac *luh lahk*

lamb l'agneau *lah-nyoh*

lamp la lampe *lah lah<u>n</u>p*

land (noun) la terre *lah tehr*

land (verb) (plane) atterrir
ah-teh-reer; débarquer *day-bahr-kay*

landing l'atterrissage (m.)
lah-teh-ree-ssahzh; le
débarquement *luh
day-bahrk-mah<u>n</u>*

lane la ruelle *lah rew-ehl*

language la langue *lah lah<u>n</u>g*

last (adj.) dernier(ière)
dehr-nyay(nyehr)

last (verb) durer *dew-ray*

late tard *tahr*; **(to be) late** (être)
en retard *ah<u>n</u> ruh-tahr*

laugh rire *reer*

launderette la laverie automatique
lah lah-vree oh-toh-mah-teek

laundering le blanchissage *luh
blah<u>n</u>-shee-ssahzh*

laundry la blanchisserie *lah blahn-sheess-ree*

learn apprendre *ah-prahn-druh*

least: at least au moins *oh mwan*

leather le cuir *luh kweer*

leave (behind) laisser *leh-ssay*

leave (depart) partir *pahr-teer;* **to go out** sortir *sohr-teer;* **to leave + (place or person)** quitter *kee-tay*

left gauche *gohsh;* **to the left** à gauche *ah gohsh*

leg la jambe *lah zhahnb*

lemon le citron *luh see-trohn*

lemonade la citronnade *lah see-troh-nahd*

lend prêter *preh-tay*

less moins *mwan*

letter la lettre *lah leh-truh*

lettuce la laitue *lah leh-tew*

library la bibliothèque *lah bee-blee-oh-tehk*

life la vie *lah vee*

life preserver la ceinture de sauvetage *lah san-tewr duh sohv-tahzh*

light (noun) la lumière *lah lew-myehr*

light (color) clair(e) *klehr*

light (weight) léger(ère) *lay-zhay(zhehr)*

light (verb) allumer *ah-lew-may*

lighter le briquet *luh bree-keh*

like (prep.) comme *kohm*

like (verb) aimer *eh-may*

lime la limette *lah lee-meht*

line la ligne *lah lee-nyuh;* la voie *lah vwah*

line (of people) la queue *lah kuh;* **form a line** faire la queue *fehr lah kuh*

linen (cloth) le lin *luh lan*

lip la lèvre *lah leh-vruh*

lipstick le rouge à lèvres *luh roozh ah leh-vruh*

list la liste *lah leesst*

listen écouter *ay-koo-tay*

little (adj.) petit(e) *puh-tee(t);* **(adv.)** peu (de) *puh (duh)*

live vivre *vee-vruh*

live in demeurer *duh-muh-ray;* habiter *ah-bee-tay*

liver le foie *luh fwah*

lobster le homard *luh oh-mahr*

lock (noun) la serrure *lah seh-rewr*

lodging le logis *luh loh-zhee*

long long, longue *lohn, lohng*

look at regarder *ruh-gahr-day*

look for chercher *shehr-shay*

lose perdre *pehr-druh*

loss la perte *lah pehrt*

lost: get lost s'égarer *say-gah-ray*

lot beaucoup de *boh-koo duh*

loudspeaker le haut-parleur *luh oh pahr-luhr*

love (noun) l'amour (m.) *lah-moor*

love (verb) aimer *eh-may*

low bas(se) *bah(ss)*

luck la chance *lah shahnss;* **Good luck!** Bonne chance! *bohn shahnss*

lunch (noun) le déjeuner *luh day-zhuh-nay*

lunch (verb) déjeuner *day-zhuh-nay*

lung le poumon *luh poo-mohn*

luxurious luxueux(euse) *lewk-ssew-uh(uhz)*

luxury le luxe *luh lewkss*

M

magazine le magazine *luh mah-gah-zeen*

mail le courrier *luh koo-ryay*

mailbox la boîte à lettres *lah bwaht ah leh-truh*

mailman le facteur *luh fahk-tuhr*

make faire *fehr*

man l'homme (m.) *lohm*

manager le gérant *luh zhay-rahn*

mango la mangue *lah mahng*

many beaucoup de *boh-koo duh*; **too many** trop de *troh duh*

map la carte *lah kahrt*; **road map** la carte routière *lah kahrt roo-tyehr*

March mars *mahrss*

margarine la margarine *lah mahr-gah-reen*

market le marché *luh mahr-shay*

marvelous merveilleux(euse) *mehr-veh-yuh(z)*

match (noun) l'allumette (f.) *lah-lew-meht*

material le tissu *luh tee-ssew*

matter (noun) l'affaire (f.) *lah-fehr*; **it doesn't matter** n'importe *nan-pohrt*; **What's the matter?** Qu'est-ce qu'il y a? *Kchss keel yah*

May mai *meh*

may (verb) pouvoir *poo-vwahr*

maybe peut-être *puh-teh-truh*

mayonnaise la mayonnaise *lah may-yoh-nehz*

meal le repas *luh ruh-pah*

mean (verb) vouloir dire *voo-lwahr deer*; signifier *see-nee-fyay*

mean (adj.) méchant(e) *may-shahn(t)*

meaning la signification *lah see-nee-fee-kah-ssyohn*

measure (noun) la mesure *lah muh-zewr*

measure (verb) mesurer *muh-zew-ray*

meat la viande *lah vee-ahnd*

meatballs les boulettes *lay boo-leht*

mechanic le mécanicien *luh may-kah-nee-ssyan*

medicine la médecine *lah mayd-sseen*

medium (cooking) à point *ah pwan*

meet rencontrer *rahn-kohn-tray*

meeting le rendez-vous *luh rahn-day-voo*

melon le melon *luh muh-lohn*

merchandise la marchandise *lah mahr-shahn-deez*

merchant le marchand *luh mahr-shahn*

mezzanine le parterre *luh pahr-tehr*

middle le milieu *luh meel-yuh*; **in the middle of** au milieu de *oh meel-yuh duh*

midnight minuit *mee-nwee*

milk le lait *luh leh*

milk shake le frappé *luh frah-pay*

million le million *luh mee-lyohn*

minute la minute *lah mee-newt*

mirror le miroir *luh mee-rwahr*; la glace *lah glahss*

miss (verb) manquer *mahn-kay*

miss mademoiselle *mahd-mwah-zehl*

mistake la faute *lah foht*; l'erreur (f.) *leh-ruhr*; **make a mistake** se tromper *suh trohn-pay*

mister monsieur *muh-ssyuh*

misunderstanding le malentendu *luh mahl-ahn-tahn-dew*

modify modifier *moh-dee-fyay*

Monday lundi *luhn-dee*

money l'argent (m.) *lahr-zhahn*

money (coins) la monnaie *lah moh-nay*

month le mois *luh mwah*

monthly mensuel(le) *mahn-sswehl*

morning le matin *luh mah-tan*

mosque la mosquée *lah mohss-kay*

mother la mère *lah mehr*

motor le moteur *luh moh-tuhr*

mountain la montagne *lah mohn-tah-nyuh*

mouth la bouche *lah boosh*

mouthwash le dentifrice *luh dahn-tee-freess*

movies le cinéma *luh see-nay-mah*

Mr. monsieur *muh-ssyuh*

Mrs. madame *mah-dahm*

museum le musée *luh mew-zay*

mushroom le champignon *luh shahn-pee-nyohn*

music la musique *lah mew-zeek*

mussels les moules (f. pl.) *lay mool*

mustard la moutarde *lah moo-tahrd*

mutton leg le gigot *luh zhee-goh*

N

nail l'ongle *lohn-gluh*

nail file la lime à ongles *lah leem ah ohn-gluh*

name le nom *luh nohn*; **family (last) name** le nom de famille *luh nohn duh fah-mee*; **first name** le prénom *luh pray-nohn*; **last name** le surnom *luh sewr-nohn*; **My name is** Je m'appelle *Zhuh mah-pehl*

napkin la serviette *lah sehr-vyeht*; **sanitary napkin** la serviette hygiénique *lah sehr-vyeht ee-zhyay-neek*

nationality la nationalité *lah nah-ssyohn-nah-lee-tay*

nausea la nausée *lah noh-zay*

near (to) près de *preh duh*

nearby proche *prohsh*

nearly presque *prehss-kuh*

necessary nécessaire *nay-sseh-ssehr*; **it is necessary** il est nécessaire *eel eh nay-sseh-ssehr*; il faut *eel foh*

neck le cou *luh koo*

necklace le collier *luh koh-lyay*

need (verb) avoir besoin de *ah-vwahr buhz-wan duh*

needle l'aiguille (f.) *lay-gwee*

neighbor le voisin *luh vwah-san*; la voisine *lah vwah-zeen*

never jamais *zhah-meh*; ne . . . jamais *nuh . . . zhah-meh*

new nouveau (m.), nouvelle (f.) *noo-voh, noo-vehl*

newspaper le journal *luh zhoor-nahl*

next prochain(e) *proh-shan(shehn)*

night la nuit *lah nwee*

night club la boîte de nuit *lah bwaht duh nwee*

nine neuf *nuhf*

nineteen dix-neuf *deez nuhf*

ninety quatre-vingt-dix *kah-truh van deess*

no non *nohn*

noisy le bruit *luh brwee*

no longer ne . . . plus *nuh . . . plew*

none ne . . . aucun(e) *nuh . . . oh-kuhn(kewn)*

nonsmokers nonfumeurs *nohn few-muhr*

noon midi *mee-dee*

north le nord *luh nohr*

nose le nez *luh nay*

not ne . . . pas *nuh . . . pah*

not any ne . . . aucun(e) *nuh . . . oh-kuhn(kewn)*

notebook le cahier *luh kah-yay*

nothing ne . . . rien *nuh . . . ryan*

notice (noun) l'avis (m.) *lah-vee*

notice (verb) remarquer *ruh-mahr-kay*

novel le roman *luh roh-mahn*

novelty la nouveauté *lah noo-voh-tay*

now maintenant *mant-nahn*

number le numéro *luh new-may-roh*

number (quantity) le nombre *luh nohn-bruh*

nurse l'infirmière (f.) *lan-feer-myehr*

nut la noix *lah nwah*

nylon le nylon *luh nee-lohn*

O

observe observer *ohb-zehr-vay*

obtain obtenir *ohp-tuh-neer*

ocean l'océan (m.) *loh-ssay-ahn*

of de *duh*

of course bien entendu *byan nahn-tahn-dew*

offer offrir *oh-freer*

office le bureau *luh bew-roh*; **box office** le bureau de location *luh bew-roh duh loh-kah-ssyohn*; **exchange office** le bureau de change *luh bew-roh duh shahnzh*; **post office** le bureau de poste *luh bew-roh duh pohsst*

often souvent *soo-vahn*

oil l'huile (f.) *lweel*

O.K. d'accord *dah-kohr*

old vieux (m.), vieille (f.) *vyuh, vyay*; **How old are you?** Quel âge avez-vous? *kehl ahzh ah-vay voo?*

old-fashioned démodé(e) *day-moh-day*

olive l'olive (f.) *loh-leev*

olive oil l'huile d'olive *lweel doh-leev*

omelet l'omelette (f.) *lohm-leht*

on sur *sewr*

one un (m.), une (f.) *uhn, ewn*

onion l'oignon (m.) *loh-nyohn*

only ne . . . que *nuh . . . kuh*; seulement *suhl-mahn*

only (adj.) seul(e) *suhl*; unique *ew-neek*

open (verb) ouvrir *oo-vreer*

open (adj.) ouvert(e) *oo-vehr(t)*

opera l'opéra (m.) *loh-pay-rah*

operator la téléphoniste *lah tay-lay-foh-neesst*

opportunity l'occasion (f.) *loh-kah-zyohn*

opposite (noun) le contraire *luh kohn-trehr*

opposite (prep.) en face de *ahn fahss duh*

optician l'opticien (m.) *lohp-tee-ssyan*

or ou *oo*

orange l'orange (f.) *loh-rahnzh*

orangeade l'orangeade (f.) *loh-rahnzh-ahd*

orchestra l'orchestre (m.) *lohr-kehss-truh*

order (noun) la commande *lah koh-mahnd*

order (verb) commander *koh-mahn-day*

other autre *oh-truh*

outside dehors *duh-ohr*

over dessus *duh-ssew*

overcoat le manteau *luh mahn-toh*; le pardessus *luh pahr-duh-ssew*

overseas outre-mer *oo-truh mehr*

owe devoir *duh-vwahr*

own posséder *poh-ssay-day*

owner le propriétaire *luh proh-pree-ay-tehr*

oyster l'huître (f.) *lwee-truh*

P

package le paquet *luh pah-keh*; le colis *luh koh-lee*

pad (writing) le bloc *luh blohk*

pain la douleur *lah doo-luhr*

painting le tableau *luh tah-bloh*

pair la paire *lah pehr*

palace le palais *luh pah-leh*

panties la culotte *lah kew-loht*

pants le pantalon *luh pahn-tah-lohn*

panty hose les collants (m. pl.) *lay koh-lahn*

paper le papier *luh pah-pyay*; **toilet** le papier hygiénique *luh pah-pyay ee-zhyay-neek*; **typing** le papier à machine *luh pah-pyay ah mah-sheen*; **wrapping** le papier d'emballage *luh pah-pyay dahn-bah-lahzh*; **writing** le papier à lettres *luh pah-pyay ah leh-truh*

park (noun) le parc *luh pahrk*

park (verb) garer *gah-ray*; stationner *stah-ssyoh-nay*

part la partie *lah pahr-tee*

pass (verb) passer *pah-ssay*

pastry la pâtisserie *lah pah-teess-ree*

pay payer *peh-yay*

pear la poire *lah pwahr*

peas les pois (m. pl.) *lay pwah*

pedestrian le piéton *luh pyay-tohn*

pen la plume *lah plewm*; **ball-point** le stylo à bille *luh stee-loh ah bee*

penalty l'amende (f.) *lah-mahnd*

pencil le crayon *luh kreh-yohn*; **pencil sharpener** le taille-crayon *luh tahy kreh-yohn*

people les gens *lay zhahn* [adj. before (f.); adj. after (m.)]

people (nation) le peuple *luh puh-pluh*

pepper le poivre *luh pwah-vruh*

perfect parfait(e) *pahr-feh(t)*

performance la représentation *lah ruh-pray-zahn-tah-ssyohn*

perfume le parfum *luh pahr-fuhn*

perhaps peut-être *puh-teh-truh*

permanent permanent(e) *pehr-mah-nahn(t)*

permanent press infroissable *an-frwah-ssah-bluh*

permit (noun) le permis *luh pehr-mee*

permit (verb) permettre *pehr-meh-truh*; **permitted** permis *pehr-mee*

person la personne *lah pehr-ssohn*

persuade persuader *pehr-sswah-day*

pharmacy la pharmacie *lah fahr-mah-ssee*

photograph (noun) la photo *lah foh-toh*

photograph (verb) photographier *foh-toh-grah-fyay*

pickle le cornichon *luh kohr-nee-shohn*

picture (art) le tableau *luh tah-bloh*

pie la tarte *lah tahrt*

piece le morceau *luh mohr-ssoh*

pill la pilule *lah pee-lewl*

pillow l'oreiller (m.) *loh-reh-yay*

pin l'épingle (f.) *lay pan-gluh*

pineapple l'ananas (m.) *lah-nah-nah*

pink rose *rohz*

pipe (smoking) la pipe *lah peep*; **pipe tobacco** le tabac pour pipe *luh tah-bah poor peep*

pitcher la cruche *lah krewsh*

place (noun) l'endroit (m.) *lahn-drwah*; le lieu *luh lyuh*

plaid le tartan *luh tahr-tahn*

plan le plan *luh plahn*; **plan of the city** le plan de ville *luh plahn duh veel*

plate l'assiette (f.) *lah-ssyeht*

platform le quai *luh kay*

platinum le platine *luh plah-teen*

play (noun) la pièce *lah pyehss*

play (verb) jouer *zhoo-ay*; **play (a game)** jouer à *zhoo-ay ah*; **play (an instrument)** jouer de *zhoo-ay duh*

please s'il vous plaît *seel voo pleh*

pleasure le plaisir *luh pleh-zeer*

plum la prune *lah prewn*

pocket la poche *lah pohsh*

pocketbook le sac *luh sahk*

policeman l'agent (m.) de police *lah-zhahn duh poh-leess*; le gendarme *luh zhahn-dahrm*

police station le commissariat *luh koh-mee-ssah-ryah*

polka-dotted à pois *ah pwah*

polyester synthétique *san-tay-teek*

poor pauvre *poh-vruh*

pork le porc *luh pohr*

portable portatif(tive) *pohr-tah-teef(teev)*

porter le porteur *luh pohr-tuhr*

possess posséder *poh-ssay-day*

postcard la carte postale *lah kahrt pohss-tahl*

poster l'affiche (f.) *lah-feesh*

postman le facteur *luh fahk-tuhr*

post office la poste *lah pohsst*; le bureau de poste *luh bew-roh duh pohsst*

postpone remettre *ruh-meh-truh*

potato la pomme de terre *lah pohm duh tehr*

pottery la poterie *lah poh-tree*

pound (meas.) la livre *lah lee-vruh*

practice (noun) l'usage (m.) *lew-zahzh*

prefer préférer *pray-fay-ray*; aimer mieux *eh-may myuh*

prepare préparer *pray-pah-ray*

prescription l'ordonnance (f.) *lohr-doh-nahnss*

pretty joli(e) *zhoh-lee*

price le prix *luh pree*

private privé(e) *pree-vay*

prize le prix *luh pree*

profession la profession *lah proh-feh-ssyohn*

prohibit interdire *an-tehr-deer*; **prohibited** interdit(e) *an-tehr-dee(t)*

promise (verb) promettre *proh-meh-truh*

promise (noun) la promesse *lah proh-mehss*

pronounce prononcer *proh-nohn-ssay*

property la propriété *lah proh-pree-ay-tay*

protect protéger *proh-tay-zhay*

protest (verb) protester *proh-tehss-tay*

prune le pruneau *luh prew-noh*

public public(ique) *pew-bleek*

pull tirer *tee-ray*

purchase (noun) l'achat (m.) *lah-shah*

purple violet *vee-oh-leht*

purse le porte-monnaie *luh pohrt moh-nay*

push pousser *poo-ssay*

put mettre *meh-truh*; **to put on** mettre *meh-truh*; **put back** remettre *ruh-meh-truh*

pyjamas le pyjama *luh pee-zhah-mah*

Q

quality la qualité *lah kah-lee-tay*

quantity la quantité *lah kahn-tee-tay*

quarter le quart *luh-kahr*

question la question *lah kehss-tyohn*

quickly vite *veet*; rapidement *rah-peed-mahn*

quickness la vitesse *lah vee-tehss*

R

rabbit le lapin *luh lah-pan*

radio la radio *lah rah-dyoh*

radish le radis *luh rah-dee*

railroad le chemin de fer *luh shuh-man duh fehr*

railroad station la gare *lah gahr*

rain la pluie *lah plwee*

raincoat l'imperméable (m.) *lan-pehr-may-ah-bluh*

rare rare *rahr*

rare (meat) saignant *seh-nyahn*

raspberry la framboise *lah frahn-bwahz*

rate le tarif *luh tah-reef*

rate of exchange le cours du change *luh koor dew shahnzh*

rather plutôt *plew-toh*

raw cru(e) *krew*

razor le rasoir *luh rah-zwahr*

read lire *leer*

ready prêt(e) *preh(t)*

really vraiment *vreh-mahn*

reason la raison *lah reh-zohn*

reasonable raisonnable *reh-zoh-nah-bluh*

receipt le reçu *luh ruh-ssew*

receive recevoir *ruh-ssuh-vwahr*

recently récemment *ray-sseh-mahn*

recommend recommander *ruh-koh-mahn-day*

record le disque *luh deessk*

recover (health) se remettre *sul ruh-meh-truh*

recuperate récupérer *ray-kew-pay-ray*

red rouge *roozh*

reduction le rabais *luh rah-beh*

refreshments les rafraîchissements (m. pl.) *lay rah-freh-sheess-mahn*

refund rembourser *rahn-boor-ssay*

refuse (verb) refuser *ruh-few-zay*

regret regretter *ruh-greh-tay*

regular régulier(ière) *ray-gew-lyay(yehr)*

regularly régulièrement *ray-gew-lyehr-mahn*

reimburse rembourser *rahn-boor-ssay*

remain rester *rehss-tay*

remedy le remède *luh ruh-mehd*

remember se rappeler *suh rah-play*; se souvenir de *suh soo-vuh-neer duh*

rent (noun) le loyer *luh lwah-yay*

rent (verb) louer *loo-ay*

repair (verb) réparer *ray-pah-ray*

repeat répéter *ray-pay-tay*

replace remplacer *rahn-plah-ssay*

resemble ressembler à *ruh-ssahn-blay ah*

reservation la réservation *lay ray-zehr-vah-ssyohn*

reserve réserver *ray-zehr-vay*

resolve résoudre *ray-zoo-druh*

responsible responsable *rehss-pohn-ssah-bluh*

rest (noun) le repos *luh ruh-poh*

rest (verb) se reposer *suh ruh-poh-zay*

restaurant le restaurant *luh rehss-toh-rahn*

result le résultat *luh ray-zewl-tah*

retain retenir *ruh-tuh-neer*

return (verb) retourner *ruh-toor-nay*; **return (give back)** rendre *rahn-druh*

reward (noun) la récompense *lah ray-kohn-pahnss*

reward (verb) récompenser *ray-kohn-pahn-ssay*

rice le riz *luh ree*

right: to be right avoir raison *ah-vwahr reh-zohn*

right (direction) droit *drwah*; **to the right** à droite *ah drwaht*

ring (noun) la bague *lah bahg*

ring (verb) sonner *soh-nay*

river le fleuve *luh fluhv*; la rivière *lah ree-vyehr*

road le chemin *luh shuh-man*

roast (adj.) rôti(e) *roh-tee*

roll le petit pain *luh puh-tee pan*

roof le toit *luh twah*

room la pièce *lah pyehss*; la salle *lah sahl*; la chambre *lah shahn-bruh*; **single room** une chambre à un lit *ewn shahn-bruh ah uhn lee*; **double room** une chambre à deux lits *ewn shahn-bruh ah duh lee*

round rond(e) *rohn(d)*

route la route *lah root*

row (noun) le rang *luh rahn*

rubber le caoutchouc *luh kah-oo-tshoo*; **rubbers** les caoutchoucs *lay kah-oo-tshoo*

rug le tapis *luh tah-pee*

rule la règle *lah reh-gluh*

ruler la règle *lah reh-gluh*

run courir *koo-reer*

runway la piste *lah peesst*

S

sad triste *treesst*

safe (strongbox) le coffre-fort *luh koh-fruh fohr*

sale la vente *lah vahnt*; **for sale** en vente *ahn vahnt*

sale (bargain) les soldes (m. pl.) *lay sohld*

salesman le vendeur *luh vahn-duhr*

saleswoman la vendeuse *lah vahn-duhz*

salmon le saumon *luh soh-mohn*

salt le sel *luh sehl*

salted salé *sah-lay*

sand le sable *luh sah-bluh*

same même *mehm*

sample l'échantillon (m.) *lay-shahn-tee-yohn*

sardine la sardine *lah sahr-deen*

satin le satin *luh sah-tan*

satisfied satisfait(e) *sah-teess-feh(t)*

Saturday samedi *sahm-dee*

sauerkraut la choucroute *lah shoo-kroot*

sausage la saucisse *lah soh-sseess*

say dire *deer*

scarf l'écharpe (f.) *lay-shahrp*

schedule l'horaire (m.) *loh-rehr*

school l'école (f.) *lay-kohl*

scissors les ciseaux (m. pl.) *lay see-zoh*

scrambled brouillé(e) *broo-yay*

sea la mer *lah mehr*

seafood les fruits (m. pl.) de mer *lay frwee duh mehr*

season la saison *lah seh-zohn*

seasoned assaisonné *ah-sseh-zoh-nay*

seat la place *lah plahss*; le siège *luh syehzh*

secondhand usagé *ew-zah-zhay*

secondhand goods la marchandise d'occasion *lah mahr-shahn-deez doh-kah-zyohn*

security la sécurité *lah say-kew-ree-tay*

see voir *vwahr*

seem sembler *sahn-blay*; avoir l'air de *ah-vwahr lehr duh*

sell vendre *vahn-druh*

send envoyer *ahn-vwah-yay*; **send for** faire venir *fehr vuh-neer*; **send back** renvoyer *rahn-vwah-yay*

sentence la phrase *lah frahz*

serious sérieux(ieuse) *say-ryuh(z)*; grave *grahv*

serve servir *sehr-veer*

service le service *luh sehr-veess*

service station la station service *lah stah-ssyohn sehr-veess*

settle régler *ray-glay*; **settle an affair** régler une affaire *ray-glay ewn ah-fehr*

seven sept *seht*

seventeen dix-sept *dee seht*

seventy soixante-dix *swah-ssahnt deess*

several plusieurs *plew-zyuhr*

sew coudre *koo-druh*

shade l'ombre (f.) *lohn-bruh*

share partager *pahr-tah-zhay*

shark le requin *luh ruh-kan*

shave (verb) raser *rah-zay*

shawl le châle *luh shahl*

she elle *ehl*

sheet la feuille *lah fuhy*

shelf le rayon *luh reh-yohn*

shellfish le coquillage *luh koh-kee-yahzh*

sherbet le sorbet *luh sohr-beh*

shine (verb) cirer *see-ray*

shirt la chemise *lah shuh-meez*

shoe le soulier *luh soo-lyay*; la chaussure *lah shoh-ssewr*

shoelaces les lacets (m. pl.) *lay lah-sseh*

shoemaker le cordonnier *luh kohr-doh-nyay*

shop (noun) la boutique *lah boo-teek*

shop (verb) faire des achats *fehr day zah-shah*; faire des emplettes *fehr day zahn-pleht*

shop window la vitrine *lah vee-treen*

shore (bank) la rive *lah reev*

short court(e) *koor(t)*

shorts (briefs) le caleçon *luh kahl-ssohn*

short story le conte *luh kohnt*

shoulder l'épaule (f.) *lay-pohl*

show (verb) montrer *mohn-tray*

show (noun) le spectacle *luh spehk-tah-kluh*

shower la douche *lah doosh*

shrimp la crevette *lah kruh-veht*

sick malade *mah-lahd*

sickness la maladie *lah mah-lah-dee*

side le côté *luh koh-tay*

sidewalk le trottoir *luh troh-twahr*

sightseeing le tourisme *luh too-reess-muh*

sign (noun) l'enseigne (f.) *lahn-sseh-nyuh*

sign (verb) signer *see-nyay*

silk la soie *lah swah*

silver l'argent (m.) *lahr-zhahn*

since depuis *duh-pwee*

since when depuis quand *duh-pwee kahn*

sing chanter *shahn-tay*

single (unmarried) célibataire *say-lee-bah-tehr*

sir monsieur *muh-ssyuh*

sister la soeur *lah suhr*

sit s'asseoir *sah-sswahr*

six six *seess*

sixteen seize *sehz*

sixty soixante *swah-ssahnt*

size la taille *lah tahy*

ski le ski *luh skee*; **water skis** les skis nautiques *lay skee noh-teek*

ski lift le téléski *luh tay-lay-sskee*

ski slope la piste de ski *lah peesst duh skee*

skin la peau *lah poh*

skirt la jupe *lah zhewp*

sky le ciel *luh syehl*

skyscraper le gratte-ciel *luh graht syehl*

sleep (verb) dormir *dohr-meer*

sleep, sleepiness le sommeil *luh soh-mehy*; **to be sleepy** avoir sommeil *ah-vwahr soh-mehy*; **sleeping car** le wagon-lit *luh vah-gohn lee*; **sleeping pill** le somnifère *luh sohm-nee-fehr*

sleeve la manche *lah mahnsh*

slice la tranche *lah trahnsh*

slide (pictures) la diapositive *lah dee-ah-poh-zee-teev*

slip (clothing) la combinaison *lah kohn-bee-neh-zohn*; le jupon *luh zhew-pohn*

slippers les pantoufles (f. pl.) *lay pahn-too-fluh*

slow (adj.) lent(e) *lahn(t)*

slowly (adv.) lentement *lahnt-mahn*

small petit(e) *puh-tee(t)*

smoke fumer *few-may*

smoker le fumeur *luh few-muhr*

snail l'escargot (m.) *lehss-kahr-goh*

snow (noun) la neige *lah nehzh*

snow (verb) neiger *neh-zhay*

so alors *ah-lohr*

soap le savon *luh sah-vohn*; **a bar of soap** la savonnette *lah sah-voh-neht*

socket la prise de courant *lah preez duh koo-rahn*

socks les chaussettes (f. pl.) *lay shoh-sseht*

soda le soda *luh soh-dah*

soft doux, douce *doo(ss)*

softly doucement *dooss-mahn*

sole (fish) la sole *lah sohl*

solid (colored) uni (e) *ew-nee*

some quelques *kehl-kuh*

some du *dew*; de la *duh lah*; de l' *duhl*; des *day*

someone quelqu'un *kehl-kuhn*

something quelque chose *kehl-kuh shohz*

sometimes quelquefois *kehl-kuh fwah*

somewhere quelque part *kehl-kuh pahr*

son le fils *luh feess*

song la chanson *lah shahn-ssohn*

soon bientôt *byan-toh*; **see you soon** à bientôt *ah byan-toh*

sore throat le mal de gorge *luh mahl duh gohrzh*

sorry: to be sorry être désolé(e) *eh-truh day-zoh-lay*; regretter *ruh-greh-tay*

soup la soupe *lah soop*; le potage *luh poh-tahzh*

south le sud *luh sewd*

space l'espace (m.) *lehss-pahss*

speak parler *pahr-lay*

speed la vitesse *lah vee-tehss*

spell épeler *ay-play*

spend (money) dépenser *day-pahn-ssay*

spend (time) passer *pah-ssay*

spinach les épinards (m. pl.) *lay zay-pee-nahr*

spoon la cuiller *lah kwee-yehr*; **teaspoon** la cuiller à café *lah kwee-yehr ah kah-fay*; **tablespoon** la cuiller à soupe *lah kwee-yehr ah soop*; **teaspoonful** la cuillerée à café *lah kwee-yuh-ray ah kah-fay*; **tablespoonful** la cuillerée à soupe *lah kwee-yuh-ray ah soop*

spouse l'époux (m.), l'épouse (f.) *lay-poo, lay-pooz*

spring le printemps *luh pran-tahn*

square (adj.) carré(e) *kah-ray*

square (public) la place *lah plahss*

stadium le stade *luh stahd*

stain la tache *lah tahsh*

staircase l'escalier (m.) *lehss-kah-lyay*

stamp le timbre *luh tan̲-bruh*

stand (noun) le kiosque *luh kee-ohssk*; **newsstand** le kiosque à journaux *luh kee-ohssk ah zhoor-noh*

state l'état (m.) *lay-tah*

station la gare *lah gahr*

stay, sojourn le séjour *luh say-zhoor*

stay (verb) rester *rehss-tay*

stay at loger *loh-zhay*

steak le bifteck *luh beef-tehk*

steal voler *voh-lay*

steering wheel le volant *luh voh-lahn̲*

stew le ragoût *luh rah-goo*

stewardess l'hôtesse de l'air *loh-tehss duh lehr*

still encore *ahn̲-kohr*

stockings les bas (m. pl.) *lay bah*

stock market la bourse *lah boorss*

stomach l'estomac (m.) *lehss-toh-mah*; le ventre *luh van̲-truh*

stone la pierre *lah pyehr*

stop (noun) l'arrêt (m.) *lah-reh*

stop (verb) arrêter *ah-reh-tay*

stop light le feu *luh fuh*

store le magasin *luh mah-gah-zan̲*; **book** la librairie *lah lee-breh-ree*; **camera** le magasin de photographie *luh mah-gah-zan̲ duh foh-toh-grah-fee*; **clothing** le magasin de vêtements *luh mah-gah-zan̲ duh veht-mahn̲*; **department** le grand magasin *luh grahn̲ mah-gah-zan̲*; **drug** la pharmacie *lah fahr-mah-ssee*; **grocery** l'épicerie (f.) *lay-peess-ree*; **hardware** la

quincaillerie *lah kan̲-kahy-ree*; **jewelry** la bijouterie *lah bee-zhoo-tree*; **liquor** le magasin de spiritueux *luh mah-gah-zan̲ duh spee-ree-tew-uh*; **record** le magasin de disques *luh mah-gah-zan̲ duh deessk*; **shoe** le magasin de chaussures *luh mah-gah-zan̲ duh shoh-ssewr*; **tobacco** le bureau de tabac *luh bew-roh duh tah-bah*; **toy** le magasin de jouets *luh mah-gah-zan̲ duh zhoo-eh*

storm la tempête *lah tahn̲-peht*; l'orage (m.) *loh-rahzh*

story l'histoire (f.) *leess-twahr*

straw la paille *lah pahy*

strawberry la fraise *lah frehz*

stream la rivière *lah ree-vyehr*

street la rue *lah rew*

string la ficelle *lah fee-ssehl*

string beans les haricots (m. pl.) verts *lay ah-ree-koh vehr*

stripe la rayure *lah rah-yewr*; **striped** à rayures *ah rah-yewr*

strong fort(e) *fohr(t)*

stuffed farci(e) *fahr-ssee*

style la mode *lah mohd*; **in style** à la mode *ah lah mohd*

subtitles les sous-titres (m. pl.) *lay soo-tee-truh*

suburb la banlieue *lah bahn̲-lyuh*; le faubourg *luh foh-boor*

subway le métro *luh may-troh*

suede le daim *luh dan̲*

sugar le sucre *luh sew-kruh*

suit (man's) le complet *luh kohn̲-pleh*; **(woman's)** le tailleur *luh tah-yuhr*

suitcase la valise *lah vah-leez*

sum total le montant *luh mohn̲-tahn̲*

summer l'été (m.) *lay-tay*

sun le soleil *luh soh-lehy*

sunburn les coups (m. pl.) de soleil *lay kood soh-lehy*

Sunday dimanche *dee-mahnsh*

sunglasses les lunettes (f. pl.) de soleil *lay lew-neht duh soh-lehy*

suntan lotion la lotion à bronzer *lah loh-ssyohn ah brohn-zay*

supermarket le supermarché *luh sew-pehr-mahr-shay*

supper le dîner *luh dee-nay*; le souper *luh soo-pay*; **to have supper** dîner *dee-nay*; souper *soo-pay*

sure sûr(e) *sewr*

surfboard la planche de surf *lah plahnsh duh sewrf*

surgeon le chirurgien *luh sheer-ewr-zhyan*

sweater le chandail *luh shahn-dahy*

sweet doux, douce *doo, dooss*

swim nager *nah-zhay*

swimming pool la piscine *lah pee-sseen*

synagogue la synagogue *lah see-nah-gohg*

synthetic synthétique *san-tay-teek*

T

table la table *lah tah-bluh*

tablet (pill) le comprimé *luh kohn-pree-may*

tailor le tailleur *luh tah-yuhr*

take prendre *prahn-druh*

take off (clothing) ôter *oh-tay*; enlever *ahn-luh-vay*

tampon le tampon périodique *luh tahn-pohn pay-ree-oh-deek*

tangerine la mandarine *lah mahn-dah-reen*

taste (noun) le goût *luh goo*

taste (verb) goûter *goo-tay*

taxi le taxi *luh tahk-ssee*

tea le thé *luh tay*; **iced** le thé glacé *luh tay glah-ssay*; **with lemon** au citron *oh see-trohn*; **with milk** au lait *oh leh*; **with sugar** sucré *sew-kray*

team l'équipe (f.) *lay-keep*

telegram le télégramme *luh tay-lay-grahm*

telephone le téléphone *luh tay-lay-fohn*; **telephone book** l'annuaire (m.) *lah-new-ehr*; **telephone booth** la cabine téléphonique *lah kah-been tay-lay-foh-neek*; **telephone call** le coup de téléphone *luh koo duh tay-lay-fohn*; **to call** donner un coup de téléphone *doh-nay uhn koo duh tay-lay-fohn*

television la télévision *lah tay-lay-vee-zyohn*

tell raconter *rah-kohn-tay*

temporary provisoire *proh-veez-wahr*

ten dix *deess*

tent la tente *lah tahnt*

terrific formidable *fohr-mee-dah-bluh*

terrycloth le tissu-éponge *luh tee-ssew ay-pohnzh*

thank remercier *ruh-mehr-ssyay*

thanks to grâce à *grahss ah*

thank-you merci *mehr-ssee*

that ça *sah*; cela *suh-lah*

the le(m.), la (f.), les (m./f. pl.) *luh, lah, lay*

there là *lah*; **over there** là-bas *lah bah*

there is, are il y a *eel yah*; voilà *vwah-lah*

they ils (m. pl.) *eel*, elles (f. pl.) *ehl*

thief le voleur *luh voh-luhr*

thin mince *manss*

thing la chose *lah shohz*

think penser *pahn-ssay*

thirst la soif *lah swahf*; **be thirsty** avoir soif *ah-vwahr swahf*

thirteen treize *trehz*

thirty trente *trah__nt__*

this ceci *suh-ssee*

thousand mille *meel*

three trois *trwah*

throat la gorge *lah gohrzh*

through à travers *ah trah-vehr*

thumb le pouce *luh pooss*

Thursday jeudi *zhuh-dee*

ticket le billet *luh bee-yeh*; **entrance ticket** le billet d'entrée *luh bee-yeh dah__n__-tray*

ticket collector le contrôleur *luh koh__n__-troh-luhr*

ticket window le guichet *luh gee-sheh*

tie (neck) la cravate *lah krah-vaht*

time l'heure (f.) *luhr*; le temps *luh tah__n__*; **at what time?** à quelle heure? *ah kehl uhr*; **on time** à l'heure *ah luhr*

time (in a series) la fois *la fwah*; **one time** une fois *ewn fwah*; **two times** deux fois *duh fwah*

timetable l'horaire (m.) *loh-rehr*; l'indicateur (m.) *la__n__-dee-kah-tuhr*

tip (end) le bout *luh boo*

tip (gratuity) le pourboire *luh poor-bwahr*

tire (car) le pneu *luh pnuh*

tire (verb) fatiguer *fah-tee-gay*

tired fatigué(e) *fah-tee-gay*

tiring fatigant(e) *fah-tee-gah__n__(t)*

tissue le mouchoir en papier *luh moo-shwahr ah__n__ pah-pyay*

title le titre *luh tee-truh*

to à *ah*

toast le pain grillé *luh pa__n__ gree-yay*

tobacco le tabac *luh tah-bah*

today aujourd'hui *oh-zhoor-dwee*

toe l'orteil (m.) *lohr-tehy*

together ensemble *ah__n__-ssah__n__-bluh*

toilet la toilette *lah twah-leht*

token le jeton *luh zhuh-toh__n__*

tolerate supporter *sew-pohr-tay*

tomato la tomate *lah toh-maht*

tomorrow demain *duh-ma__n__*

tonsilitis l'amygdalite (f.) *lah-meeg-dah-leet*

tooth la dent *lah dah__n__*; **toothache** le mal de dent *luh mahl duh dah__n__*

toothpaste la pâte dentifrice *lah paht dah__n__-tee-freess*

toothpick le cure-dent *luh kewr dah__n__*

touch toucher *too-shay*

tourist le touriste *luh too-reesst*

tourist office le syndicat d'initiative *luh sa__n__-dee-kah dee-nee-ssyah-teev*

towards vers *vehr*

towel la serviette *lah sehr-vyeht*

tower la tour *lah toor*

town hall la mairie *lah meh-ree*

track la voie *lah vwah*

traffic la circulation *lah seer-kew-lah-ssyoh__n__*

traffic light le feu *luh fuh*

train le train *luh tra__n__*

translate traduire *trah-dweer*

travel (verb) voyager *vwah-yah-zhay*

travel agency l'agence (f.) de voyage *lah-zhah__nss__ duh vwah-yahzh*

treatment le traitement *luh treht-mah__n__*

tree l'arbre (m.) *lahr-bruh*

trick (verb) tromper *troh__n__-pay*

trip le voyage *luh vwah-yahzh*; l'excursion (f.) *lehkss-kewr-zyoh__n__*; **business trip** le voyage d'affaires *luh vwah-yahzh dah-fehr*

trouble la difficulté *lah dee-fee-kewl-tay*

trout la truite *lah trweet*

truck le camion *luh kah-myohn*

true vrai(e) *vreh*

trunk la malle *lah mahl*; **car trunk** la malle arrière *lah mahl ah-ryehr*

truth la vérité *lah vay-ree-tay*

try (to) essayer (de) *eh-sseh-yay duh*

try (on) essayer *eh-sseh-yay*

Tuesday mardi *mahr-dee*

tuna fish le thon *luh tohn*

turkey la dinde *lah dand*

turn (noun) le tour *luh toor*

turn (verb) tourner *toor-nay*

twelve douze *dooz*

twenty vingt *van*

two deux *duh*

U

ugly laid(e) *leh(d)*

umbrella le parapluie *luh pah-rah-plwee*

unbearable insupportable *an-ssew-pohr-tah-bluh*

unbelievable incroyable *an-krwah-yah-bluh*

undecided indécis(e) *an-day-ssee(z)*

under sous *soo*; dessous *duh-ssoo*

undershirt le maillot de corps *luh mah-yoh duh kohr*

understand comprendre *kohn-prahn-druh*

underwear les sous-vêtements (m. pl.) *lay soo veht-mahn*

unfair injuste *an-zhewsst*

unhappy malheureux(euse) *mahl-uh-ruh(z)*

unimportant insignifiant(e) *an-ssee-nee-fee-ahn(t)*

United States les États-Unis *lay zay-tah zew-nee*

until jusqu'à *zhewss-kah*

up, upstairs en haut *ahn oh*

urgent urgent(e) *ewr-zhahn(t)*; **urgently** (d'urgence) *dewr-zhahnss*

us nous *noo*

use (verb) utiliser *ew-tee-lee-zay*; employer *ahn-plwah-yay*

use (noun) l'emploi (m.) *lahn-plwah*

used up épuisé(e) *ay-pwee-zay*

useful utile *ew-teel*

useless inutile *een-ew-teel*

V

vacation les vacances (f. pl.) *lay vah-kahnss*

valid valable *vuh-lah-bluh*

value la valeur *lah vah-luhr*

varied varié(e) *vah-ree-yay*

veal le veau *luh voh*

vegetable le légume *luh lay-gewm*

velvet le velours *luh vuh-loor*

very très *treh*

vest le gilet *luh zhee-leh*

vicinity les environs (m. pl.) *lay zahn-vee-rohn*

view la vue *lah vew*

village le village *luh vee-lahzh*

vinegar le vinaigre *luh vee-neh-gruh*

vitamin la vitamine *lah vee-tah-meen*

W

waist la taille *lah tahy*

waiter le garçon *luh gahr-ssohn*

wait for attendre *ah-tahn-druh*

waiting room la salle d'attente *lah sahl dah-tahnt*

waitress la serveuse *lah sehr-vuhz*

walk (noun) la promenade *lah prohm-nahd*; **to take a walk** faire une promenade *fehr ewn prohm-nahd*

walk (verb) marcher *mahr-shay*

wall le mur *luh mewr*

wallet le portefeuille *luh pohr-tuh-fuhy*

want désirer *day-zee-ray*; vouloir *voo-lwahr*; avoir envie de *ah-vwahr ahn-vee duh*

war la guerre *lah gehr*

warm chaud *shoh*

wash laver *lah-vay*; **wash oneself** se laver *suh lah-vay*

wash and wear ne pas repasser *nuh pah ruh-pah-ssay*

washroom le lavabo *luh lah-vah-boh*

watch (noun) la montre *lah mohn-truh*

watch (verb); (look at) regarder *ruh-gahr-day*; **(supervise)** surveiller *sewr-veh-yay*

watchmaker's shop l'horlogerie (f.) *lohr-lohzh-ree*

waterfall la cascade *lah kahss-kahd*

water l'eau *loh*

watermelon la pastèque *lah pahss-tehk*

way le moyen *luh mwah-yan*; la façon *lah fah-ssohn*

weak faible *feh-bluh*

wear porter *pohr-tay*

weather le temps *luh tahn*

Wednesday mercredi *mehr-kruh-dee*

week la semaine *lah suh-mehn*

weigh peser *puh-zay*

weight le poids *luh pwah*

welcome: you're welcome de rien *duh ryan*; il n'y a pas de quoi *eel nyah pah duh kwah*

well bien *byan*

well-done (cooking) bien cuit *byan kwee*

west l'ouest (m.) *lwehsst*

wet mouillé(e) *moo-yay*

what que, quoi *kuh, kwah*

when quand *kahn*

where où *oo*

which quel(le) *kehl*

white blanc(he) *blahn(sh)*

who qui *kee*

whole entier(ière) *ahn-tyay (ahn-tyehr)*

why pourquoi *poor-kwah*

wife la femme *lah fahm*

willingly volontiers *voh-lohn-tyay*

win gagner *gah-nyay*

wind le vent *luh vahn*

window la fenêtre *lah fuh-neh-truh*; **ticket window** le guichet *luh gee-sheh*

window display l'étalage (m.) *lay-tah-lahzh*

windshield wipers les essuie-glaces (m.) *lay zeh-sswee glahss*

wine le vin *luh van*; **red** rouge *roozh*; **rosé** rosé *roh-zay*; **sparkling** mousseux *moo-ssuh*; **white** blanc *blahn*

wine merchant le négociant en vins *luh nay-gohss-yahn ahn van*

wine waiter le sommelier *luh soh-muh-lyay*

winter l'hiver (m.) *lee-vehr*

wish (verb) désirer *day-zee-ray*; vouloir *voo-lwahr*; avoir envie de *ah-vwahr ahn-vee duh*

wish (someone something) souhaiter *sweh-tay*

with   avec *ah-vehk*

without   sans *sahn*

woman   la femme *lah fahm*

wood(s)   le(s) bois *luh (lay) bwah*

wool   la laine *lah lehn*

word   le mot *luh moh*

work (noun)   le travail *luh
trah-vahy*

work (verb)   travailler *trah-vah-yay*;
  function   fonctionner
  fohnk-ssyoh-nay; marcher
  mahr-shay

workshop   l'atelier (m.)
  lah-tuh-lyay

world   le monde *luh mohnd*

worn out (things)   usé(e) *ew-zay*;
  (people)   épuisé(e) *ay-pwee-zay*

wound (noun)   la blessure *lah
bleh-ssewr*

wound (verb)   blesser *bleh-ssay*

wounded   blessé *bleh-ssay*

wrapper   l'enveloppe (f.) *lahn-vlohp*

wrap up   emballer *ahn-bah-lay*;
  envelopper *ahn-vloh-pay*

wrist   le poignet *luh pwah-nyeh*

write   écrire *ay-kreer*

wrong: to be wrong   avoir tort
  ah-vwahr tohr

X

X-ray   la radio *lah rah-dyoh*

Y

year   l'an (m.) *lahn*, l'année (f.)
  lah-nay

yellow   jaune *zhohn*

yes   oui *wee*

yesterday   hier *yehr*

yet   encore *ahn-kohr*

yogurt   le yaourt *luh yah-oort*

you   tu *tew*; vous *voo*

young   jeune *zhuhn*

Z

zero   zéro *zay-roh*

zipper   la fermeture éclair *lah
fehr-muh-tewr ay-klehr*

zone   la zone *lah zohn*

zoo   le zoo *luh zoh*; le jardin
  zoologique *luh zhahr-dan
  zoh-oh-loh-zheek*

FRENCH-ENGLISH DICTIONARY

A

à to, at; **à peu près** about, approximately; **à prix fixe** fixed price meal; **à travers** across, through

abricot (m.) apricot

accord (m.) agreement; **d'accord** agreed, O.K.

accrocher to hang up

achat (m.) purchase

acheter to buy

addition (f.) check, restaurant bill

adresse (f.) address

affaire (f.) matter, concern

affiche (f.) poster

agence (f.) agency, bureau; **une agence de voyage** travel agency

agent (de police) (m.) policeman

agneau (m.) lamb

aider to help

aiguille (f.) needle

ail (m.) garlic

ailleurs elsewhere

aimer to like, love; **aimer mieux** to prefer

ajouter to add

alcool (m.) alcohol

aliments (m.pl.) food

aller to go; **aller à** to fit

allumer to light

allumette (f.) match

alors then

amande (f.) almond

ambulance (f.) ambulance

amende (f.) fine, penalty

amer, amère bitter

ami(e) (m./f.) friend

amour (m.) love (noun)

ampoule (f.) bulb (electric)

amygdalite (f.) tonsilitis

an (m.) year

ananas (m.) pineapple

ancien(ne) former, old

anglais (m.) English

année (f.) year

anniversaire (m.) birthday

annonce (f.) advertisement

annuaire (m.) telephone book

antiseptique (m.) antiseptic

août August

appareil de photo (m.) camera

appartenir to belong

appeler to call; **s'appeler** to be called, named

appendicite (f.) appendicitis

apporter to bring

apprendre to learn

après after; **après-demain** day after tomorrow; **après-midi** afternoon

arbre (m.) tree

argent (m.) money, silver

armoire (f.) closet

arranger to adjust

arrêt (m.) a stop; **arrêt obligatoire** regular bus stop

arrêter to stop

arrière back; **en arrière** backward, behind

arrivée (f.) arrival

artichaut (m.) artichoke

ascenseur (m.) elevator

asperge (f.) asparagus

assaisonné(e) seasoned

asseoir (s' . . .) to sit down; **asseyez-vous** sit down

assez (de) enough

assiette (f.) plate

assurance (f.) insurance

assurer (faire assurer) to insure

atelier (m.) workshop, studio

attendre to wait for

attention caution

atterrir to land (plane)

atterrissage (m.) landing (plane)

attraper to catch

au to the; **au lieu de** instead of; **au milieu de** in the middle of; **au moins** at least; **au secours** help

auberge (f.) inn; **auberge de jeunesse** youth hostel

aubergine (f.) eggplant

aucun(e) any; **ne (verb) aucun(e)** not any

aujourd'hui today

aussi also, too

auteur (m.) author

autoroute (f.) highway

autour de around

autre other

aux to the

avant (de, que) before; **avant-hier** day before yesterday; **en avant** forward, ahead

avec with

avion (m.) airplane; **par avion** air mail, by plane

avis (m.) notice

avocat (m.) lawyer

avoir to have; **avoir l'air de** to seem to; **avoir besoin de** to need; **avoir chaud** to be hot;

avoir envie de to want to; **avoir faim** to be hungry; **avoir froid** to be cold; **avoir peur de** to be afraid of; **avoir raison** to be right; **avoir soif** to be thirsty; **avoir sommeil** to be sleepy; **avoir tort** to be wrong

B

bague (f.) ring

baguette (f.) French bread

baigner (se . . .) to bathe

bain (m.) bath

balcon (m.) balcony

ballet (m.) ballet

banane (f.) banana

banc (m.) bench

bande (f.) bandage

banlieue (f.) suburb

banque (f.) bank

bas (m. pl.) stockings

bas (se) low; **en bas** downstairs

bateau (m.) boat

bâtiment (m.) building

batterie (f.) battery (car)

beau (m.) beautiful

beaucoup (de) many, much, a lot, a great deal of

belle (f.) beautiful

besoin (m.) need; **avoir besoin de** to need

betterave (f.) beet

beurre (m.) butter

bibliothèque (f.) library

bien well; **bien entendu** of course

bientôt soon; **à bientôt** see you soon

bière (f.) beer

bifteck (m.) steak

bijou (m.) jewel

bijouterie (f.) jewelry shop

bijoutier (m.) jeweler

billet (m.) ticket; **billet d'entrée** admission ticket

biscuit (m.) cookie

bistro (m.) bar, tavern, saloon

blanc(he) white

blanchissage (m.) laundering, washing

blanchisserie (f.) laundry

blessé(e) wounded

blesser to wound, hurt

blessure (f.) wound

bleu(e) blue

bloc (m.) writing pad

blouse (f.) blouse

boeuf (m.) beef, ox

boire to drink

bois (m.) wood; **bois (m. pl.)** woods

boisson (f.) drink; **une boisson non-alcoolisée** soft drink

boîte (f.) box; **boîte aux lettres** mailbox; **boîte de nuit** nightclub

bon(ne) good

bonjour hello

bon marché cheap

bouche (f.) mouth

boucherie (f.) butcher shop

boucle (f.) curl; **boucles d'oreille** earrings

bougie (f.) candle, spark plug

bouilli(e) boiled

boulangerie (f.) bakery

boulette (f.) meatball

bourse (f.) stock market

bout (m.) tip, point, end

bouteille (f.) bottle

boutique (f.) shop

bouton (m.) button

braisé(e) braised

bras (m.) arm

brioche (f.) breakfast bun

briquet (m.) cigarette lighter

briser to break

brosse (f.) brush; **brosse à dents** toothbrush

brosser (se , . .) to brush

brouillé(e) scrambled; **les oeufs brouillés** scrambled eggs

bruit (m.) noise

brûler to burn

brûlure (f.) a burn

brun(e) brown

bureau (m.) office, desk; **bureau de location** theater box office; **bureau d'objets trouvés** lost and found; **bureau de poste** post office; **bureau de renseignements** information desk; **bureau de tabac** tobacconist shop

C

ça that; **ça ne fait rien** it doesn't matter

cabine téléphonique (f.) telephone booth

cadeau (m.) gift, present

café (m.) coffee, cafe; **café au lait** coffee with milk; **café crème** coffee with cream; **café express** espresso; **café glacé** iced coffee; **café noir** black coffee

cahier (m.) notebook

caisse (f.) cash register

caissier (m.) cashier

caleçon (m.) men's shorts, undergarments

camion (m.) truck

campagne (f.) country (outside city)

canard (m.) duck

caoutchouc (m.) rubber; caoutchoucs (m. pl.) rubbers

carburateur (m.) carburetor

carotte (f.) carrot

carré(e) square

carreaux (à carreaux) checked (material)

carrefour (m.) crossroad

carte (f.) map, card; cartes à jouer playing cards; carte de crédit credit card; carte postale post card; carte routière road map

cas (m.) case; en cas d'urgence in case of emergency

cascade (f.) waterfall

casser to break; casser la croûte to get a bite to eat

cave (f.) cellar

ceci this, it

ceinture (f.) belt; ceinture de sauvetage life preserver; ceinture de sécurité seat belt

célibataire single (unmarried)

cendrier (m.) ashtray

cent one hundred

cerise (f.) cherry

chacun(e) each one

chaînette (f.) chain (jewelry)

chaise (f.) chair

châle (m.) shawl

chaleur (f.) heat

chambre (f.) room; chambre à coucher bedroom; chambre à un lit single room; chambre à deux lits double room

champignon (m.) mushroom

champ (m.) field

chance (f.) luck; Bonne chance! Good luck!

chandail (m.) sweater

changement (m.) change

changer to change

chanson (f.) song

chanter to sing

chaque each

charcuterie (f.) cold cuts, delicatessen

chasseur (m.) bellboy, bellhop

chat (m.) cat

château (m.) castle

chaud hot; avoir chaud to be hot (person); faire chaud to be hot (weather)

chauffage (m.) heating

chauffer to heat

chaussettes (f.) socks

chaussures (f.) shoes

chemin (m.) road, way

chemin de fer (m.) railway, railroad

chemise (f.) shirt

chèque (m.) check; toucher un chèque to cash a check

cher, chère dear, expensive

chercher to look for

cheval (m.) (pl. chevaux) horse

cheveux (m. pl.) hair

cheville (f.) ankle

chez at the house (shop, business) of

chien (m.) dog

chirurgien (m.) surgeon

choisir to choose

chose (f.) thing

chou (m.) cabbage

choucroute (f.) sauerkraut

choux de Bruxelles (m. pl.) Brussel sprouts

ciel (m.) sky

cigare (m.) cigar

cigarette (f.) cigarette

cil (m.) eyelash

cimetière (m.) cemetery

cinéma (m.)　movies

cinq　five

cinquante　fifty

cintre (m.)　hanger

circulation (f.)　traffic

cirer　to shine, wax

ciseaux (m. pl.)　scissors

citron (m.)　lemon

citronnade (f.)　lemonade

clair(e)　clear, light (color)

clef (f.)　key

client (m.)　customer

climatiseur (m.)　air conditioner

cloche (f.)　bell

coco (m.)　coconut

coeur (m.)　heart

coffre-fort (m.)　safe, strong-box

coiffeur (m.)　barber

coin (m.)　corner

col (m.)　collar

colis (m.)　package, parcel

collants (m. pl.)　panty hose

colle (f.)　glue

collier (m.)　necklace

combien (de)　how much, how many

combinaison (f.)　slip (clothing)

commande (f.)　order

commander　to order

comme　like, as

commencer　to begin

comment　how

commissariat (m.)　police station

compagnie (f.)　company

complet (m.)　suit (man's)

comprendre　to understand

comprimé (m.)　tablet

compris(e)　included

compter　to count

concert (m.)　concert; la salle de concert　concert hall

concierge (m. or f.)　house porter, caretaker, doorman

concombre (m.)　cucumber

conduire　to drive, take a person somewhere

confiserie (f.)　confectionery store

confiture (f.)　jam, marmalade

connaître　to know, be acquainted with

conseil (m.)　advice

consigne (f.)　baggage checkroom

consommation (f.)　drink

contagieux (ieuse)　contagious

conte (m.)　short story

contenir　to contain

contenu (m.)　contents

contraire (m.)　opposite

contre　against

contrôleur (m.)　ticket collector

contusion (f.)　bruise

coquillage (m.)　shellfish

cordonnier (m.)　shoemaker

cornichon (m.)　pickle

corps (m.)　body

costume (m.)　suit (woman's)

côte (f.)　coast

côté (m.)　side; à côté de　beside, next to

côtelette (f.)　cutlet, chop

coton (m.)　cotton

cou (m.)　neck

couche (f.)　diaper

couchette (f.)　berth

coude (m.)　elbow

coudre　to sew

couleur (f.)　color

coup de téléphone (m.)　phone call

coupe de cheveux (f.)　haircut

coupe de glace (f.)　sundae

couper　to cut

cour (f.)　courtyard

courir to run

courrier (m.) mail

cours du change (m.) exchange rate

court(e) short

couteau (m.) knife

coûter to cost

coûteux (euse) costly

couvert (m.) cover charge

couverture (f.) blanket

couvrir to cover

crabe (m.) crab

crampe (f.) cramp

cravate (f.) tie

crayon (m.) pencil

crème (f.) cream; la crème anglaise custard; la crème fouettée whipped cream

crêpe (f.) thin French pancakes

crevette (f.) shrimp

cric (m.) jack (auto)

croire to believe

croisement (m.) intersection

croissant (m.) crescent-shaped breakfast pastry

croûte (f.) crust; casser la croûte to get a bite to eat

cru(e) raw, uncooked

cruche (f.) pitcher

cuiller (f.) spoon; cuiller à soupe tablespoon; cuiller à café teaspoon

cuillerée (f.) spoonful; cuillerée à soupe tablespoonful; cuillerée à café teaspoonful

cuir (m.) leather

cuisine (f.) cooking, kitchen

cuisinier (m.) the cook

cuisse (f.) thigh; les cuisses de grenouille frog's legs

cuit(e) cooked

cure-dent (m.) toothpick

D

d'abord at first

d'accord agreed, O.K.

daim (m.) suede

dans in

danse (f.) the dance

danser to dance

date (f.) date

datte (f.) date (fruit)

de of; de bonne heure early

débarquement (m.) landing (boat)

débarquer to land (boat)

décider to decide

déclarer to declare

déçu(e) disappointed

dedans inside

défendre to forbid; défense de cracher no spitting; défense d'entrée no entry; défense de fumer no smoking

défendu(e) forbidden

dehors outside

déjà already

déjeuner (m.) lunch

déjeuner to eat lunch

demain tomorrow

demander to ask (for)

demeurer to live, reside

demi(e) half

démodé(e) old-fashioned

dent (f.) tooth; mal (m.) de dent toothache

dentelle (f.) lace

dentifrice (m.) mouthwash; la pâte dentifrice toothpaste

déodorant (m.) deodorant

dépêcher (se . . .) to hurry up; dépêchez-vous hurry up

dépenser to spend money

déranger to bother

dernier(ière) last

derrière behind

des some

descendre to go down, get off

désirer to desire, wish, want

désolé(e) sorry; **être désolé(e)** to be sorry

dessous under, beneath

dessus over, above

deux two

devant in front of

devenir to become

devoir to owe, have to, ought to

diapositive (f.) slide (photo)

dictionnaire (m.) dictionary; **dictionnaire de poche** pocket dictionary

Dieu God

différent(e) different

difficile difficult

dimanche Sunday

diminuer to diminish

dinde (f.) turkey

dîner (m.) dinner

dîner to dine

dire to say

discothèque (f.) discotheque

dispute (f.) dispute, argument

disque (m.) record

dix ten

dix-huit eighteen

dix-neuf nineteen

dix-sept seventeen

docteur (m.) doctor

doigt (m.) finger

donner to give

dormir to sleep

dos (m.) back

douane (f.) customs

douanier (m.) custom's official

doucement softly

douche (f.) shower

douleur (f.) pain

doux, douce sweet, mild, soft

douzaine (f.) dozen

douze twelve

droit (m.) right; **à droite** to the right

du some

durer to last

E

eau (f.) water; **eau courante** running water; **eau chaude** hot water; **eau froide** cold water; **eau glacée** ice water; **eau minérale** mineral water

échanger to exchange

échantillon (m.) sample

écharpe (f.) scarf

école (f.) school

écouter to listen to

écrire to write

égarer (s' . . .) to lose one's way, to get lost

église (f.) church

elle she

elles they

emballer to wrap up

embrasser to kiss

emploi (m.) employ, use

employer to use

emporter to carry, take away

emprunter to borrow

en in; **en arrière** behind; **en avant** ahead; **en bas** downstairs; **en ce moment** right now; **en face de** opposite, facing; **en retard** late; **en voiture** all aboard

encore yet, still; **encore une fois** again

endosser to endorse

endroit (m.) place

enfant (m./f.) child

ennuyer to annoy, bother

enregistrer to check bags

enseigne (f.) sign

ensemble together

entendre to hear

entier (entière) entire, whole

entre between

entrée (f.) entrance

entrer to enter

enveloppe (f.) envelope, wrapper, cover

envelopper to wrap up

environ about

environs (m. pl.) vicinity

envoyer to send

épaule (f.) shoulder

épeler to spell

épicerie (f.) grocery store

épinards (m. pl.) spinach

épingle (f.) pin

époux (épouse) spouse

épuisé(e) exhausted, used up

équipe (f.) team

escalier (m.) stairs

escargot (m.) snail

espace (f.) space

espérer to hope

essayer (de) to try (to)

essence (f.) gas; **le réservoir à essence** gas tank

essuie-glaces (m. pl.) windshield wipers

est (m.) east

estomac (m.) stomach

et and

étage (m.) story, floor

étalage (m.) window display

état (m.) state

États-Unis (m. pl.) United States

été (m.) summer

étiquette (f.) label

étranger(ère) foreign; **à l'étranger** abroad

être to be; **être d'accord** to agree; **être de retour** to be back; **être en difficulté** to be in trouble

éviter to avoid

excellent(e) excellent

excursion (f.) excursion, trip

exemple (m.) example; **par exemple** for example

express (m.) express

F

facile easy

façon (f.) way, style, fashion

facteur (m.) mailman

facture (f.) bill, invoice

faible weak

faim (f.) hunger; **avoir faim** to be hungry

faire to make, do; **faire beau** to be beautiful weather; **faire chaud** to be hot weather; **faire des achats** to go shopping; **faire des emplettes** to go shopping; **faire du soleil** to be sunny; **faire du vent** to be windy; **faire froid** to be cold weather; **faire la connaissance de** to make the acquaintance of; **faire la correspondance** to change trains or planes; **faire la queue** to form a line; **faire une promenade** to take a walk; **faire venir** to send for

fait(e) à la main handmade

famille (f.) family

farci(e) stuffed

fatigant(e) tiring
fatigué(e) tired
fatiguer to tire
faubourg (m.) suburb
faut: il faut it is necessary
faute (f.) mistake, error
faux, fausse false
félicitations (f.) congratulations
femme (f.) woman, wife; **femme de chambre** chambermaid
fenêtre (f.) window
fer (m.) iron
ferme (f.) farm
fermer to close
fermeture éclair (f.) zipper
fête (f.) festival, feast, holiday
feu (m.) fire, traffic light
feuille (f.) sheet, leaf
feutre (m.) felt
février February
ficelle (f.) string
fiche (f.) form
fièvre (f.) fever
figue (f.) fig
figure (f.) face
fille (f.) girl, daughter
film (m.) film
fils (m.) son
fin (f.) end
finir to finish, end
flan (m.) custard
flanelle (f.) flannel
fleur (f.) flower
fleuriste (m.) florist
fleuve (m.) river
foie (m.) liver
foire (f.) fair, market
fois (f.) time in a series; **une fois** one time, once; **deux fois** two times, twice
foncé(e) dark (color)

fonctionner to function, work
fontaine (f.) fountain
forêt (f.) forest
formidable terrific
formule (f.) form
fort(e) strong
fourchette (f.) fork
frais, fraîche fresh
frais (m. pl.) expense, charge, cost
fraise (f.) strawberry
framboise (f.) raspberry
français (m.) French
frappé (m.) milk shake
frapper to knock, hit, strike
freins (m. pl.) brakes
frère (m.) brother
frit(e) fried
froid (m.) cold; **avoir froid** to be cold (person); **faire froid** to be cold (weather)
fromage (m.) cheese
front (m.) forehead
frontière (f.) border
fruit (m.) fruit
fruits de mer (m. pl.) seafood
fumer to smoke
fumeur (m.) smoker, smoking compartment

G

gabardine (f.) gabardine
gagner to earn, win
gant (m.) glove
garçon (m.) boy, waiter
garder to keep
gare (f.) station
garer to park a car
gare routière (f.) bus station
gâteau (m.) cake

gauche left; **à gauche** to the left

gencives (f. pl.) gums

gendarme (m.) policeman

gêner to bother, annoy

genou (m.) knee

gens (m./f. pl.) people

gérant (m.) manager

gibier (m.) game (meat)

gigot (m.) leg of mutton

gilet (m.) vest

glace (f.) ice, ice cream

glacé(e) iced

glaçon (m.) ice cube

gomme (f.) eraser

gorge (f.) throat; **avoir mal à la gorge** to have a sore throat

goût (m.) taste

goûter to taste

goyave (f.) guava

grâce à thanks to

grand(e) big

gratte-ciel (m.) skyscraper

gratuit(e) (adj.) free

gratuitement (adv.) free of charge

grave grave, serious

grillé(e) grilled, broiled

gris(e) gray

gros(se) fat

guerre (f.) war

guichet (m.) ticket window

guide (m.) guide; **guide touristique** tourist guide

H

habiller (s' . . .) to dress oneself

habiter to live in

habits (m. pl.) clothes

hamburger (m.) hamburger

hanche (f.) hip

hareng (m.) herring; **hareng fumé** smoked herring

haricot (m.) bean

haricots verts (m. pl.) string beans

haut(e) high

hauteur (f.) height, elevation

haut-parleur (m.) loudspeaker

herbe (f.) grass

heure (f.) hour; **à l'heure** on time; **de bonne heure** early

heureux(euse) happy

hier yesterday

histoire (f.) story

hiver (m.) winter

homard (m.) lobster

homme (m.) man

hôpital (m.) hospital

horaire (m.) schedule, timetable

horloge (f.) clock

horlogerie (f.) watchmaker's shop

hôte (m.) host

hôtel (m.) hotel

hôtesse (f.) hostess

huile (f.) oil; **l'huile d'olive** olive oil

huit eight

huître (f.) oyster

I

ici here

il he

île (f.) island

ils they

il y a there is, are; **il y a + time** ago

immédiatement immediately

imperméable (m.) raincoat

important(e) important

impossible impossible

imprécis(e) indefinite
incapable incapable
incendie (m.) fire
incroyable unbelievable
indécis(e) undecided
infection (f.) infection
infirmière (f.) nurse
infroissable permanent press
injuste unfair
insignifiant(e) unimportant
insomnie (f.) insomnia
insuffisant(e) insufficient
insupportable unbearable
intelligent(e) intelligent
interdire to prohibit, forbid
interdit(e) prohibited, forbidden
intéressant(e) interesting
interprète (m./f.) interpreter
interpréter to interpret
inutile useless
inviter to invite
invraisemblable improbable, unlikely
itineraire (m.) itinerary, route
ivre drunk

J

jamais never; **ne . . . jamais** never
jambe (f.) leg
jambon (m.) ham
janvier January
jardin (m.) garden
jarre (f.) jar
jaune yellow
je I
jeton (m.) token
jeu (m.) game
jeudi Thursday

jeune young
joli(e) pretty
joue (f.) cheek
jouer to play; **jouer à** to play a game, sport; **jouer de** to play a musical instrument
jour (m.) day
journal (m.) newspaper
juge (m.) judge
juger to judge
juillet July
juin June
jupe (f.) skirt
jupon (m.) slip
jus (m.) juice
jusqu'à until

K

ketchup (m.) ketchup
kiosque (m.) stand; **le kiosque à journaux** newsstand
klaxon (m.) horn

L

là there; **là-bas** over there
lac (m.) lake
lacet (m.) lace (shoe)
laid(e) ugly
laine (f.) wool
laisser to let, leave behind
lait (m.) milk
laitue (f.) lettuce
lampe (f.) lamp; **la lampe de poche** flashlight
langue (f.) language, tongue
lapin (m.) rabbit

laque (f.) hairspray

lard (m.) bacon

lavabo (m.) washroom

laver to wash; **se laver** to wash oneself

laverie automatique (f.) launderette

léger(ère) light (weight)

légume (m.) vegetable

lent(e) slow

lentement slowly

lettre (f.) letter

lever: se lever to get up

lèvre (f.) lip; **rouge à lèvres (m.)** lipstick

librairie (f.) bookstore

libre free

ligne (f.) line

limette (f.) lime

lin (m.) linen (material)

lire to read

liste (f.) list

lit (m.) bed

livre (m.) book

livre (f.) pound (weight)

livrer to deliver

loger to stay at

logis (m.) lodging

loin far; **loin de** far from

long(ue) long

lotion (f.) lotion; **la lotion à bronzer** suntan lotion

louer to rent, hire

loyer (m.) the rent

lumière (f.) light

lundi Monday

lunettes (f. pl.) eye glasses; **les lunettes de soleil** sunglasses

luxe (m.) luxury

luxueux(euse) luxurious

lycée (m.) high school

M

macédoine de fruits (f.) fruit salad

mâchoire (f.) jaw

madame Mrs.

mademoiselle Miss

magasin (m.) store; **de chaussures** shoe store; **de disques** record store; **un grand magasin** department store; **de jouets** toy store; **de photographie** camera store; **de souvenirs** gift shop; **de spiritueux** liquor store; **de vêtements** clothing store

magazine (m.) magazine

mai May

maillot (m.) de bain bathing suit; **de corps** undershirt

main (f.) hand

maintenant now

mairie (f.) town hall

mais but

maïs (m.) corn

maison (f.) house; **à la maison** at home

mal (m.) ache; **mal de dents** toothache; **mal d'estomac** stomachache; **mal de gorge** sore throat; **mal de tête** headache

malade sick

maladie (f.) sickness, illness

malentendu (m.) misunderstanding

malgré in spite of

malheureux(euse) unhappy

malle (f.) trunk; **malle arrière** auto trunk

manche (f.) sleeve
mandarine (f.) tangerine
manger to eat
mangue (f.) mango
manque (m.) lack
manquer to lack, miss
manteau (m.) overcoat
marchand (m.) merchant
marchandise (f.) merchandise
marché (m.) market
marcher to walk
mardi Tuesday
margarine (f.) margarine
mari (m.) husband
marque (f.) brand (of product)
marron brown
marron (m.) chestnut
mars March
matin (m.) morning
mauvais(e) bad
mayonnaise (m.) mayonnaise
mécanicien (m.) mechanic
médecin (m.) doctor
médecine (f.) medicine
meilleur(e) better (adj.)
melon (m.) melon
même same; **le/la même** the same
menton (m.) chin
mer (f.) sea; **au bord de la mer** at the seashore
merci thank-you
mercredi Wednesday
mère (f.) mother
mériter to deserve
merveilleux(euse) marvelous
mesure (f.) measurement
mesurer to measure
métro (m.) subway
mettre to put, put on

meublé(e) furnished
midi noon
mieux better (adv.)
milieu (m.) middle; **au milieu de** in the middle of
mille thousand
million (m.) million; **un million de + noun** a million
mince thin
minuit midnight
minute (f.) minute
miroir (m.) mirror
mode (f.) style; **à la mode** stylish, in style
modifier to modify, change
moins less
mois (m.) month
moitié (f.) half
monde (m.) world; **tout le monde** everybody.
monnaie (f.) coin money, change
monsieur (m.) mister, Mr., sir
montagne (f.) mountain
montant (m.) sum total
monter to go up
montre (f.) watch
montrer to show
morceau (m.) piece
mosquée (f.) mosque
mot (m.). word
moteur (m.) motor
mouchoir (m.) handkerchief; **le mouchoir en papier** tissue
mouillé(e) wet
moule (f.) mussel
mousseline de soie (f.) chiffon
moutarde (f.) mustard
moyen (m.) way
mur (m.) wall
musée (m.) museum
musique (f.) music

N

nager to swim

nationalité (f.) nationality

nausée (f.) nausea

ne; ne . . . aucun(e) not . . . any; **ne . . . jamais** never; **ne . . . pas** not; **ne . . . plus** no longer, not . . . any more; **ne . . . que** only; **ne . . . rien** nothing

nécessaire necessary

neige (f.) snow

neiger to snow

nettoyer to clean

nettoyer à sec to dry clean

neuf nine

nez (m.) nose

noir(e) black

noix (f.) nut

nom (m.) name; **nom de famille** family name; **prénom (m.)** first name; **surnom (m.)** last name, nickname

nombre (m.) number (quantity)

non no

non-fumeurs non-smoking

nord (m.) north

note (f.) bill (hotel)

nourriture (f.) food

nous us

nouveau (m.) new

nouveauté (f.) novelty

nouvelle (f.) new

nuit (f.) night

numéro (m.) number; **le numéro de téléphone** telephone number

nylon (m.) nylon

O

observer to observe

obtenir to obtain

occasion (f.) opportunity, bargain; **marchandise d'occasion (f.)** secondhand (used) goods; **une véritable occasion** a genuine bargain

occupé(e) busy

océan (m.) ocean

oeil (m.) eye; **(pl.) les yeux** eyes

oeuf (m.) egg; **au plat** fried; **brouillé** scrambled; **dur** hard-boiled; **frit** fried; **mollet** soft-boiled; **poêlé** sunny-side up

offrir to offer

oie (f.) goose

oignon (m.) onion

olive (f.) olive; **l'huile (f.) d'olive** olive oil

ombre (f.) shade (tree)

omelette (f.) omelet; **l'omelette norvégienne** baked Alaska

omnibus (m.) local bus

ongle (m.) nail (finger); **la lime à ongle** nail file

onze eleven

opéra (m.) opera, opera hall

opticien (m.) optician

or (m.) gold; **en or** of gold

orage (m.) storm

orange (f.) orange

orangeade (f.) orangeade

orchestre (m.) orchestra

ordonnance (f.) prescription

oreille (f.) ear; **boucle (f.) d'oreille** earring

oreiller (m.) pillow

orteil (m.) toe

os (m.) bone

ôter to take off, remove

ou or

où where

ouate (f.) absorbent cotton

oublier to forget

ouest (m.) west

oui yes

outre-mer overseas

ouvert(e) open (adj.)

ouvrir to open

P

paille (f.) straw (material)

pain (m.) bread; **baguette (f.)** French bread; **pain blanc** white bread; **pain bis** pumpernickel; **pain de froment** whole wheat; **pain grillé** toast; **pain de seigle** rye bread; **petit pain** roll

paire (f.) pair

palais (m.) palace

palourde (f.) clam

pamplemousse (m.) grapefruit

panier (m.) basket

panne (f.) breakdown, mishap; **en panne** broken down

pantalon (m.) pants

pantoufle (f.) slipper

papier (m.) paper; **papier à lettres** note paper; **papier à machine** typing paper; **papier d'emballage** wrapping paper; **papier hygiénique** toilet paper

paquet (m.) package

par by; per; **par avion** air mail, by plane; **par exemple** for example; **par ici** this way; **par jour** per day

parapluie (m.) umbrella

parc (m.) park

parce que because

pardessus (m.) overcoat

pardon excuse me

pardonner to excuse

parfait(e) perfect

parfum (m.) perfume, flavor

parler to speak

parmi among

partager to share

parterre (m.) mezzanine

partie (f.) part

partir to leave

partout everywhere

pastèque (f.) watermelon

pâte (f.) paste; **la pâte dentifrice** toothpaste

pâtisserie (f.) pastry, pastry shop

patron (m.) boss

pauvre poor

payer to pay

pays (m.) country (nation)

paysage (m.) countryside

peau (f.) skin

pêche (f.) peach; fishing

pêcher to fish

peigne (m.) comb

pellicule (f.) roll of film

pendant during

pendule (f.) clock

penser to think

pension (f.) boardinghouse

perdre to lose

père (m.) father

permanent(e) permanent

permettre to permit; **permis** permitted

permis (m.) permit

personne (f.) person

persuader to persuade

perte (f.) loss

peser to weigh

petit(e) small

petit déjeuner (m.) breakfast

peu (adv.) little, not much

peuple (m.) people (nation)

peur (f.) fear; **avoir peur de** to be afraid of

peut-être maybe, perhaps

phare (m.) headlight

pharmacie (f.) pharmacy

photo (f.) photograph

photographier to photograph

phrase (f.) sentence

pièce (f.) room, play

pied (m.) foot; **à pied** on foot

pierre (f.) stone

piéton (m.) pedestrian

pilule (f.) pill

pipe (f.) pipe; **le tabac pour pipe** pipe tobacco

piscine (f.) swimming pool

piste (f.) runway; **piste de ski** ski slope

place (f.) square (public); seat in conveyance

plafond (m.) ceiling

plage (f.) beach

plainte (f.) complaint

plaisanterie (f.) joke

plaisir (m.) pleasure

plan (m.) plan; **plan de ville** street map of city; **plan à vue d'oiseau** bird's-eye view of the city

planche de surf (f.) surfboard

plancher (m.) floor

plat (m.) dish of food

plat(e) flat

platine (f.) platinum

pleurer to cry

pluie (f.) rain

plume (f.) pen

plusieurs several

plutôt rather

pneu (m.) tire; **pneu crevé** flat tire

poche (f.) pocket; **livre de poche** paperback

poids (m.) weight

poignet (m.) wrist

poire (f.) pear

pois (m.) pea; **pois chiches (m. pl.)** chick-peas; **à pois** polka-dotted

poisson (m.) fish

poitrine (f.) chest

poivre (m.) pepper

pomme (f.) apple

pomme de terre (f.) potato

pont (m.) bridge

porc (m.) pork

portatif(ive) portable

porte (f.) door

porte-bonheur (m.) charm

portefeuille (m.) wallet

porte-monnaie (m.) purse

porter to carry, wear

porteur (m.) porter

posséder to possess, own

poste (f.) post office; **poste aérienne** air mail

poste (m.) station; **poste d'essence** gas station

potable drinkable; **eau potable** drinking water

potage (m.) soup

poterie (f.) pottery

pouce (m.) thumb

poulet (m.) chicken

poumon (m.) lung

pour for, in order to

pourboire (m.) tip (gratuity)

pourquoi why

pousser to push

pouvoir to be able to, can

préférer to prefer

premier(ière) first; **premier secours (m.)** first aid

prendre to take

prénom (m.) first name

préparer to prepare

présenter to present, introduce
préservatif condom
presque almost
pressé(e) hurried, rushed
prêt(e) ready
prêter to lend
printemps (m.) spring
prise de courant (f.) socket
privé(e) private
prix (m.) price, prize
prochain(e) next
proche near, neighboring
profession (f.) profession
promenade (f.) walk; **faire une promenade** to take a walk
promesse (f.) promise
promettre to promise
prononcer to pronounce
propre clean
propriétaire (m.) owner
propriété (f.) property
protéger to protect
protester to protest
provisoire temporary
provisoirement temporarily
prudence (f.) carefulness
prune (f.) plum
pruneau (m.) prune
public(ique) public
pyjama (m.) pyjamas

Q

quai (m.) platform
qualité (f.) quality
quand when
quantité (f.) quantity
quarante forty
quart (m.) quarter
quartier (m.) district

quatorze fourteen
quatre four
quatre-vingt-dix ninety
quatre-vingts eighty
que that
que? what?
quel(le) which
quelque chose something
quelquefois sometimes
quelque part somewhere
quelques some
quelequ'un someone
question (f.) question
queue (f.) line (of people); tail; **faire la queue** to form a line
qui who
quincaillerie (f.) hardware store
quinze fifteen
quitter + place or person to leave
quoi what
quotidien(ne) daily

R

rabais (m.) reduction
raconter to tell
radio (f.) radio, X-ray
radis (m.) radish
rafraîchissements (m. pl.) refreshments
ragoût (m.) stew
raifort (m.) horseradish
raisin (m.) grape
raison (f.) reason; **avoir raison** to be right
raisonnable reasonable
rang (m.) row
rapide fast, express train
rapidement quickly

rappeler: se rappeler to remember

rare rare

raser: se raser to shave oneself

rasoir (m.) razor; **le rasoir électrique** electric razor

rayon (m.) shelf; department (of a store)

rayure (f.) stripe; **à rayures** striped

récemment recently

recevoir to receive

réclame (f.) advertisement

recommander to recommend

récompense (f.) reward

récompenser to reward

reçu (m.) receipt

récupérer to recuperate

refuser to refuse

regarder to look at

règle (f.) rule, ruler

régler to settle, adjust, regulate; **régler une affaire** to settle an affair

regretter to regret, be sorry

regulier(ière) regular

regulièrement regularly

relier to connect

remarquer to notice

rembourser to reimburse, refund

remède (m.) remedy

remercier to thank

remettre to put back; **se remettre** to recover (health)

remplacer to replace

remplir to fill (out)

rencontrer to meet

rendez-vous (m.) meeting

rendre to return, give back

renseignement (m.) a piece of information; **les renseignements** information

renvoyer to send back

réparer to repair

repas (m.) meal

repasser to iron; **ne pas repasser** wash and wear

répéter to repeat

répondre to answer

réponse (f.) the answer

repos (m.) rest, relaxation

reposer: se reposer to rest

représentation (f.) performance

requin (m.) shark

réservation (f.) reservation

réserver to reserve

résoudre to resolve

responsable responsible

ressembler à to resemble, look like

restaurant (m.) restaurant

rester to stay, remain

résultat (m.) result

retard (m.) delay; **en retard** late

retenir to retain

retourner to return, go back

réveil (m.) alarm clock

réveiller: se réveiller to wake up

revenir to come back, return

rez-de-chaussée (m.) ground floor

rhume (m.) cold; **rhume de cerveau** head cold; **rhume des foins** hay fever; **rhume de poitrine** chest cold

rien nothing; **ne . . . rien** nothing; **de rien** you're welcome

rire to laugh

rive (f.) bank, shore

rivière (f.) river, stream

riz (m.) rice

robe (f.) dress; **robe de chambre** bathrobe; **robe de soir** evening gown

robinet (m.) faucet

roman (m.) novel; **roman policier** detective story

rond(e) round

rose pink, rose

rôti(e) roasted

rouge red

route (f.) route, road

rue (f.) street

ruelle (f.) lane, alley

S

sable (m.) sand

sac (m.) bag, pocketbook

saignant(e) rare (food)

saison (f.) season

salade (f.) salad

sale dirty

salé(e) salted

salle (f.) room; **salle à manger** dining room; **salle d'attente** waiting room; **salle de bains** bathroom; **salle de concert** concert hall

salon (m.) **de beauté** beauty parlor

saluer to greet

samedi Saturday

sang (m.) blood

sans without

santé (f.) health

sardine (f.) sardine

satin (m.) satin

satisfait(e) satisfied

saucisse (f.) sausage

saumon (m.) salmon

savoir to know (facts)

savon (m.) soap

sec, sèche dry

sèche-cheveux (m.) hair dryer

sécher to dry

secours (m.) help; **au secours!** help!

sécurité (f.) security; **la ceinture de sécurité** seat belt

seize sixteen

séjour (m.) stay, sojourn

sel (m.) salt

selon according to

semaine (f.) week

sembler to seem

sentir: se sentir to feel

sept seven

sérieux(ieuse) serious

serrure (f.) lock

serveuse (f.) waitress

service (m.) service

serviette (f.) towel, napkin, briefcase

serviette hygiénique (f.) sanitary napkin

servir to serve

seul(e) alone, only (adj.)

seulement (adv.) only

si if; yes (to a negative question)

siège (m.) seat

signer to sign

signification (f.) meaning

signifier to mean

s'il vous plaît please

six six

ski (m.) ski; **les skis nautiques** water skis

slip (m.) panties

soda (m.) soda

soeur (f.) sister

soie (f.) silk

soif (f.) thirst; **avoir soif** to be thirsty

soin (m.) care; **avec soin** carefully

soir (m.) evening

soixante sixty

soixante-dix seventy

soldes (m. pl.) sales, bargains

sole (f.) sole, flounder

soleil (m.) sun; **il fait du soleil** it is sunny; **les coups (m. pl.) de soleil** sunburn

sommeil (m.) sleep, sleepiness; **avoir sommeil** to be sleepy

sommelier (m.) wine waiter

somnifère (m.) sleeping pill

sonner to ring

sorbet (m.) sherbert

sortie (f.) exit

sortir to leave

souhaiter to wish (someone something)

soûl(e) drunk

soulier (m.) shoe

souper (m.) supper

souper to have supper

sous under

sous-titre (m.) subtitle

sous-vêtement (m.) undergarment; **les sous-vêtements (m. pl.)** underwear

soutien-gorge (m.) bra

souvent often

spectacle (m.) show

stade (m.) stadium

station-service (f.) service station; gas station

stylo à bille (m.) ball-point pen

succursale (f.) branch of a bank, etc.

sucre (m.) sugar

sud (m.) south

suivant(e) following, next

suivre to follow

supermarché (m.) supermarket

supporter to tolerate

sur on

sûr(e) sure

surnom (m.) last name, nickname

surtout especially

surveiller to watch, supervise

synagogue (f.) synagogue

syndicat (m.) d'initiative tourist office

synthétique synthetic, polyester

T

tabac (m.) tobacco

table (f.) table

tableau (m.) picture, painting

tache (f.) stain

taille (f.) size, figure (body), waist

taille-crayon (m.) pencil sharpener

tailleur (m.) tailor, woman's suit

talon (m.) heel (of foot)

tampon (m.) périodique tampon

tapis (m.) rug

tard late

tarif (m.) rate

tartan (m.) plaid

tarte (f.) pie

tasse (f.) cup

taxi (m.) taxi

teinturerie (f.) dry cleaner's

télégramme (m.) telegram

téléphone (m.) telephone; **cabine (f.) téléphonique** telephone booth

téléphoner to call on the phone

téléphoniste (f.) operator

téléski (m.) ski lift

télévision (f.) television

tempête (f.) storm

temple (m.) church (Protestant)

temps (m.) weather, time; **de temps en temps** from time to time

tenir to hold

tente (f.) tent

terminer to finish

terrain (m.) ground; **terrain de camping** camping grounds; **terrain de golf** golf course **terrain de sport** playing field;

terre (f.) land, earth; **par terre** on the ground

tête (f.) head

thé (m.) tea; **au citron** with lemon; **au lait** with milk; **glacé** iced; **sucré** with sugar

thon (m.) tuna fish

timbre (m.) stamp

tire-bouchon (m.) corkscrew

tirer to pull

tissu (m.) material

tissu-éponge (m.) terry cloth

titre (m.) title

toit (m.) roof

tomate (f.) tomato

tomber to fall; **tomber malade** to become ill

tort: avoir tort to be wrong

tôt early

toucher to touch; **toucher un chèque** to cash a check

toujours always

tour (f.) tower

tour (m.) trip, turn

touriste (m./f.) tourist

tourner to turn

tout (m. s.); **tous** (m. pl.); **toute** (f. s.); **toutes** (f. pl.) all, every; **tous les jours** every day; **tout le monde** everybody; **tout le temps** all the time

tousser to cough

toux (f.) the cough; **la pastille contre la toux** cough drop; **le sirop contre la toux** cough syrup

traduire to translate

train (m.) train; **être en train de** to be in the act of

traitement (m.) treatment

trajet (m.) distance, journey, trip

tranche (f.) slice

travail (m.) work

travailler to work

travers: à travers across, through

traverser to cross, go across

treize thirteen

trente thirty

très very; **très bien** very well

triste sad

trois three

tromper to deceive, trick; **se tromper** to be mistaken, make a mistake

trop (de) too much, many (of)

trottoir (m.) sidewalk

trou (m.) hole

trouver to find

truite (f.) trout

tu you

U

un (m.) a, an, one

une (f.) a, an, one

uni(e) solid (color)

unique only (adj.)

urgent(e) urgent; **cas urgent** (m.) emergency; **d'urgence** urgently

usage (m.) custom, practice

usagé(e) secondhand

usé worn out, threadbare, hackneyed
usine (f.) factory
utile useful
utiliser to use

V

vacances (f. pl.) vacation
valable valid
valeur (f.) value
valise (f.) suitcase
varié(e) varied
veau (m.) veal
velours (m.) velvet; **velours côtelé** corduroy
vendeur(euse) salesman, saleswoman
vendre to sell
vendredi Friday
venir to come; **venir de** to have just; **faire venir** to send for
vent (m.) wind; **il fait du vent** it is windy
vente (f.) sale; **en vente** for sale
ventilateur (m.) fan, blower
verglas (m.) ice, frost
vérifier to check
vérité (f.) truth
verre (m.) glass; **le verre de contact** contact lens
vers towards
vert(e) green
vestiaire (m.) coat checkroom
veston (m.) jacket
vêtements (m. pl.) clothing
viande (f.) meat
vide empty
vie (f.) life

vieille (f.) old
vieux (m.) old
village (m.) village
ville (f.) city
vin (m.) wine; **vin blanc** white wine; **vin mousseux** sparkling wine; **vin rosé** rosé wine; **vin rouge** red wine; **le négociant en vins** wine merchant
vinaigre (m.) vinegar
vingt twenty
violet purple
virage (m.) turn, bend, corner
visage (m.) face
vitamine (f.) vitamin
vite quickly
vitesse (f.) speed
vitrine (f.) shop window
vivre to live
voici here is, are
voie (f.) route, path, track
voilà there is, are
voir to see
voisin(e) neighbor
voiture (f.) car
vol (m.) flight
volant (m.) steering wheel
voler to fly, steal
voleur (m.) thief, robber
volontiers gladly, with pleasure, willingly
vouloir to wish, want; **vouloir dire** to mean, signify
vous you
voyage (m.) trip; **voyage d'affaires** business trip
voyager to travel
voyageur (m.) traveller
vrai(e) true
vraiment really
vue (f.) view

W

wagon (m.)   railroad car
wagon-lit (m.)   sleeping car
wagon-restaurant (m.)   dining car
W.C.   toilet

Y

y   there
yaourt (m.)   yogurt
yeux (m. pl.)   eyes

Z

zéro   zero
zone (f.)   zone
zoo (m.)   zoo

INDEX

READY REFERENCE KEY

Here are some phrases and words from the book that you are likely to use often. For a more extensive list of phrases, refer to the appropriate chapter within the book.

SIMPLE WORDS AND PHRASES

Do you speak English?	**Parlez-vous anglais?**	*pahr-lay voo ah_n-gleh*
Do you understand?	**Comprenez-vous? (Vous comprenez?)**	*kohn-pruh-nay voo (voo kohn-pruh-nay)*
I don't speak French.	**Je ne parle pas français.**	*zhuh nuh pahrl pah frahn-sseh*
I don't understand.	**Je ne comprends pas.**	*zhuh nuh kohn-prahn pah*
Please speak slowly.	**Parlez lentement s'il vous plaît.**	*pahr-lay lahn_t-mahn_ seel voo pleh*
Please repeat.	**Répétez, s'il vous plaît.**	*Ray-pay-tay, seel voo pleh*

BEING POLITE

Please	**S'il vous plaît**	*seel voo pleh*
Thank you very much.	**Merci beaucoup**	*mehr-ssee boh-koo*
Excuse me.	**Excusez-moi.**	*ehkss-kew-zay mwah*
	Pardon	*pahr-doh_n*
Good morning (afternoon).	**Bonjour.**	*boh_n-zhoor*
Good evening (night).	**Bonsoir.**	*boh_n-swahr*
	Bonne nuit.	*boh_n nwee*

NEEDS AND WANTS

I need _____ .	**Il me faut _____ .** *eel muh foh*
We need _____ .	**Il nous faut _____ .** *eel noo foh*
I'd like _____ .	**Je voudrais _____ .** *zhuh voo-dreh*
We'd like _____ .	**Nous voudrions _____ .** *noo voo-dree-yohn*
I'm looking for _____ .	**Je cherche _____ .** *zhuh shehrsh*
Please bring me _____ .	**Apportez-moi, s'il vous plaît _____ .** *ah-pohr-tay mwah seel voo pleh*
Please show me _____ .	**Montrez-moi, s'il vous plaît _____ .** *Mohn-tray mwah, seel voo pleh*
Please send up _____ .	**Faites monter _____ s'il vous plaît** *feht mohn-tay seel voo pleh*

DIRECTIONS

I'm lost.	**Je suis perdu(e).** *zhuh swee pehr-dew*
We're lost.	**Nous sommes perdus(ues).** *noo sohm pehr-dew*
I'm looking for _____ .	**Je cherche _____ .** *zhuh shehrsh*
Where is _____ ?	**Où est _____ ?** *oo eh*
to the left	**à gauche** *ah gohsh*
to the right	**à droite** *ah drwaht*
straight ahead	**tout droit** *too drwah*
How far away is _____ ?	**À quelle distance est _____ ?** *ah kehl deess-tahnss eh*
Where is it on the map?	**Où se trouve-t-il sur la carte?** *oo suh troov teel sewr lah kahrt*

THE BASICS FOR GETTING BY

Speaker 1: Pardon, Monsieur. Pouvez-vous nous aider? Nous sommes perdus. *Pahr-don, muh-syuh. Poo-vay voo noo zeh-day? Noo sohm pehr-dew.*

Excuse me, sir. Can you help us? We're lost.

Speaker 2: Bien sûr, avec plaisir! Où allez-vous? *bee-an sewr, ah-vek pleh-zeer. Oo ahl-lay voo?*

Of course, with pleasure. Where are you going?

1: Au Louvre. C'est dans quelle direction? *Oh Loov. Seh dahn kel dee-rek-ssyon?*

To the Louvre. Which way is it?

2: Il faut prendre le métro en direction de Mairie d'Ivry. *Eel foh prahn-druh luh may-troh ahn dee-rehk-ssyon duh Mehr-ee dee-vree.*

You have to take the subway in the direction of Mairie d'Ivry.

1: Nous sommes américains. Vous parlez trop vite. Je ne comprends pas. *Noo sohm zah-may-ree-kan. Voo pahr-lay troh veet. Zhuh nuh cohn-prahn pah.*

We're Americans. You're speaking too fast. I don't understand.

2: Le métro est droit devant vous. Ou bien vous pouvez prendre un bus. Vous comprenez? *Luh may-troh eh drwah duh-vahn voo. Oo byan voo poo-vay prahn-druh uhn bewss. Voo kohn-pruh-nay?*

The subway is straight ahead. Or you can take a bus. Do you understand?

1: Je parle très peu le français. *Zhuh pahrl tray puh luh frahn-sseh.*

I speak very little French.

2: J'irai avec vous au musée. *Zhee-ray ah-vehk voo oh moo-say.*

I'll go to the museum with you.

1: Merci beaucoup. Vous êtes

Thank you very

bien aimable. *Mehr-ssee boh-koo. Voo zeht byan eh-mah-bluh.*

much! You are very kind.

2: Pas de quoi. Je suis guide touristique au Louvre. Je fais le guide... en anglais. *Pah duh kwah. Zhuh swee geed too-reess-teek oh Loov. Zhuh feh luh geed-an an-gleh.*

You're welcome. I'm a tour guide at the Louvre. I give tours—in English.

WHEN YOU ARRIVE

Speaker 1: **Bonjour, mademoiselle. Vos papiers, s'il vous plaît.** *Bohn-zhoor, mahd-mwah-zehl. Voh pah-pyay, seel voo pleh.*

Hallo, Miss. Your papers, please.

Speaker 2: **Les voici, monsieur. Mon passeport, ma déclaration de douane, mon permis de conduire, mes cartes de crédit...** *Lay vwah-ssee, muh-ssyuh. Mohn pahss-pohr, mah day-klah-rah-ssyohn duh dwahn, mohn pehr-mee duh kohn-dweer, may kahrt duh kray-dee...*

Here they are, sir. My passport, my customs declaration, my driver's license, my credit cards...

1: Ça suffit, merci. Vous resterez combien de temps en France? *Sah sew-fee, mehr-see. Voo rehss-tray kohn-byan duh tahn ahn Frahnss?*

That's enough, thank you. How long will you be staying in France?

2: Oh, je ne sais pas exactement. Un mois, peut-être. Ça dépend. *Oh, zhuh nuh say pah ehk-zahk-tuh-mahn. Uhn mwah, puh-teh-truh. Sah day-pahn.*

Oh, I don't know exactly. A month, perhaps. It depends.

1: Vous logerez où? *Voo lohzh-ray oo?*

Where will you be staying?

2: Chez mes grands-parents. *Shay may grahn-pah-rahn.*

At my grandparents' house.

1: **Pourquoi êtes-vous venue en France?** *Poor-kwah eht-voo vuh-new ahn Frahnss?*

Why did you come to France?

2: **Je suis en voyage d'affaires.** *Zhuh swee zahn vwah-yahzh dah-fehr.*

I'm on a business trip.

1: **Ah, bon? Quel genre d'affaires?** *Ah bohn? Kehl zhan-ruh dah-fehr?*

Oh, really? What type of business?

2: **Des affaires du cœur. Je cherche un mari—un beau Français.** *Day zah-fehr dew kuhr. Zhuh shersh uhn mah-ree-uhn boh frahn-sseh.*

Love [matters of the heart]. I'm looking for a husband—a handsome Frenchman!

AT THE HOTEL

Speaker 1: **Allô, monsieur le concierge. Cette chambre ne me plaît pas du tout.** *Ah-loh muh-ssyuh luh kohn-ssyerzh. Seht shahn-bruh nuh muh pleh pah dew too.*

Hello, concierge. This room doesn't please me at all.

Speaker 2: **Mais pourquoi? Quel est le problème?** *Meh poor-kwah? Kehl eh luh proh-blehm?*

But why? What's the problem?

1: **D'abord, je préfère une chambre qui donne sur la cour.** *Dah-bohr, zhuh pray-fehr ewn shahn-bruh kee dohn sewr lah koor.*

First of all, I prefer a room facing the courtyard.

2: **On peut changer votre chambre si vous voulez, mais vous avez une vue panoramique sur tout Paris!** *Ohn puh shahn-zhay voh-truh shahn-bruh see voo voo-lay, meh voo zah-vay ewn vew pah-noh-rah-meek sewr too Pah-ree.*

We can change your room if you like, but you have a panoramic view of all of Paris.

1: **Aussi, mon rasoir électrique**

Also, my electric

ne fonctionne pas. *Oh-ssee, mohn
rah-zwahr ay-lehk-treek nuh fohnk-ssyohn pah.*

razor doesn't work.

2: **Mais monsieur, notre électri-
cien vient de vérifier les prises
de courant. En êtes-vous sûr?**
*Meh, muh-ssyuhr, noh-truh ay-lehk-tree-
ssyahn vyan duh vay-ree-fyay lay preez
dew koo-rahn. Ahn eht voo sewr?*

But sir, our elec-
trician just checked
the outlets. Are you
sure about this?

1: **Mais oui!** *Meh wee.*

Yes, of course!

2: **C'est peut-être votre transformateur qui ne marche pas. Vous
en avez besoin pour adapter le
courant français aux appareils
américains.** *Seh puh-teh-truh voh-
truh trahns-fohr-mah-tuhr kee nuh
mahrsh pah. Voo-zahn ah-vay buh-swan
poor ah-dap-tay luh koo-rahn frahn-seh
oh zahp-pah-ray ah-may-ree-kahn.*

Perhaps your adaptor
isn't working. You
need it to adapt
French electric cur-
rent to American
appliances.

BANKING AND MONEY

Speaker 1: **Bonjour, monsieur. Je
voudrais toucher un chèque, s'il
vous plaît.** *Bohn-zhoor, muh-ssyuh.
Zhuh voo-dreh too-shay uhn shehk, seel
voo pleh.*

Hello, sir. I would
like to cash a check,
please.

Speaker 2: **Dans ce cas, il faut aller
chercher une banque.** *Dahn suh
kah, eel foh ahl-lay sher-shay ewn bahnk.*

In that case, you
have to go find a
bank.

1: **Où se trouve la banque la
plus proche?** *Oo suh troov lah bahnk
lah plew prohsh?*

Where is the closest
bank?

2: **À droite, en face de l'église.**
Ah drwaht, ahn fahss duh lay-gleez.

To the right, opposite
the church.

1: **Je voudrais toucher ces chèques de voyage. Quel est le cours du dollar aujourd'hui?** *Zhuh voo-dray too-shay say shehk duh vwah-yahzh. Kehl eh luh koor dew doh-lahr oh-joor-dwee?*

I'd like to cash these travelers' checks. What is the exchange rate for the dollar today?

2: **Cinq francs au dollar.** *Sank frahn oh doh-lahr.*

Five francs to the dollar.

1: **Voilà cent dollars.** *Vwah-lah sahn doh-lar.*

Here is $100.

2: **Ça fait 450 francs, alors.** *Sah feh kah-truh sahn san-kahnt frahn, ah-lohr.*

That makes 450 francs, then.

1: **Quoi? Vous faites erreur!** *Kwah? Voo feht ehr-uhr.*

What? You're mistaken!

2: **Pas du tout, monsieur. Regardez le panneau. Notre bureau de change prend une commission de 10 pour cent.** *Pah dew too, muh-ssyuh. Ruh-gahr-day luh pah-noh. Noh-truh bew-roh duh shanzh prahn ewn koh-mee-ssyohn duh deess poor sahn.*

Not at all, sir. Look at the sign. Our exchange bureau charges a 10% commission.

GETTING AROUND TOWN

Speaker 1: **Monsieur, vous avez l'air embêté. Puis-je vous aider?** *Muh-ssyuh, voo zah-vay lehr ahm-beh-tay. Pweezh voo zeh-day?*

Sir, you look confused. Can I help you?

Speaker 2: **Merci, madame. Pourriez-vous me dire comment aller à l'Opéra?** *Mehr-see, mah-dahm. Poo-ryay-voo muh deer cohm-mahn tah-lay ah loh-pay-rah?*

Yes, ma'am. Could you tell me how to get to the Opera?

1: **Oh, c'est très facile. Prenez le métro en direction de Porte**

Oh, that's easy. Take the subway in the did'Orléans. **Vous allez descendre à Réaumur-Sébastopol.** *Oh, seh treh fah-sseel. Pruh-nay luh may-troh ahn dee-rek-ssyohn duh Pohrt dohr-lay-ahn. Voo zahl-lay deh-ssahn-druh ah Ray-oh-mewr Say-bahss-toh-pohl.*

rection of Porte d'Orléans. You get off at Réaumur-Sébastopol.

2: **C'est tout? C'est facile, en effet.** *Seh too? Seh fah-sseel, ahn eh-feh.*

That's all? That really is easy.

1: **Puis ensuite, vous prenez une correspondance pour la ligne trois en direction de Pont Levallois, et vous descendez au quatrième arrêt. L'Opéra est juste là.** *Pwee ahn-sweet, voo pruh-nay ewn koh-ress-pohn-dahnss poor lah leen-yuh trwah ahn dee-rek-ssyohn duh Pohn Luh-vahl-wah, ay voo day-ssahn-day oh kah-tree-yehm ah-reh. Loh-pay-rah eh zhewst lah.*

Then you transfer for line 3 in the direction of Pont Levallois, and you get off at the fourth stop. The Opera is right there.

2: **Y a-t-il une station de taxis près d'ici?** *Ee-ah-teel ewn stah-ssyohn duh tahk-ssee preh dee-ssee?*

Is there a taxi stand round here?

PLANNING A TRIP

Speaker 1: **Quand y-a-t-il un vol de Nice à Paris?** *Kahn dee-ah-teel uhn vohl duh Neess ah Pah-ree?*

When is there a flight from Nice to Paris?

Speaker 2: **À 13 heures 45, monsieur.** *Ah trehz uhr kah-rant-sank, muh-ssyuh.*

At 1:45, sir.

1: **Y reste-t-il une place dans la section non-fumeurs?** *Ee reh-stuh-teel ewn plahss dahn lah sehk-ssyohn nohn-few-muhr?*

Is there a seat remaining in the nonsmoking section?

2: **Oui, il y en a plusieurs.** *Wee, eel yahn ah plew-zyuhr.*

Yes, there are several.

1: **Quel repas sert-on?** *Kehl ruh-pah sehr-tohn?*	What meal is being served?
2: **On n'en sert pas. Le vol est de très courte durée.** *Ohn nahn sehr pah. Luh vohl eh duh treh coort dew-ray.*	We're not serving any. The flight is very short.
1: **Je voudrais un aller et retour en seconde classe, s'il vous plaît. À quelle heure arriverons-nous à Paris?** *Zhuh voo-dreh uhn ah-lay ay ruh-toor ahn suh-gohnd klahss, seel voo pleh. Ah kehl uhr ah-reev-rohn noo ah Pah-ree?*	I'd like a round trip ticket in second class, please. What time do we get to Paris?
2: **À 14 heures 45, monsieur.** *Ah kah-tohrz uhr kah-rahnt sank, muh-ssyuh.*	At 14:45, sir.
1: **Incroyable! Impossible! De Nice à Paris, Texas?** *An-krwah-yah-bluh. Ahn-poh-ssee-bluh. Duh Neess ah Pah-ree, Tehk-ssass?*	Incredible! Impossible! From Nice to Paris, Texas?
2: **Mais non, c'est le vol pour Paris, France.** *Meh nohn. Seh luh vohl poor Pah-ree, Frahnss.*	No. It's the flight to Paris, France.

DRIVING A CAR

Speaker 1: **Bonjour, monsieur. Je voudrais louer une voiture de sport avec transmission automatique.** *Bohn-zhoor, muh-ssyuh. Zhuh voo-dreh loo-ay ewn vwah-tewr duh spohr ah-vehk trahnz-mee-ssyohn oh-toh-mah-teek.*	Good morning, sir. I'd like to rent a sports car, with automatic transmission.
Speaker 2: **Nous en avons une qui est très populaire.** *Noo zahn ah-vohn zewn kee eh treh poh-pew-lehr.*	We have one that is very popular.

1: **Quel est le tarif à la semaine?** *Kehl eh luh tah-reef ah lah suh-mehn?*

How much does it cost per week?

2: **Mille six cent cinquante francs.** *Meey ssee ssahn san-kahnt frahn.*

1650 francs.

1: **L'essence est comprise?** *Leh-ssahnss eh kohn-preez?*

Is gas included?

2: **Non, je regrette.** *Nohn, zhuh ruh-greht.*

No, I'm afraid not.

1: **Combien coûte l'assurance?** *Kohn-byan koot lah-ssew-rahnss?*

How much does insurance cost?

2: **Vingt francs à la journée.** *Van frahn ah lah zhoor-nay.*

Twenty francs a day.

1: **Acceptez-vous des cartes de crédit? Lesquelles?** *Ahk-ssehp-tay voo lay kahrt duh kray-dee? Lay-kehl?*

Do you accept credit cards? Which ones?

2: **Nous acceptons toutes les cartes principales.** *Noo zahk-ssehp-tohn toot lay kahrt prahn-ssee-pahl.*

We accept all major cards.

1: **Dois-je verser une caution?** *Dwahzh vehr-ssay ewn koh-ssyohn?*

Do I have to leave a deposit?

2: **Non, ce n'est pas nécessaire. Remplissez ces formules et la voiture est à vous.** *Nohn, suh neh pah nay-ssay-sehr. Rahn-plee-ssay say fohr-mewl ay lah vwah-tewr eh tah voo.*

No, it's not necessary. Fill out these forms and the car is yours.

COMMUNICATIONS

Speaker 1: **Vendez-vous des télécartes ici au bureau de poste?** *Vahn-day voo day tay-lay-kahrt ee-ssee oh bew-roh duh posst?*

Do you sell telephone cards here at the post office?

Speaker 2: **Oui, nous en vendons.** Yes, we sell them.
Wee, noo zahn vahn-dohn.

1: **Avec cette carte, faut-il des je-** With this card, do
tons ou de la monnaie? *Ah-vehk* you need tokens or
seht kahrt, foh-teel day zheh-tohn oo duh money?
lah moh-nay?

2: **Non, la carte suffit.** *Nohn, la* No, the card is
kahrt sew-fee. enough.

1. **Peut-on téléphoner à** Can you make a long-
l'extérieur? *Puh-tohn tay-lay-foh-* distance call?
nay ah lehks-tay-ryuhr?

2: **Oui, facilement.** *Wee,* Yes, easily.
fah-sseel-mahn.

1. **Comment est-ce qu'on utilise** How do you use this
cette carte? *Koh-mahn ehss-kohn* card?
new-tee-leez seht kahrt.

2: **Décrocher le récepteur. In-** Remove the receiver.
sérez la carte dans la fente. Insert the card in the
Attendez quelques secondes. Re- slot. Wait a few sec-
gardez votre crédit. Composez onds. Look at your
le numéro. Parlez. Après l'ap- credit. Dial your
pel, le crédit qui vous reste est number. Speak. After
indiqué. *Day-kroh-shay luh ray-* the call, the remain-
sehp-tuhr. An-ssay-ray lah kahrt dahn ing credit is
la fahnt. Ah-tahn-day kehl-kuh suh- indicated.
gohnd. Ruh-gahr-day voh-truh kray-dee.
Kohn-poh-zay luh new-may-roh. Ah-preh
lah-pehl, luh kray-dee kee voo rehst eh
tan-dee-kay.

1. **Est-ce que cette carte est** Is this card only for
uniquement pour mon usage per- my own personal
sonnel? *Ehss-kuh seht kahrt eh* use?
tew-neek-mahn poor mohn new-zahzh
pehr-soh-nehl?

2: **Non. Vous pouvez prêter ou** No. You can lend or
donner votre carte à n'importe give your card to
qui. *Nohn. Voo poo-vay preh-tay oo* anyone.
doh-nay voh-truh kahrt ah nan-pohrt kee.

1: **Excellent. J'en prendrai une. C'est le cadeau parfait pour mon petit ami, Paul. De cette façon, il peut me téléphoner plus souvent. J'en ai assez de lui téléphoner tout le temps.** *Ehk-sseh-lahn. Zhahn prahn-dray ewn. Seh luh kah-doh pahr-feh poor mohn puht-ee tah-mee, Pohl. Duh seht fah-ssohn eel puh muh tay-lay-foh-nay plew soo-vahn. Zhah nay ah-ssay duh lwee tay-lay-foh-nay too luh tahn.*

Excellent. I'll take one. It's the perfect gift for my boyfriend, Paul. This way, he can call me more often. I'm tired of calling him all the time.

2: **Bonne idée!** *Bohn ee-day!*

Good idea!

GETTING TO KNOW PEOPLE

Speaker 1: **Permettez-moi de me présenter. Je m'appelle Jean Rousseau.** *Pehr-meht-tay mwah duh muh pray-sahn-tay. Zhuh mah-pehl Zhahn Roo-ssoh.*

Allow me to introduce myself. My name is John Rousseau.

Speaker 2: **Enchantée. Moi, je m'appelle Denise Vartan. Vous me paraissez familier. Est-ce que je vous connais?** *Ahn-shahn-tay. Mwah, zhuh mah-pehl Duh-neez Vahr-tahn. Voo muh pah-rehss-ay fah-mee-lyay. Ehss-kuh zhuh voo kohn-neh?*

How do you do. My name is Denise Vartan. You look very familiar. Do I know you?

1: **Je ne crois pas. Êtes-vous ici avec votre mari?** *Zhuh nuh krwah pah. Eht-voo zee-ssee ah-vehk voh-truh mah-ree?*

I don't think so. Are you here with your husband?

2: **Non, je suis célibataire. Et vous?** *Nohn, zhuh swee say-lee-baht-ehr. Ay voo?*

No, I'm single. And you?

1: **Je suis seul. Ça vous dé-**

I'm alone. Do you

range si je fume? *Zhuh swee suhl. Sah voo day-rahnzh see zhuh fewm?*	mind if I smoke?
2: Oui, ça m'énerve. Combien de temps restez-vous à Paris? *Wee, sah may-nehrv. Kohn-byan duh tahn rehss-tay-voo ah Pah-ree?*	Yes, that bothers me. How long are you staying in Paris?
1: Deux mois, et vous? *Duh mwah, ay voo?*	Two months. How about you?
2: Un mois. Quelle est votre profession? *Uhn mwah. Kehl eh voh-truh proh-feh-ssyon?*	One month. What is your job?
1: Je suis instituteur. *Zhuh swee zahn-stee-tew-tuhr.*	I'm a teacher.
2: Je vous reconnais maintenant. Vous étiez mon prof à l'école Picard. *Zhuh voo ruh-koh-neh mant-nahn. Voo zay-tyay mohn prohf ah lay-kohl Pee-kahr.*	I recognize you now. You were my teacher at the Picard School.

ENTERTAINMENTS AND DIVERSIONS

Speaker 1: Dis donc. On va au cinéma ce soir? *Dee dohnk. Ohn vah oh see-nay-mah suh swahr?*	Say, shall we go to the movies this evening?
Speaker 2: Qu'est-ce qu'on joue aujourd'hui? *Kehss-kohn zhoo oh-zhoor-dwee?*	What's playing today?
1: Une histoire d'amour. *Ewn eess-twahr dah-moor.*	A love story.
2: Bof. Tu préfères aller au discothèque? *Bohf. Tew pray-fehr ah-lay oh deess-koh-tehk?*	Ugh. Would you rather go to a disco?
1: Je n'ai pas envie de danser. On peut aller patiner. *Zhuh nay pah*	I don't feel like dancing. We can go

ahn-vee duh dah<u>n</u>-say. Oh<u>n</u> puh ahl-lay pah-tee-nay.

skating.

2: **Non, je n'aime pas ça. Allons faire du bowling.** *Noh<u>n</u>, zhuh nehm pah sah. Ah-loh<u>n</u> fehr dew boh-leeng.*

No, I don't like that. Let's go bowling.

1: **Je le déteste. Tu veux aller nager?** *Zhuh luh day-tehst. Tew vuh ah-lay nah-zhay?*

I hate it. Do you want to go swimming?

1: **Non, c'est ennuyeux. Tiens, regardons le match de foot à la télé!** *Noh<u>n</u>, seht ah<u>n</u>-nwee-yuh. Tya<u>n</u>, ruh-gahr-doh<u>n</u> luh mahch duh foot ah lah tay-lay!*

No, that's boring. Hey, let's watch the soccer game on TV?

2: **Ça ne m'intéresse pas.** *Sah nuh ma<u>n</u>-tay-rehss pah.*

That doesn't interest me.

1: **Alors, qu'est-ce-que tu as envie de faire?** *Ah-lohr, kehss-kuh tew ah ah<u>n</u>-vee duh fehr?*

So what do you feel like doing?

2: **De dormir. C'est fatiguant de tant discuter.** *Duh dohr-meer. Seh fah-tee-gah<u>n</u> duh tah<u>n</u> dee-skew-tay.*

Sleeping. It's tiring to have all this discussion.

FOOD AND DRINK

Speaker 1: **Garçon, qu'est-ce que vous me recommandez?** *Gahr-ssoh<u>n</u>, kehss kuh voo muh ruh-koh-mah<u>n</u>-day?*

Waiter, what can you suggest to me?

Speaker 2: **Comme hors d'œuvre, les artichauts à la vinaigrette.** *Kohm ohr-duh-vruh, lay zahr-tee-shoh ah lah vee-neh-greht.*

As an appetizer, artichokes vinaigrette.

1: **Et comme plat principal? Quelle est votre spécialité?**

And as a main dish? What is your

Ay kohm plah prahn-ssee-pahl? Kehl eh voh-truh spay-ssee-ah-lee-tay?   specialty?

2: Nous servons une bouillabaisse qui est superbe. *Noo sehr-vohn zewn boo-yah-behss kee eh sew-pehrb.*   We serve a superb bouillabaisse.

1: Qu'est-ce que c'est que la bouillabaisse? *Kehss-kuh seh kuh lah boo-yah-behss?*   What's "bouillabaisse"?

2: C'est une sorte de ragoût contenant des poissons et des fruits de mer variés. *Seh tewn sohrt duh rah-goo kohn-tuh-nahn day pwah-ssohn ay day frwee duh mehr vah-ree-yay.*   It's a sort of stew containing different types of fish and seafood.

1: Excellent. Je la prends. Et que recommandez-vous comme vin? *Ehk-seh-lahn. Zhuh lah prahn. Ay kuh ruh-koh-mahn-day-voo kohm van?*   Excellent. I'll take it. And what wine do you recommend?

2: Un vin blanc—du Graves, ou peut-être du Pouilly-Fuissé. *Uhn van blahn—dew Grahv oo dew Poo-yee Fwee-ssay.*   A white wine— Graves or perhaps Pouilly-Fuissé.

1: Du Graves, s'il vous plaît. C'est tout pour le moment. *Dew Grahv, seel voo plek. Seh too poor luh moh-man.*   Graves, please. That's all for the moment.

2: D'accord. Merci. À votre service. *Dah-kohr. Mehr-ssee. Ah voh-truh sehr-veess.*   All right. Thank you. At your service.

(une demi-heure après) *(ewn duh-mee uhr ah-preh)*   (a half hour later)

1: Garçon, le poison dans cette bouillabaisse est vraiment délicieux. *Gahr-ssohn, luh pwah-zohn dahn seht boo-yah-behss eh vreh-mahn day-lee-ssyuh.*   Waiter, the poison in this bouillabaisse is really delicious.

2: Quelle horreur, madame. Nous   That's horrible,

n'empoisonons jamais nos clients.
Kehl ohr-uhr, mah-dahm. Noo nahn-pwah-zohn-ohn zhah-meh noh klee-yahn.

ma'am! We never
poison our
customers.

SHOPPING 2

Speaker 1: **Tu veux aller au concert de Jacques Lamour avec moi ce soir?** *Tew vuh ahlay oh kohn-ssehr duh Zhahk Lah-moor ah-vehk mwah suh swahr?*

Do you want to go to the Jacques Lamour concert with me this evening?

Speaker 2: **Je regrette. Je ne peux pas. Ma mère prépare un grand dîner pour un ami spécial et je dois l'aider a faire des courses.** *Zhuh ruh-greht. Zhuh nuh puh pah. Mah mehr pray-pahr uhn grahn dee-nay poor uhn nah-mee spay-ssyahl ay zhuh dwah leh-day ah fehr day koorss.*

I'm sorry. I can't. My mother is preparing a big dinner for a special friend and I have to help her do the shopping.

1: **Où vas-tu?** *Oo vah-tew?*

Where are you going?

2: **D'abord je vais à la char-cuterie acheter cinq cent grammes de jambon.** *Dah-bohr zhuh veh zah lah shahr-kew-tree ahsh-tay sank sahn grahm duh zhahn-bohn.*

First I'm going to the delicatessen to buy 500 grams of ham.

1: **Et après?** *Ay ah-preh?*

And afterwards?

2: **Je vais chez le fleuriste acheter de jolies fleurs. Puis après je vais au magasin de photos acheter deux pellicules de trente-six en couleur.** *Zhuh veh shay luh fluh-reesst ahsh-tay duh zhoh-lee fluhr. Pwee ah-preh zhuh veh zoh mah-gah-zan duh foh-toh ahsh-tay duh peh-lee-kewl duh trahnt-ssees ahn koo-luhr.*

I'm going to the florist to buy some pretty flowers. Then I'm going to the photography store to buy two rolls of color film with 36 exposures.

1:	**C'est tout?** *Seh too?*	Is that all?
2:	**Non. Finalement je vais au magasin de disques acheter les derniers succès de Jacques Lamour.** *Nohn. Fee-nahl-mahn zhuh veh oh mah-gah-zan duh deessk ahsh-tay lay dehr-nyay sewk-ssay duh Zhahk Lah-moor.*	No. Finally I'm going to the record store to buy Jacques Lamour's latest hits.
1:	**Pourquoi? Qui est cet ami spécial de ta mère?** *Poor-kwah? Kee eh seht ah-mee spay-ssyahl duh tah mehr?*	Why? Who is this special friend of your mother's?
2:	**C'est Jacques Lamour. Il était son petit ami lorsqu'ils étaient au collège Goncourt ensemble. Il vient chez nous après le concert.** *Seh Zhahk Lah-moor. Eel ay-teh sohn puh-tee tah-mee lohrss-keel zay-teh toh kohl-lehzh Gohn-koor ahn-sahn-bluh. Eel vyan shay noo ah-preh luh kohn-ssehrt.*	It's Jacques Lamour. He was her boyfriend when they were at Goncourt College together. He's coming to our house after the concert.

GENERAL INFORMATION

Speaker 1:	**Quel jour est-ce** *Kehl zhoor ehss?*	What day is this?
Speaker 2:	**C'est mercredi.** *Seh mehr-kruh-dee.*	It's Wednesday.
1:	**Quelle heure est-il?** *Kehl uhr eh-teel?*	What time is it?
2:	**Il est neuf heures moins le quart.** *Eel eh nuh vuhr mwan luh kahr.*	It's a quarter to nine.
1:	**Quelle saison est-ce?** *kehl seh-zohn ehss?*	What season is this?

2: **C'est l'été.** *Seh lay-tay.*

It's summer.

1: **Quel temps fait-il?** *Kehl tan feh-teel?*

What's the weather?

2: **Il fait très chaud. Le soleil brille très fort.** *Eel feh treh shoh. Luh soh-lay breey treh fohr.*

It's very hot. The sun is shining very brightly.

1: **Quelle est la température?** *Kehl eh lah tahn-pay-rah-tewr.*

What's the temperature?

2: **Il fait trente degrés. Pourquoi me posez-vous des questions tellement bêtes?** *Eel feh trahnt duh-gray. Poor-kwah muh poh-zay voo day kehss-tyohn tehl-mahn beht?*

It's 30 degrees (centigrade). Why are you asking me such stupid questions?

1: **Je viens de passer trois mois de vacances au Brésil, où tout est à l'envers—les saisons, le temps, l'heure. Je suis toujours dans les nuages et je ne me suis pas encore réhabituée à la vie française.** *Zhuh vyan duh pah-ssay trwah mwah duh vah-kahnss oh Bray-zeel oo too teh tah lahn-vehr—lay seh-zohn, luh tahn, luhr. Zhuh swee too-zhoor dahn lay new-ahzh ay zhuh nuh muh swee pah zahn-kohr ray-ah-bee-tew-ay ah lah vee frahn-ssehz.*

I just spent three months of vacation in Brazil where everything is backwards—the seasons, the weather, the time. I'm still very confused (up in the clouds) and I haven't readjusted to life in France yet.

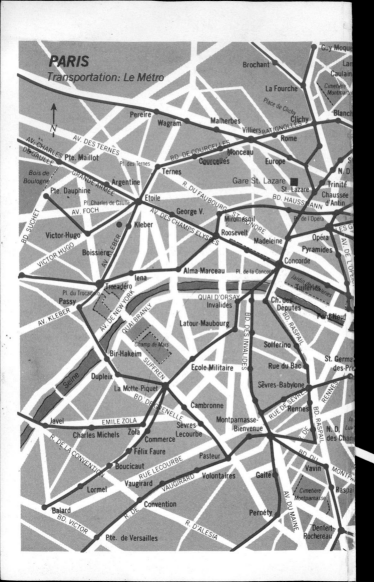